TOM WALSH'S OPERA
The History of the Wexford Festival, 1951–2004

Tom Walsh as 'Marco' in *The Gondoliers*, 1930

Tom Walsh's Opera

A HISTORY OF THE WEXFORD FESTIVAL

1951–2004

KARINA DALY

FOUR COURTS PRESS

This book was typeset in 11.5 on 15 pt Adobe Caslon
by Susan Waine for
FOUR COURTS PRESS LTD
7 Malpas Street, Dublin 8, Ireland
e-mail: info@four-courts-press.ie
and in the United States for
FOUR COURTS PRESS
c/o International Specialised Book Services,
920 N.E. 58th Avenue, Suite 300, Portland, OR 97213

A catalogue record for this title is available from the British Library.

ISBN 1-85182-878-8

Printed in England by
MPG Books Ltd, Bodmin, Cornwall.

Contents

Acknowledgements

Putting together the history of Wexford's Opera Festival has been an exciting and fascinating journey. There are many, many people who have played key roles in bringing this journey to the conclusions I have reached – Gillian Brennan helped me to start the process of turning my research into a logical story; Ger Lawlor, and David Graham of Lewes, kindly restored and reproduced old photographs; Denise O'Connor-Murphy, Derek Speirs and John Ironside have allowed me to use photographs to bring some of the story to life; the *Irish Times,* Bord Fáilte and Tom Mooney of the *Echo* have also been most generous with photographic material; Gráinne Doran of Wexford County Library was always willing to help; Nicky Cleary sorted through all the photographs, naming each and every opera and singer; Ted Howlin, Jerome Hynes and Phil Keeling kindly answered queries and gave me access to the Festival's newly-constituted archive; Paul Hennessy offered unlimited help with access issues. A special word of thanks must go to Jim Golden, who was completely selfless with his time – Jim read drafts of my book and was a source of reality and perspective which was crucial to a balanced story.

Many people shared their own experiences of the Festival with me, including the late Moran Caplat, the late Terry Sheehy, Luigi Ferrari and Alan Wood. Others very kindly agreed to partake in the journey by writing down their experiences which are included in the epilogue – Harry White, Peter Ebert, Bryan Balkwill and Lord Briggs. Their participation has meant so much to me and has added hugely to this book.

The person who inspired me to write this history – Richard Aldous – played an integral part in the process of completing this book. He has been a mentor, an editor and a friend. I am indebted to him for his kindness in making time to answer my every query and read my every chapter.

I cannot emphasize enough how much Victoria Walsh-Hamer has helped me. She has read endless drafts and commented on each one at length. She very kindly gave me access to her father's material – something that was crucial to ensure a rounded version of the story. I can never hope to repay her kindness. I only hope that she has enjoyed the journey and the memories.

Special thanks also to John who has encouraged my every endeavour since we studied together at University College Dublin. He is a true optimist and has instilled in me the notion that anything is possible when you focus your mind.

Finally, I would like to make special mention to my parents, Michael and Irene. I cannot say how much their help, support and generosity has contributed to this and all my endeavours. My mother read and commented on many drafts. My father was always on hand with practical advice. I can never fully express my gratitude to them.

This book is dedicated to my parents, Michael and Irene.

Prologue by Bernard Levin

writing in the 1989 Festival Programme Book

If you are reading this, you are holding in your hands the Wexford Festival Programme Book, as the orchestra tunes. If Tom Walsh had not lived, you would not be, because there would be no Wexford Festival Programme Book, because there would be no Wexford Festival. It is as simple as that.

Mind you, it wasn't at first. Tom thought there should be an opera festival in Wexford, and when he mentioned the subject, other music-lovers agreed. But when he made clear that he was going to create one, in a town of 11,000 people, and a town very far from prosperous, too, heads were shaken, temples tapped, smiles hidden behind hands. Tom was written off as a visionary.

So he was; he had seen a vision. But his enthusiasm, his energy, his silver tongue, his unwavering determination, his implacable unwillingness to accept defeat – these combined to keep his vision clear and bright. All he had to do then was to raise the money, prepare the theatre, find the artists, engage the orchestra and tell the world. A madman, certainly: but what are you holding in your hands? ...

The Festival opened, on time. It continued, it waxed, it became known, it became *well* known, it became famous. Tom's enchanting smile grew wider – not from the knowledge of his operatic paternity, but for the joy he had brought to so many visitors. All music festivals have their 'regulars', who return every year; it is probable that the proportion of regulars at Wexford is greater than any other in the world.

Why? Because Tom built to last. His greatest magic was to inspire the town to spread happiness before its visitors like a red carpet before royalty. In Wexford at Festival time you cannot go round a corner without meeting an old friend, nor round another without making a new one, and Irish hospitality is at its warmest in this town of tiny streets and great hearts ...

A man like Tom Walsh cannot be lost by death; his spirit will live on in the town he loved, the town he taught the world to love, too, and his achievement, the Wexford Festival, is now deep-rooted and will endure.

The tuning is finished. The lights will soon go down. Close the book. *Si monumentum requires, circumspice.*

The most ambitious venture in years

'My own favourite festival is Wexford,' wrote William Mann in the *Times*.

> The town is small, as is the opera house. That, straight away, means that it is very select and catering for a small public. But the operatic repertory is wide, French, German, Italian. The productions are tasteful and immaculate. It's small scale but totally delectable. The place is small enough to surround you with new friends all the time, if you were sociable. Food, drink and gossip are everywhere on tap at all times. Salzburg in the early 1920s must have been like this. It is how an opera festival should be.[1]

It has been the source of utter amazement to those who visit the Festival on an annual basis that it has survived and prospered in a town like Wexford. Even more amazing is the fact that it was set up in the first place – for Dr T.J. Walsh created an opera festival in a land without classical music.

In mid-twentieth century Ireland, grand opera was associated with the old values of the Ascendancy and the Anglo-Irish. Much of the Irish population did not care for an operatic tradition and were even against the idea of introducing any art that had filtered through to Ireland from Britain. Opera formed no part of the Irish character. There had been few important Irish composers. Even those whose music still survived, like Vincent Wallace of Waterford and Michael Balfe of Dublin had aimed primarily at an audience outside of Ireland. Opera houses themselves were hard to come by, as many had been turned into cinema houses or theatres to entertain a greater demand.[2]

This was partly explained by the Irish political situation. After Independence in 1922, Ireland entered a period of cultural decline. There was a sense of anti-intellectualism, even. The arts in particular suffered as they were seen as an elite pastime and at worst, as 'anti-Irish'. As John F. Larchet, Professor of Music at University College Dublin from 1921 to 1958, wrote of Dublin:

> It possesses no concert hall, good or bad, and no permanent orchestra which could be called a symphony orchestra … Most of the people have no knowledge of Strauss, Brahms, and the great volume of modern orchestral music. Few are acquainted with any important works of later date than Wagner's *Ring of the Nibelungen*.
>
> Little interest is taken in chamber music or choral music; a large percentage of music lovers in Dublin have never heard a string quartet … In such circumstances, it is inevitable that Dublin should contribute nothing to the support or progress of music.[3]

Imagine, then, what it was like in Wexford. It was against this backdrop of cultural stagnation that T.J. Walsh introduced opera to provincial Wexford.

Walsh was born in 6 Upper George Street, Wexford, in 1911. Educated at the town's Christian Brothers School, he began his medical studies at the University College Dublin in 1930. He did not qualify until 1944, his time at college being disrupted, firstly due to the death of his father, a local publican, and then because Walsh himself developed tuberculosis. He then married Eva Cousins, a lady considerably older than himself and a leading member of the local light opera society. She was well off and a member of a family who owned a mineral water business in Wexford town. Eva was a skilled pianist, and her love of music naturally complemented her husband's interest in starting an opera festival. During his time at University College Dublin, Walsh studied singing with the prestigious A.G. Viani at the Royal Irish Academy of Music. This served him very well indeed, particularly with regard to his acute ability later on to recognize the potential of singers for productions at Wexford. Viani, an Italian-born music teacher, was one of the leading figures in the establishment of the Dublin Operatic Society in 1928 and was responsible for the performance of opera at the Gaiety Theatre until 1936.

According to Nellie Walsh, her brother's love of music and opera began at an early age, when both of them used to listen to opera on gramophone records and, later, on the radio. Walsh was a member of the Wexford Musical Society and had taken part in many local productions.[4] His memories of Wexford were that it was a 'dull country town' and he said that he was lured to the local theatre because 'there was light there'. The first opera he remembered attending was *Rigoletto*. It had been produced in Wexford in 1921 by a touring company, and it had left an indelible mark on his taste for opera, because, as he admitted, he had nothing to compare it to at that stage.[5]

When Walsh came home to work as a medical doctor following his studies in Dublin, he kept up his favourite pastime of listening to opera. Friends began to call around to his house when they realized what an impressive collection of gramophone recordings he had built up. Although this was only a hobby, being a man of serious ambition, Walsh was not satisfied with this arrangement. He wanted to extend the gathering to offer other opera lovers the opportunity to listen to such music.

In 1950, he set up the Wexford Opera Study Circle to bring opera lovers together. The Circle was merely an extension of the gatherings at his home.[6]

Walsh's love of opera was so intense that he was not content with simply listening to recordings. He was deeply knowledgeable about singers and opera and he wanted to stage his own production in his own town. This was a crazy idea, but Walsh had seen what his music teacher in Dublin, Viani, had achieved with the founding of the Dublin Operatic Society.

Walsh was not alone in his enthusiasm once he discussed his proposal with some close friends – Eugene McCarthy, the owner of White's Hotel, Wexford; Seamus O'Dwyer, a postman; Dr Jim Liddy and Dr Des Ffrench, who were both medical doctors. Walsh's wife, Eva, was also extraordinarily optimistic that her husband's dream could be achieved. The group met often to discuss their project, each time becoming more and more convinced that it was feasible. While all this was going on, Walsh was holding down a full-time job as a general practice doctor, and was at the same time acting as anaesthetist to the Wexford county hospital.

In a Wexford Arts Newsletter of 1977, Walsh wrote an article on his memories of how the project began. The inspiration came from an old programme of Benjamin Britten's Aldeburgh Festival which he found in Foyle's Bookshop in London. It was not the Aldeburgh Festival itself that inspired Walsh, but merely the image of the boats at Aldeburgh that reminded him of similar scenes at Wexford.

The fact that Aldeburgh had begun a festival from very humble beginnings gave Walsh the confidence to discuss his proposal with Sir Compton Mackenzie, the famous editor of *Gramophone* magazine. In 1950 he wrote to Mackenzie, describing himself as 'an amateur of opera endeavouring to revive an interest in the art, traditional to our town up to the year 1938, since when the old touring companies have ceased to visit us.'[7]

He invited Mackenzie to give the opening lecture to the Wexford Opera Study Circle. Mackenzie consented and went on to become the president of the Wexford Festival of Music and the Arts in its inaugural year and an invaluable source of publicity for the Festival in England.[8] It was interesting that the first president of the Festival was not an Irishman, but was British. Mackenzie had suggested to Walsh that the Festival should perhaps have a local, or at least an Irish president. Walsh disagreed with him, later commenting that 'we owe a deep debt to Sir Compton. He was a political friend of this country when it was neither popular nor profitable to be so, and as long as we have a festival Sir Compton will be its president.'[9]

Although Mackenzie was enthusiastic, interest was not forthcoming locally. Walsh and his aides began by finding out how many local businesses and local people would become subscribers to the projected Festival. The target was 500 guineas but only 200 guineas were collected. Walsh later recalled that

> to a man everybody voted against it, on the perfectly sensible grounds that there was obviously insufficient interest in the project to make it a success. Whereupon, I decided we would hold the Festival anyhow.[10]

Throughout the summer of 1951, leading up to the first Festival, Walsh admitted that he was at times unsure as to how the venture would be received publicly. 'In fact, thinking back on it the reaction of most of the townspeople was to look upon the whole business as a joke, and outside Wexford, nobody [had] even heard of us,'[11] he said, smiling.

Walsh was certainly ambitious. He set out to enlist the help of the English conductor Sir Thomas Beecham. Beecham was at first baffled that a medical doctor should be so enthusiastic about opera. This was strangely ironic because Beecham himself was essentially an amateur musician, although he was a world-famous one by 1951. 'But you are a doctor, why are you so interested in opera?' Walsh recalled Beecham asking him. 'Sir Thomas, do you ever go to football matches?' Walsh retorted. Instantly he realized what Walsh meant and, as Walsh relayed, 'his eyes twinkled and, poking me in the chest with his finger, he said, "With your team winning? I know, I know!"'

Walsh had taken the important decision of choosing the opera for his so-

1   Des Ffrench and Sir Compton Mackenzie, 1951
2   Eugene McCarthy and TJW

called Festival – Balfe's *The Rose of Castile*.[12] The opera told the story of conspiracy and intrigue with a classic twist of romantic fate. Walsh explained that he had chosen *The Rose* for its melodious music so as to attract an Irish operatic audience. Besides, he knew that Balfe had had connections with Wexford, having spent part of his early life there, and the fact that performance of the said opera was a rarity heightened its interest factor for Walsh, who wanted to present a little-known work.[13] *The Rose of Castile* had been first produced at Drury Lane in October 1857.

Walsh then set about putting together the production, beginning with the chorus; the chorus started out as an entirely amateur and entirely local group (apparently many of them could not even read music)[14] – a fact which led people to think that Walsh might be taking on too much. For the orchestra, he managed to convince Radio Éireann, the national broadcaster, to provide its Light Orchestra. The decision to seek help from a public, professional organization such as Radio Éireann marked the start of a trend in the history of the Festival.

Walsh's relationship with the broadcasting administrators was a difficult one. They came to describe him as 'a martinet and ruthless perfectionist, who because of fiery temperament enjoys a love-hate relationship with journalists'.[15] They appeared to respect the work he was doing in the organization of the Festival, but they were wary of the amateur nature of the project. Still, the Wexford Festival, soon came to rely on successful local collaboration with this national and professional institution. Contact had been made as early as February 1951. Walsh suggested in a letter to Fachtna Ó hAnnracháin, Director of Music, that the principal artists would come from London and Dublin, and the chorus would be local; and he asked if the orchestra might be the Radio Éireann Light Orchestra. He also indicated that the producer would perhaps come from London and the scenery and costumes would be specially designed for the production. He pointed out to Ó hAnnracháin that 'neither expense or trouble will be spared to make this an artistic venture of national importance'.[16]

Although opera was to be the prominent attraction of the Festival, a number of other entertainments were being arranged to fill the daytime before evenings of operatic performance. Recitals would be given by violinist Jaroslav Vaněček and pianist Joseph Weingarten, and the Director of the National Gallery had consented to loan paintings to the Festival for an exhibition. An exhibition of rare gramophone records and prints of famous singers would also be on display, prepared by the National Museum.[17]

Clearly very confident about what he expected to achieve, Walsh tried to impress his professional attitude upon Ó hAnnracháin. He even calculated for Ó hAnnracháin the expected loss of the venture, stating that it would be in the region of £250 to £500, which he predicted would be covered by local subscriptions. He hoped that the Director of Music would agree to one or two broadcasts as a means of promoting the Festival. Failing this, he requested the recording of a performance from the fringe events. This recording was to be broadcast at a later date, so as not to run the risk of people simply staying at home and waiting for the broadcast version.[18] Ó hAnnracháin was quick to point that if Radio Éireann did get involved, the station must have full rights of broadcasting or recording for broadcasting at a later date.[19]

Because the Festival had been guaranteed against loss of up to £350 and with that in mind, Ó hAnnracháin considered it relatively safe for Radio Éireann to cooperate. Further, he agreed to make enquiries to help the Festival council find suitable singers, and to obtain the orchestral music that was available from the agents Goodwin and Tabb in London. He seemed content with the arrangement between himself and the council, in view of the fact that, as he recalled, the organizers were willing to pay for a good team of soloists as well as a first-class producer.[20] But their commitment was equivocal.

Seamus O'Dwyer, a postman who was working closely with Walsh on the Festival project, suggested that Radio Éireann give Walsh himself the chance of a short broadcast, in the form of an interview, to help promote the Festival.[21] Yet Radio Éireann declined, saying that they could possibly include a 5–7 minute script by Walsh in a fortnightly series due to begin in October, entitled *Music Magazine*.[22] It was obvious at this early stage that Radio Éireann was not entirely comfortable with its association with this proposed Festival.

By May 1951 Walsh had secured Ria Mooney as producer for the opera and Michael O'Herlihy as designer of the sets. (Mooney was a distinguished Abbey Theatre actress, who, in the period 1943–8, produced new plays at the Gaiety Theatre, Dublin. She subsequently worked at the Abbey again as a producer from 1948 to 1963.) The problems of obtaining soloists had not yet been solved, but Walsh had placed advertisements in the daily papers in the hope of uncovering some more possibilities.[23]

By June, the principal roles for *The Rose of Castile* had still not been filled. It was not until July that Walsh managed to get an agreement from Maureen Springer to sing one of the principal roles. She, in turn, helped Walsh to contact her agents, Harold Holt Ltd, London, to find suitable candidates for the other roles. Ironically, given her later involvement, Veronica Dunne was turned down for the main part of Elvira, because Walsh believed her to be 'a lyrico-spinto rather than a coloratura', while also stressing that his council was 'anxious to have at least one "Star" name on the bill.'[24]

Getting these 'star' names led to the first disagreements between Walsh and Ó hAnnracháin. Ó hAnnracháin told him disdainfully that he seemed

to imply that we are trying to keep the 'Star' names out of the bill; whereas, I have been insisting from the beginning that all solo parts should be given to really good singers only. Unless, therefore, we have your written agreement that in the event of our failure to secure satisfactory singers locally, suitable singers will be found elsewhere, we cannot see our way to proceed in the projected collaboration.[25]

3 Frank Stafford and James White at the art exhibition during the 1951 Festival
4 Murray Dickie, Dermot O'Hara and Maureen Springer, 1951

Walsh was exasperated by Radio Éireann's attitude. The broadcasting station was trying to take over, and he was far from ready to relinquish control. Ó hAnnracháin also insisted the Walsh consult Mairéad Pigott, Radio Éireann's assistant for Vocal Programmes, before making any offers of solo parts. The auditions were to begin at the Radio Éireann premises in Dublin without further delay. At this point, Radio Éireann was not sure if the Wexford project would ever be launched and its directors were not keen about the idea of being part of an enterprise that was doomed to fail.

Walsh insisted that he had not, in fact, implied that Radio Éireann had wanted to exclude 'star' names from the cast, but went on to declare, during a meeting at which Dermot O'Hara, Ria Mooney, Michael O'Herlihy, and Walsh himself had been present at on 29 June, that it had been decided that 'it was better policy to engage, let us say – second rate Irish artists than third raters and "has beens" from England'.[26]

Walsh was concerned lest English singers might arrive at the Festival with a very 'imperfect knowledge' of their parts or, worse still, that they might break their contracts altogether. Most of the singers would be unfamiliar with Balfe's opera and may not have thought it worth their while learning the

parts. Walsh, however, stressed to Ó hAnnracháin that the council had managed to secure prestigious artists such as Joseph Weingarten and Jaroslav
Vaněček. Moreover, the National Gallery had, for the first time, agreed to
loan pictures for an Irish exhibition, and this exhibition would be part of the
Wexford Festival. Walsh was trying to impress upon Ó hAnnracháin that the
Wexford enterprise would in fact succeed and that Radio Éireann's efforts on
their behalf would not be wasted. This was evident in his explanation of the
work done thus far:

> For our opera we have engaged one of the best producers in Ireland, with set-
> tings and costumes designed by an artist who has been described as Ireland's
> leading theatre designer. To my knowledge no operatic production in this
> country has had scenery and costumes specially designed for it by an artist of
> Mr O'Herlihy's calibre for well over a hundred years.[27]

The engagement of singers continued to cause immediate problems for Walsh
and the Festival council. Walsh even suggested to Ó hAnnracháin that he
would contact the Dublin Operatic Society, whose season would occur before
the Wexford one, to enquire about whether Wexford could retain some of
their artists.[28] He also indicated his intention to investigate what singers were
available for principal roles in Ireland itself.[29] (At this stage, Walsh and his
front men were unsure as to how to go about finding suitable singers. It was
even suggested that music teachers be contacted to identify appropriate
singers.)

Because of its involvement in the Festival, Radio Éircann wanted the right
to choose singers but Walsh was keen to keep its involvement to a minimum.
Walsh did not need someone from Dublin to tell him how to run his Festival:
'We fully understand the enterprise we have undertaken,' he told Ó
hAnnracháin angrily, 'and we have no intention of mounting any production
that will not alone bring credit to Radio Éireann and to Wexford but honour
to Ireland.'[30]

By the late summer of 1951, preparations of the first Wexford Festival were
in place. The principal artists had at last been decided upon – Maureen
Springer, coloratura soprano at the Edinburgh Festival, along with Murray
Dickie, a tenor who had excelled in opera at Covent Garden, Glyndebourne
and Rome.[31] An agreement had been drawn up regarding the performance of
the Radio Éireann Light Orchestra for the first opera season that was to take

place between 1 and 4 November. It was very specific. On behalf of the Minister for Posts and Telegraphs, the Director of Broadcasting, C.E. Kelly, agreed to provide not less than thirty members of the Radio Éireann Light Orchestra and a conductor. Tucked away in the contract was the condition that the opera, *The Rose of Castile*, must be put on by a professional producer and that the chosen primary artists be acceptable to the Director of Broadcasting himself. Even as late as September, this was still causing stress. Ó hAnnracháin was adamant that Walsh's choice of producer – an amateur – was unacceptable. Further, Radio Éireann had full permission to record any or all of the performances of the opera and the concert free of charge as it so wished. Although the Broadcasting Service was providing the orchestra free of charge, the Festival was responsible for the covering of any travelling or hotel expenses of the orchestra and conductor. The number of rehearsals, their duration and the actual personnel of the orchestra were to be decided upon jointly by Radio Éireann and the Festival council.[32]

Walsh visited Ó hAnnracháin in Dublin to discuss the production of *The Rose of Castile*. Radio Éireann settled upon John Stephenson as producer.[33] Walsh was dissatisfied with this decision being taken by Radio Éireann after he had personally approved Ria Mooney for the position. But Radio Éireann had made its point about a professional producer clear. However, when Stephenson was approached, he turned Wexford down flat; '£40' he said, was a fee that 'no professional producer would accept'; he was insulted by the fact that he was being treated more like an amateur than a professional. He added sarcastically that he was sorry not to come in order 'to learn all Doctor Walsh has to show me about the "style of Operatic Production at the Opéra Comique Paris", and to incorporate these ideas as far as possible into the production of *The Rose of Castile*'.[34]

Stephenson's rejection raised tensions between Radio Éireann and Walsh, not least because Walsh was now threatening to take charge of the production himself. Ó hAnnracháin wrote to the council on 20 September, stridently setting out Radio Éireann's position:

> I feel that I must point out that I made it quite clear to Dr Walsh when he first discussed the project of the Wexford Festival with me that Radio Éireann could collaborate only on the assurance that a professional producer of standing would be engaged. I was rather amazed yesterday therefore, to learn

that Dr Walsh had proposed to undertake the responsibility of production himself without even mentioning the matter to me … I should be grateful if in all future notices you would use the words Radio Éireann Light Orchestra and not Radio Éireann Orchestra … Naturally [Dermot O' Hara, conductor] will not go to Wexford again until the question of production is solved to the mutual satisfaction of the Wexford Festival Organising Committee and Radio Éireann.[35]

Walsh relented, and at the end of the month engaged Powell Lloyd to produce *The Rose of Castile*. Lloyd had been resident producer at Sadler's Wells from 1941 to 1945 and producer-designer with the Dublin Grand Opera Society in 1948, 1949 and 1950.[36] Although Radio Éireann were clearly against the idea of having anything to do with an amateur organization and wished to maintain as much control as possible, there could be no opposition towards the employment of Lloyd.

The rows continued in the weeks leading up to the first night. Just days before the opening night, the Director of Broadcasting, C.E. Kelly, told the Wexford Festival council that the pit was too small for the agreed 30 players in the small theatre and that a lesser number would be used.[37] Walsh was furious, believing it would compromise the power of the performance. But while Radio Éireann continued its lukewarm support, public interest at home and abroad was growing. Was it really possible that a small harbour town in the southeast of Ireland was about to put on its own opera festival?

As early as 9 October 1951, the London *Times* music critic, Frank Howes, announced that he was coming over to Wexford to witness the atmosphere of the Festival for himself. Ironically, it was the English press which first printed news of the Wexford Festival of Music and the Arts. On 11 October, the *Times* had reported news of the Festival and immediately the Irish correspondent of the *Times* contacted Walsh for the story. The *Evening Herald* in Dublin tried to justify their delay in reporting the events at Wexford, by declaring that

the remarkable feature of the event is the silence, almost secrecy, with which the plans were conceived and brought along to fruition. Too often have we trumpeted about our inherent love of music and culture, but the only suitable notes to comfort our efforts in most cases would be 'The Last Post.'[38]

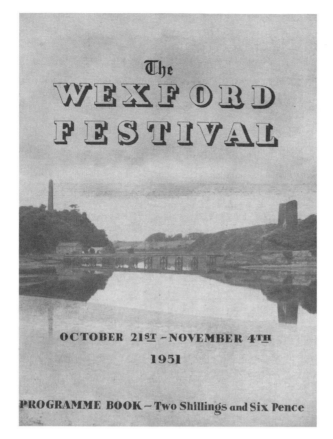

Perceval Graves, who had been the one to tip-off the London *Times* about Walsh's plan, was busy trying to promote the Festival in England. He wrote to Seamus O'Dwyer on 13 September, asking about the possibility of 'circularising the various Dominions Agents-General in London about the Festival'.[39] Graves had initially contacted Walsh to request information on the composer Michael Balfe on whom he intended to give a lecture.

The English press was clearly intrigued by this opera festival, which, until after the first season, they knew very little about. Perhaps they realized that it had the potential to be of an international standard, but it is more likely that they were surprised that the European and English trend of private opera production should have reached Ireland.

One of the aspects that the press picked up on was the importance of the Festival at Wexford as an educational aid to children. Schoolchildren were to attend a concert held by Radio Éireann Light Orchestra, as part of the Festival activities. The Department of Education deduced that since the con-

6   Poster for the 1951 Festival

7

8

7   Elsie Martin and Nellie Walsh in *The Rose of Castile*, 1951
8   TJW, Eva Walsh, Sir Compton Mackenzie and Erskine Childers, 1951
9   Audience, including Sir Compton Mackenzie, at the first performance of *The Rose of Castile*, 1951
10   Erskine Childers addresses the audience on the opening night, 1951

9   10

11   Erskine Childers with cast of *The Rose of Castile*, 1951

cert was being given on a Saturday morning, no problem would arise in this respect since it was outside of primary school hours. With regard to secondary schools, which did hold classes on Saturdays, the decision was left to the discretion of the managers and likewise in the vocational schools, where the Vocational Education Committee would decide permission of attendance. It was even agreed by the Department of Education that the Inspector of Music in the Secondary branch of the Department, Peadar Ó Collín, would attend the concert and give a short lecture to the students.

Yet despite all the hard work, preparations for the first Festival had not been without their problems. Experience of organization was minimal. The Wexford Festival council's knowledge of how to approach certain situations was pitiful. The 1951 Festival programme book, for example, boasted glamorously of acquiring Joan Denise Moriarty – the 'prima ballerina'.[40] Moriarty felt she was treated as anything but an important member of the cast. She aired her discontent in a letter to the council:

The dance which I had composed had to be entirely scrapped for lack of space on the stage, and it seemed clear from the beginning that no dancing was wanted by the producer in the opera. As a result only improvisation was possible; for the few minutes of my appearance I had to forgo an entire week's work in Cork so that the fee originally agreed upon could be no source of profit, apart from the worry and disappointment of the whole engagement.[41]

Walsh did his best to appease the cast in the days leading up to the opening night, but there was so much going on and it was difficult to stay on top of all matters. The press was beginning to ask Walsh what his association with the tourist industry was, seeing as the Festival had the potential to attract tourists to this small seaside town. He was quick to dispel the notion that the Festival was somehow an attempt to promote tourism in Wexford: 'I don't know how people come to think I'm in the tourist business,' he declared:

> but I'm not interested in tourism at all. I have enough on my plate trying to bring the opera. Let somebody else bring the tourists. I'm sure the Festival [will help] the tourist industry – how much or how little, is not my pigeon. I just want to put on opera.[42]

Finally, after all the preparations, the Wexford Festival of Music and the Arts opened on 1 November. It was a marvellous occasion: opera goers arrived to the narrow street that housed the Theatre Royal donned in black tie; artists scurried up the street and into the theatre already in costume, as the dressing room space in the theatre was entirely inadequate. Children were draped from every window in this tiny street to catch a glimpse of the unusual and entirely novel creatures that were congregating in the theatre across the street from where they lived. The sound of English accents was audible and caused further excitement. Doubtless those who came to investigate the situation did not recognize the Musical Director of Radio Éireann, Fachtna Ó hAnnracháin, or the Director of Broadcasting, C.E. Kelly. Lt.-Col. Bill O'Kelly, chairman of the Dublin Grand Opera Society, was also present. Erskine Childers, the then Minister for Posts and Telegraphs and later President of Ireland, had also made his way to Wexford for the great occasion.

The Rose of Castile was a successful choice. The performances lasted from 1 to 4 November. As Walsh appeared on the stage following the performance on each of the four nights, the audience sprang to their feet spontaneously to show their appreciation for what he had achieved. He was naturally delighted. The press was bemused by the entire affair, recognizing that it had been an outstanding amateur success, yet not quite knowing how it had come about. Perhaps one of the most gratifying compliments came from that great arbiter of taste in England, and the Festival's president, Sir Compton Mackenzie, when he declared that 'the Festival [has] ended in glory as indeed it deserved to ... At the rate you are going you'll be competing with Salzburg before long.'[43] He congratulated Walsh personally on the positive financial result of the Festival, which Mackenzie described as 'remarkable'.[44]

The first Wexford Festival of Music and the Arts received acclaim from all over the world. At home, the *Evening Herald* commented that:

> the town of Wexford has shot into the limelight, having planned a Festival on an ambitious scale ... Their courage and determination should not go unapplauded by the rest of the country.[45]

The *Irish Independent* followed in November 1951, by declaring that:

> Wexford has just given a lead which could with great cultural benefit be followed by other towns throughout this country ... Those towns which are prepared to show as much enterprise ... may confidently expect support from the directors of the National Gallery, from the controllers of the Radio Éireann Orchestra, and from singers, speakers, and lecturers of the distinguished calibre of those who graced the Wexford Festival.[46]

The London *Times* described it as:

> the most ambitious venture of its kind in years. Mr Compton Mackenzie, the Festival President, is to be there this week. He should be not a little tickled at the thought that a talk on opera that he gave in Wexford last winter planted the seed that has brought forth so flourishing a cultural plant.[47]

News of the Festival even reached the United States. The *Boston Globe* reported that

> Wexford's Festival of Music and Art ... was so great a success and its promise for the future is so encouraging that Irish art circles hold it to have been

the most constructive cultural step taken by the nation since the founding of the Abbey Theatre 50 years ago.[48]

Help from other sources was highlighted in the acknowledgments of the first Wexford Festival Programme. The Festival council expressed its appreciation to the Minister for Posts and Telegraphs, for allowing the Radio Éireann Light Orchestra to perform for the operas. Other members of the broadcasting team who were singled out for thanks were C.E. Kelly, Margaret Pigott, and Fachtna Ó hAnnracháin, Director of Music.[49]

This had been a triumph for Walsh. He had the ruthless personality needed to make a cultural venture succeed in Ireland in the 1950s. As the journalist Fanny Feehan pointed out:

> It takes a remarkable and strong personality to achieve anything in Ireland if it is of a cultural nature; and then he needs the gods on his side. If it is to happen in the provinces a monstrous determination is needed to combat the lethargy and inertia.[50]

He may well have been a 'martinet and ruthless perfectionist',[51] but it was that authoritarian personality that would turn his amateur and private festival in the southeast corner of Ireland into a world-acclaimed festival.

∞ **2** ∞

An amateurish affair

It was almost taken for granted that the Festival would continue into its second year. The 1952 programme incorporated four operatic nights of Donizetti's *L'Elisir d'Amore*, with the Radio Éireann Light Orchestra conducted again by Dermot O'Hara. Peter Ebert, son of the prestigious Carl Ebert of Glyndebourne fame, was the producer, Joseph Carl as the designer.[1] It was to be Dermot O'Hara's last year to work at Wexford, apparently following an episode where he requested the curtain to be lifted after one night's production and he proceeded to blame the local chorus for not knowing their music in front of an audience that was just beginning to leave the theatre.[2]

As Walsh himself admitted, *The Rose of Castile* had been presented the previous year amid much criticism. Some people questioned his choice of opera, suggesting that *Maritana* might have been a more popular choice. But Walsh was not interested in popular opera. This was soon understood with the production of *L'Elisir d'Amore*. Walsh himself admitted that his choice of opera 'nearly broke the Festival'. Only on the last night was the theatre full, and this was because of the talent of the tenor chosen by Walsh, Nicola Monti.[3] With the engagement of four Italian singers, three of whom boasted La Scala reputations,[4] Walsh ensured that Wexford would be included on the international circuit of opera festivals.[5]

Following the success of another season, the Minister for Posts and Telegraphs, Erskine Childers, commented that Radio Éireann's involvement with the Wexford Festival was its most important function outside of Dublin. He praised the initiative of Walsh and his friends and said that the Festival was comparable to other significant cultural events that were taking place on the Continent. Childers further intimated that he would like to see other counties in Ireland taking the lead from Wexford. He promised that Radio Éireann would give any enterprise as much help and support as possible. The Wexford Festival, he noted, had already acquired a positive reputation for standards achieved, and he hoped that it would continue on into the future.[6]

12   Nicola Monti in *L'Elisir d'Amore*, 1952
13   Peter Ebert and Bryan Balkwill address the cast of *Don Pasquale*, 1953

And continue it did. The conductor for the 1953 season was Bryan Balkwill, a man who described his experience at Wexford as 'a pioneering job'. Balkwill commented later on that he had taken the job because, in his opinion, Wexford already had a good name. The sense of being in on something from the beginning added to the whole experience for Balkwill. He had worked at Glyndebourne, as had Peter Ebert the producer, and he noted that Walsh had been extremely impressed with the results at Glyndebourne.[7] This third season witnessed again certain strains between the Festival council and Radio Éireann. Walsh had requested a concert on the opening night of the Festival. Ó hAnnracháin told him that the Light Orchestra was available for the 1953 season, but that Radio Éireann would not guarantee their services for further festivals;[8] Radio Éireann was evidently still unsure about the future of the Festival and had no inclination to be associated indefinitely with a faltering scheme.

For this season also, Radio Éireann agreed to provide its Symphony Orchestra for a concert,[9] with a possible children's concert on the Saturday

14 Cristiano Dalamangas, Nicola Monti, Afro Poli and Elvina Ramella in *Don Pasquale*, 1953

morning, provided it did not upset travel arrangements and did not exceed the allocated one hour and thirty minutes.[10]

Donizetti's *Don Pasquale* was the opera chosen, but Walsh diplomatically indicated that Dermot O'Hara would no longer be welcome to conduct at Wexford.

> In a conversation we had last year with Mr O'Hara he mentioned that he would prefer not to be associated with our Opera production this year. Consequently we have engaged Bryan Balkwill, who has had considerable experience both at the Cambridge Theatre with Peter Ebert, our producer, and on the Continent.[11]

Nellie Walsh was clear that the reason why O'Hara had not been asked to return was his behaviour the previous year.

By the end of April, relations between Radio Éireann and the Festival council had worsened. Disagreements arose over the matter of allowing the

15 Nicola Monti, Anthony Besch, Thetis Blacker, Gwyn Griffiths and Peter Ebert, 1954
16 Sir Compton Mackenzie and the cast of *La Sonnambula*, 1954

17

18

17 Bryan Balkwill, Peter Ebert and the cast of *La Sonnambula*, 1954
18 Bryan Balkwill, Nicola Monti and the cast of *La Sonnambula*, 1954
19 Halinka de Tarczynska, Gwyn Griffiths, Marilyn Cotlow, Nicola Monti and Thetis Blacker, 1954

19

Wexford public into the theatre to view the dress rehearsals of the operas. Ó hAnnracháin registered his opposition to this practice and added that arrangements needed to be made for the acoustic treatment of the pit as had been done for the 1952 season.[12] He obviously did not realize the significance of allowing local people to attend the dress rehearsals. Wexford needed the operatic dress rehearsals to gain support, financial and otherwise, for the enterprise locally, but Ó hAnnracháin appeared to be taking charge of the Radio Éireann involvement in the Festival, thus making life very difficult for the amateur Festival council.

Walsh was naturally extremely anxious about this objection put forward by Radio Éireann:

> I am considerably worried at your suggestion that members of the public cannot attend at any rehearsal of our Opera. As you are undoubtedly aware, we charge a small fee to the public for our dress rehearsal, which enables us to make a little extra money, which I am sure you can understand, we particularly need in running our Festival. I cannot understand your objection to this and must point out that both myself, and, I am satisfied, the Festival Council, will protest strongly against this new arrangement. What is your objection to it?[13]

Of course Ó hAnnracháin's objection was obvious to any musical man, and Walsh must surely have seen it too. Ó hAnnracháin made the point that it would nearly always be necessary to stop during an operatic dress rehearsal in order to tweak the production. The conductor or producer would often feel it necessary to make comment to a performer – which would not be appropriate in front of an audience. Singers, too, might well prefer not to 'sing out' during a rehearsal, that is, give of their best, and this privilege would be lost if an audience was present. Of the previous season's example, Ó hAnnracháin said:

> Last year's dress rehearsal in Wexford showed clearly how impossible it is to rehearse satisfactorily with the Theatre full of people. Your point about enabling 'the poorer people' of the town to hear first class opera can hardly have been put forward seriously and if it is a question of money we think some other way must be found.[14]

This was a huge difference of opinion that needed to be overcome before the Festival could presume to continue. After all, the principal artists had already been engaged and it was not feasible to cancel the production if there were insurmountable differences between the amateurs at Wexford and the professionals in Dublin.[15] Walsh replied to Ó hAnnracháin in the same irritated tone he had used in his argument about public dress rehearsals. He did not agree that the dress rehearsal would be ineffective if an audience was present; the public were fully aware of the possible necessity to stall the performance at any stage. And, although the Italians were noted for merely 'marking' their parts at a rehearsal, under the agreement at Wexford each singer had given a guarantee that he or she would sing out fully at the rehearsal performance.[16] Walsh stressed the importance to the town of allowing the local public to sample opera at a cut of the normal price:

> The question of money for the dress rehearsal is naturally of importance to us but is one which can be surmounted. My point about the poorer people of the town hearing first class opera is however insurmountable; in fact, so important is it that if the dress rehearsal is not open to them at these nominal prices so great would be the ill-feeling in the town that it would mean the end of the Wexford Festival. As one who saved pennies to hear opera in Wexford I would think it a most despicable business that people in the town who could never have the opportunity of hearing a great tenor such as Monti should be precluded from doing so *for no reason whatsoever.* I would further point out that when entering into your agreement with us this year as in the two previous years you made no mention of this very important new factor. If you had, we could then have decided if it were feasible to hold our Festival.[17]

Walsh went on to say that the dress rehearsal would go ahead on 26 October, whether the Radio Éireann Light Orchestra would participate or not. A compromise was consequently reached, with both parties agreeing to add an extra dress rehearsal, for the benefit of the public.[18] An overt clash had been averted, but even so, Ó hAnnracháin managed to undermine Walsh's authority. The Music Director insisted that he had spoken to soloists about the arrangement of allowing the public to attend the dress rehearsal, and that they agreed that they had never come across such an arrangement before.[19] He furthermore commented that

> surely a rehearsal which is likely to be full of imperfections and lacking in

continuity should not be described as first class opera and furthermore the 'poorer people of the town' (as you choose to describe them) are surely as worthy of the best as any other section of the community.[20]

One the 1953 principal artists, Nicola Monti, was requested by Radio Éireann to perform with the Radio Éireann Symphony Orchestra for a concert to be held in Dundalk and also in its Promenade Concert on 8 November.[21] Walsh had written to Monti on behalf of Radio Éireann, but noted in a letter to Ó hAnnracháin that the Wexford Festival council had booked the services of Monti as early as the Festival the previous year and that he may not have been available at such short notice, due to his growing popularity on the Continent.[22] In the event, Monti agreed to assist Radio Éireann, for a fee of £100 for each performance.[23]

The 1953 Wexford Festival of Music and the Arts was another success. Patrick J. Little, who had been Minister for Posts and Telegraphs from 1943 to 1948, opened the Festival proceedings. It was significant that a political figure had agreed to do so: it showed a growing confidence in the enterprise, even at this early stage. Little was also chairman of the Arts Council at the time. 'I think the people of Wexford have come to recognise the festival as not only good for the town and county, but for the country as a whole,' Walsh told the press in the same year.[24] The *Irish Independent* made the important point that the Festival had already become an outstanding event in Irish cultural life. Compton Mackenzie told the audience at a Festival Forum, in reply to a query about the future of the Festival, that

> it is something so alive and so big, like living poetry, that nothing can interfere with it now. It is an idle question to ask if it will go on. Of course it will go on, and I am as proud of the honour of being President as I am of anything in my whole career.[25]

Mackenzie paid tribute again to the Festival from the theatre stage following the final performance of *Don Pasquale*:

> I want to pay tribute to this magnificent company. Watching the opera tonight, I could not help feeling that we were linked with Europe and the opera houses of Italy. I can't think of a single town in Scotland, Wales or England, which could carry off such an achievement as we have seen tonight.[26]

By 1954 things seemed to be on a sure footing. There were no particular problems that threatened the Festival's immediate existence. The opera chosen was *La Sonnambula* by Vincenzo Bellini. There was no change in either conductor, producer or designer in that year. [27] The *Irish Press* summed up the curious success of opera in a town like Wexford:

> In Wexford things are different. Here a real war for decent values has begun, and with real prospects of success because the people behind it know what the fight is all about. People elsewhere have been content to follow the pattern of what has been done before, so there are pleasant drama festivals in many small towns around the country, with the usual plays, many of which in their time were box office stuff and are still capable of drawing the crowd, but most of which have little artistic value and very little relation at all to life in Ireland … [But] Wexford puts the standard first.

The Radio Éireann Light Orchestra again took part, despite its scepticism the year before, and Wexford enjoyed four operatic nights and a public dress rehearsal for a local paying audience.

By this stage, the full enormity of Walsh's success was being recognized at home and abroad. An extract from the periodical *Creation* paid tribute to what Walsh had achieved:

> [Walsh] combines genuine devotion to music – and [Wexford] – with an encyclopaedic knowledge of opera, tremendous drive, and a single- minded tenacity of purpose. It may be several generations before the people of Ireland fully recognise and appreciate all he has done to bring international prestige to the little town of Wexford.
>
> Dr Walsh has in fact achieved the impossible. And he has wrought this miracle in the face of true Irish scepticism.

As Walsh himself declared in 1954, 'The first year it was a joke. The second year it was no longer a joke – it was impossible.[28]

At this stage it was still the valuable cultural aspect of the Festival that occupied the thoughts of those at the fore. Financial considerations were dealt with more as a necessity rather than as an issue central to the success of the Festival. An expenditure account of the 1955 season indicated that the bulk of the money spent on production by the Festival council went to the producer, conductor and designer, and the artists themselves. This amounted to £4,150, nearly half of the overall expenditure for the season. In total, taking into consideration the opera performances, the Radio Éireann Symphony Concert, recitals, exhibitions and lectures, along with advertising and administration, the expenditure account totalled at £8,350.[29] The receipts for the income account signified that members' subscriptions accounted for over one third of the total income to the Festival. The deficit for 1955 was £2900, [30] obviously not a crippling amount, as the council prepared for its coming year.

For the first time ever at Wexford, the 1955 Festival managed to combine two operas into an extended season of two weeks. It was certainly an achievement, and the council deserved more than a little recognition, not only for maintaining the high standard of the festival, but also for expanding its seasons' repertoire. The operas were alternated every second night, beginning on 30 October with *Manon Lescaut* by Puccini and followed by Lortzing's *Der Wildschütz*. Anthony Besch produced both operas, while the designer, Peter Rice, had the responsibility for both works.[31]

The Wexford Festival chorus had remained a loyal and valuable part of the productions, and Walsh, though not always on amicable terms with the Music Director of Radio Éireann, managed to secure the services of the Radio Éireann Light Orchestra for each consecutive year.[32] From a peripheral perspective, the continued success was both astounding and baffling:

> Like its founder, the festival is indeed somewhat eccentric, a mixture of fashion and familiarity, high professional quality and endearingly homespun. It began against all the odds, but has survived and prospered. And the town has prospered around it. Wexford has never become an imitation of other glossier European festivals,[33]

the *New York Times* said later although the notion was particularly apt in 1955.

Walsh was honest about the amount of help he had received from Glyndebourne and what an inspiration Glyndebourne had been as Wexford planned its own Festival. To those who were not aware of any connections, Walsh declared that

> since I had first visited Glyndebourne Festival Opera before the war I had recognised from what I had seen there that opera was not just a platform for singers, but an art form in which singers, chorus, orchestra, production,

20 21

20 Elizabeth Lindermeier, Monica Sinclair and Thomas Hemsley in *Der Wildschütz*, 1955
21 Esther Réthy in *Manon Lescaut*, 1955
22 Nellie Walsh and chorus of *Der Wildschütz*, 1955

22

scenery, costumes and lighting all had their place in creating what in Germany they call 'gesamtkunstwerk' – a total work of art.[34]

Walsh and his council had managed to keep very quiet about the fact that the Wexford Festival was helped enormously by the Glyndebourne Opera Festival, especially by what Walsh himself had learned from the East Sussex experience. Ireland in the 1950s was still showing signs of retaining suspicions about high culture, but Glyndebourne became the name immediately associated with the Wexford Festival. Carl Ebert said of Wexford that it was

> just like Glyndebourne at the beginning. Nobody then believed that we could successfully run an opera festival just two hours journey from London. The success of Wexford, is of course, due to the passion and artistic knowledge of its director Dr Tom Walsh, plus the wonderful support which it gets from the local people.[35]

With Carl Ebert's son, Peter Ebert, producing three of the operas so far between 1951 and 1955, it was obvious that a Glyndebourne influence was infiltrating into the make-up of the Wexford productions. In musical and operatic circles, it was not a problem but an honour to be associated with such a prestigious organization, even if it was English. But some voiced strong objection to the very hint of a connection:

> In Tom Walsh's day many of us felt, and sometimes said, that he was slightly prejudiced against things Irish and tended to rely too much upon people from England. To what extent that impression was a matter of his personality, and to what extent a basic logistic necessity of Walsh-standard opera, is un-discoverable. But this dependence upon England seems to be increasing,

Charles Acton remarked in a newspaper article entitled 'Wexford needs to stress Irishness.'[36]

Although most of the correspondence between Glyndebourne and Wexford was not preserved at Wexford,[37] information from the Glyndebourne side makes for interesting reading and serves to highlight the fact that Wexford and Glyndebourne were joined closely in cultural circles and benefited greatly from each other's assistance. In 1955, Moran Caplat, who had become general manager at Glyndebourne in 1945, commented that he was immensely impressed with what he saw at Wexford.

23   Moran Caplat and TJW, 1960s

> I enjoyed myself very much and I congratulate you all not only on the success but on the vitality of the Wexford Festival ... I shall look forward to seeing you at Glyndebourne,

he wrote in the wake of the 1955 season.[38] Caplat was a contributor to the Festival Forum and was particularly useful in promoting the Wexford Festival in England, sometimes through the requests of the council. For the 1956 Festival Forum, the host, Fintan O'Connor, requested that Caplat put forward some possible questions for discussion. John Raymond of the *New Statesman* was to accompany Caplat and Mackenzie onto the Forum platform for 1956.[39]

Another thing on which Wexford had sought Glyndebourne's help was the formation of Loc Garmain [*sic*] Enterprises in 1955, which became, the following year, Wexford Festival Limited. The Festival council had agreed that it would be in their best interest to form 'a limited liability company', to be called 'The Wexford Festival Limited'; it was aware that Glyndebourne had formed two organizations, a limited company and also a trust. O'Connor wrote to Caplat to request permission to view the memorandum and articles of association of the company and the trust document.[40] Glyndebourne readily shared its experience with Walsh and Eugene McCarthy, who were named as the original shareholders and directors of Wexford Festival Limited, with one share each.[41]

The press soon picked up on the negative aspects of Wexford's relationship with Glyndebourne. Charles Acton noted that Wexford had been described as 'the Irish Glyndebourne', and he went on to say:

> There is this danger that the image and feel of Wexford Opera should come to have some of the cosiness and smugness that some people associate with Glyndebourne, so that in Ireland, and even more in England, Wexford should be thought of, rightly or wrongly, as Glyndebourne's provincial branch.[42]

This was not a criticism of the operatic performances or indeed any aspect of the Festival. It was the association with a type of aristocratic Englishness that was viewed with suspicion.

A criticism that was made of Wexford's association with Glyndebourne was the fact that using artists from abroad inevitably reduced Wexford's own involvement in the production of the operas. 'Wexford's super-dependence on the Glyndebourne connection [is] both convenient and administratively useful', wrote John Mulcahy, 'but it inevitably replaces the search for local talent and the fostering of native resources'.[43]

Still, the chorus was mainly local, the voluntary workers were local, and the Radio Éireann Light Orchestra was based in Dublin.

Minutes of the council meetings indicate that the number of local members of the chorus had dropped and was continuing to do so, forcing a greater reliance on members of the Glyndebourne chorus to fill the places. This fall-off in local help was inevitable, however: the Wexford voluntary chorus could not indefinitely commit to the Festival as a firm commitment would mean surrendering much time to rehearsals each year. On the other hand, the Glyndebourne chorus were paid for their efforts.[44] Walsh was fortunate to have such a strong relationship with Glyndebourne which essentially allowed the Wexford Festival to progress year after year. The *RTÉ Guide* was quick to pick up on this fact:

Glyndebourne early on took an interest in Wexford, and their help, in many little ways, was undoubtedly a prerequisite for Wexford's continuing success. And after all, Glyndebourne did for opera in England before the war what Wexford has done for opera in Ireland – shown just what good opera can really be ... That Wexford could be mentioned in the same breath as Glyndebourne and that Glyndebourne would go talent-spotting in Wexford had a lot to do with Ireland becoming known on the operatic map of the world.[45]

❦ 3 ❦

The burden of carrying it on

Preparations for this annual Festival continued on into 1956 with the production of *Martha* by Friedrich von Flotow and *La Cenerentola* by Gioacchino Rossini. Bryan Balkwill conducted both operas, and the designer was Joseph Carl. Peter Potter, a new addition to the Wexford Festival staff, produced *Martha* and Peter Ebert returned after a year's interlude to produce *La Cenerentola*.[1] Mackenzie had promised to write an article about the Festival for the publicity department of the Tourist Board in England and wrote to Walsh in April to request specific details about the coming festivities.[2]

Although the operas continued to be successful and their popularity was reflected in the admirable attendance at each performance, a considerable loss was incurred in 1956. On 7 January 1957, the accountant and auditor, Joseph Busher had produced a balance sheet which showed the deficit for 1956 to be at £2,900,[3] which was not a huge amount, and the words of Mackenzie on this subject served as some condolence for those working so hard, yet struggling to keep the financial side afloat.

> I am sorry to hear you had such a loss – though in fact it is very little for what was achieved. Edinburgh loses £30,000 last year. Anyway I am sure you will override all difficulties.[4]

At a council meeting on 20 June 1956, Walsh made the claim that the Wexford Opera Festival had managed to become the third largest festival in England, Ireland, Scotland and Wales, preceded only by Edinburgh and Glyndebourne. The Festival must be run 'on business lines', he argued; otherwise its future would be in jeopardy. He also pointed out that the entire liability of the Festival was being carried solely by Walsh himself, Eugene McCarthy and Des Ffrench.

24

25

26

27

Members of the cast of *La Cenerentola*, 1956:

24 Patricia Kern
25 April Cantelo
26 Patricia Kern, Barbara Howitt and
    April Cantelo
27 Paolo Pedani
28 Patricia Kern and Paolo Pedani

28

29 Josef Traxel in *Martha*, 1956
30 Gisella Vivarelli and Constance Shacklock in *Martha*, 1956

The question of how to finance the growing amateur venture was a real concern. Further, how was the Festival going to progress from here? The proposed solution to the financial question was to find at least twenty people who were willing to guarantee £50 towards liability. It was decided that since the Festival had achieved so much for the county, if the local people wished for the prosperity to continue they should agree to guarantee the money. As an incentive to those who would contribute, they would automatically become members of the council. At this point, Walsh, McCarthy, Jim Liddy and Des Ffrench put their names forward as guarantors. It was also decided that each member of the council should try to enlist another person as guarantor of the Festival.[5] Walsh enlisted his wife, Eva, who then automatically became a council member.[6]

31   TJW and Eugene McCarthy at a London press conference

Another pressing issue was the poor condition of the Theatre Royal. The issues of rain leaking through the roof and the condition of seating needed to be addressed. As Walsh warned, '[the] dressing rooms are in such poor condition that it is difficult to get artists to come and sing in the place'.[7]

The problems with the theatre had temporary solutions, each year the roof being repaired and the seating attended to for use during Festival week. But a limited liability company, Theatrical Entertainments Ltd, owned the theatre and could not afford major renovations. A local timber company had, however, agreed to take care of the repairs for the 1956 season free of charge. These offers of help were vital. A suggestion was made that the Wexford Festival should seek assistance from Bord Fáilte for the permanent renovation of the theatre. A loan of £5,000 was sought.[8]

In October 1956 a letter was received from the Director General of Bord Fáilte Éireann stating that they would be willing to mak a grant of £1,000 for the renovation of the Theatre Royal.[9] This news was welcomed; however, the success and even continuance of the Festival still depended to a large extent

32 Mario Spina, Bryan Balkwill, Patricia Kern, Graziella Sciutti and Peter Ebert in *La Figlia del Reggimento*, 1957

33 Patricia Kern, Graziella Sciutti, Geraint Evans and cast in *La Figlia del Reggimento*, 1957

34   Mario Spina, Jeannie Reddin, Paolo Montesolo, Gwyn Griffiths, Paolo Pedani, Patricia Kern,
     April Cantelo and Barbara Howitt, 1957
35   Barbara Howitt in *L'Italiana in Algeri*, 1957
36   TJW share certificate, 1958

on its 'wealthy admirers', as admitted by Walsh in 1956. These supporters of Walsh's efforts offered to buy the plot of land at the back of the theatre for the benefit of the Festival. Walsh was also offered £250 on the assumption that the council could provide a further £800 for the renovation of the theatre.[10] But the council was naturally not prepared to spend large sums of money on a theatre that might not be available for their use in the future. As they could obviously not afford to purchase the building, it was suggested that Wexford Festival Limited obtain a long lease of the theatre from Theatrical Entertainments (Wexford) Ltd, thereby ensuring that any money spent on its renovation would benefit the Festival in the future.

The council's time was increasingly taken up with the important issue of financing the coming season. The cost of producing opera was increasing steadily. In 1956, the notion of insuring the artists was discussed. It was agreed that insurance was an absolute necessity to guard against the failure of artists to perform.[11] This served as an added expense for the council – an expense that had not been considered in the earlier years. Eva, Walsh's wife, had even suggested that funding could be raised by the setting up of a 'Silver Circle' that involved collecting money locally in Wexford but also from the rest of the country.[12] Schemes to extract money from the community were generally high on the agenda at the council meetings, but realistically the bulk of the income was donated by the council members and private sponsors at this stage. Little reference was made to the Arts Council subsidy; nevertheless it continued to contribute annually.

The council was promised a subsidy from the German government in December 1956, in the form of part-payment of the artists' fees.[13] This was because Wexford was employing German musicians. Walsh, moreover, received a letter from the editor of the German magazine, *Festival*, stating that a number of staff members were interested in visiting the Wexford Festival, with a view to writing it up and doing a piece on cultural life in Ireland generally. No doubt it served the Festival well to be deemed a representative of progressive cultural life in Ireland. On receiving the letter, Walsh immediately contacted Bord Fáilte Éireann who was the sponsor of visiting journalists to Ireland.[14]

In 1956, too, officers of Bord Fáilte in Britain began to take a real interest in the Festival. Terry Sheehy, who was general manager of Bord Fáilte in Britain at the time, recalled a meeting held at the Café Royal in London to publicize and promote the Festival; the meeting which took the form of a type of conference or luncheon, was attended by Walsh, Eugene McCarthy, with Mackenzie in the chair. This panel was joined by the top music critics in Britain. London editors of papers such as the *Irish Times*, the *Irish Press* and the *Cork Examiner* were also present. Considering the power and prestige of Britain's music critics, this was a huge affair, essentially creating for Walsh and Wexford the ambience of importance which they so richly deserved.

The BBC had a keen interest in the affairs at Wexford, and ran programmes about the Wexford Festival. Sir Huw Wheldon, who later became managing director of BBC Television, had personally visited Wexford to experience the Festival, thus lending weight and credence to the enterprise. The Irish Tourist Board paid for other invited guests to attend.

The Irish Tourist Board in London set up a 'Wexford Festival window' for the purpose of promoting the venture. Sheehy later pointed out that the Dublin Grand Opera Society was *not* aided by the Tourist Board for the simple fact that it held no international attraction on account of it being introverted: it was just a typical opera society, unlike Wexford, where the unusual location, budget, management and local chorus gave weight to the claims that it was a unique event.[15] As Moran Caplat of Glyndebourne pointed out, 'the venerable Dublin Grand Opera Society was in the habit of hiring established productions from abroad and slapping them on, miserably unrehearsed, with singers ranging from the excellent to the execrable'.[16]

The *Wexford People* claimed in October 1959 that

> the Tourist Board had made it clear to them that they were not particularly interested in the work of the Festival as a promoter of the arts, but, they were more concerned with encouraging a bigger flow of people to this country from abroad.[17]

But Sheehy himself refuted this, and declared that Wexford had brought out the cultural side of Ireland. Intellectuals were going there to see opera, and it had waves of meaning for the country.[18]

The Wexford Festival council had managed to uphold its policy of producing rare operas, or certainly ones that had not been produced elsewhere in Ireland or Britain. Of course, this constituted much of the charm at Wexford for the visitors, and undoubtedly there were many who were assured that they would not be able to witness the same performance at Glyndebourne or

Covent Garden. For 1957 the council had chosen another Rossini opera, this time *L'Italiana in Algeri* and also Gaetano Donizetti's *La Figlia del Reggimento*.[19] The council were particularly proud of the fact that the earl and countess of Harewood attended this year's festival.[20]

With the deficits incurred increasing each year, it was becoming more likely that the Festival would be forced to fold. This was alluded to in the council minutes where it was requested that discussions regarding the possibility of not holding a Festival in 1957 should not be mentioned to the public.[21] It was at this point that the first indication of Walsh's intention to resign became evident. Just as the musical repertoire had reached a solid point, financial troubles were beginning to take hold. Work was being carried out on the theatre for a new season but Walsh was reluctant to utilize the funding by donors for a project that might not reach fruition. It was reported that

> owing to the question of future Festivals being in doubt [Walsh] did not want to involve the Donors into a liability if the Festival were to cease this year. As the offer had been made by the donors to him, Dr Walsh considered that the responsibility was on him to see that the deal would only be carried out if the Festival were to continue.[22]

It is significant that at this juncture, the first signs of division in the council became apparent. Walsh requested that a professional organizer be appointed for the 1958 Festival, and also threatened his resignation. He was persuaded, however, to reconsider, given that the council did intend to employ someone to aid Walsh with the direction of the Festival. Meanwhile, every option was considered with regard to extra funding and there was an ongoing application for funding from the Shaw Trust.[23] Sir Alfred Beit, a former Conservative MP now living at Russborough, Co. Wicklow,[24] was investigating the possibility of obtaining a grant for the Festival from the Gulbenkian Foundation.[25]

Beit's interest in the Festival marked an important turning point in its affairs. He was an extremely wealthy man and had come to live in Ireland in 1952, where he housed a remarkable collection of paintings at his home. His knowledge and interest in opera was immense, beginning, like Walsh, when he was ten years old. Beit had a high regard for Verdi and Puccini and also for French and German composers.[26] He had moved to Co. Wicklow to retire from active political life.[27]

37 Paolo Pedani in *I Due Foscari*, 1958   38 Plinio Clabassi in *Anna Bolena*, 1958

Nineteen fifty-eight was another successful year in ticket sales, with the production of *I Due Foscari*, composed by Verdi and *Anna Bolena*, by Donizetti.[28] Manchester's Hallé Orchestra had been invited over to perform in concert and the orchestra's performance was very well received.[29] It was no surprise to anyone that Walsh was beginning to feel the strain. He was tired of the financial burden of the Festival. Money issues were arising year in, year out, but were never resolved. Described by the *Evening Herald* as a 'star matador', he attended a press conference in July 1958, only to be described as embodying 'the bland expression of one who knows that the Press must have their little fling; his the face that launched a thousand Press conferences.'[30]

The confidence of achievement and sense of purpose of the man who had launched such an important cultural event, no longer carried the same air of optimism. Each new idea and new season was fraught with financial strain. Of course, the financial accounts of the Wexford council were not publicly known and therefore the press continued in its praise of the festival.

But there was a more personal reason for Walsh's 'bland expression' at this time – the death of his wife. It was no surprise that Festival activity was not Walsh's priority at this time following the loss of his beloved wife. Eva had complemented Walsh's role in the Festival, playing a very active part. She too, had a musical background, and she had played hostess to many who had visited the Festival since 1951. The Reverend M.J. O'Neill paid tribute to her enormous influence on her husband's Festival.

Eight years ago in those first uncertain years of Festival planning – or perhaps one should say – improvisation, when friends were few, Eva rallied to her husband's side and by her encouragement and prudent, practical judgement helped to make the venture possible. To fit an International Festival of Music and the Arts into Wexford was, indeed, a difficult undertaking. With Tom she realised that artistic standards must be raised to the highest level, but she also realised – with that feminine intuition, which husbands rarely appreciate, but always use – that high standard alone would not assure success. She foresaw that what Wexford lacked by way of a Vienna Staatsoper or a Salzburg Felsenreitschule must be masked by establishing a genuine Irish spirit of friendliness and hospitality, so that celebrities, patrons and all visitors would be made to feel at home when they came here.[31]

Compton Mackenzie, who had known Eva well through his association with the Festival, echoed these sentiments:

Tom Walsh has been the dynamo of the Festival, but he could never have achieved what he has so remarkably achieved without the help of his wife, and to lose her like this is a heartbreak for him and for all those who loved her.[32]

Grief dimmed Walsh's enthusiasm as the next season loomed. At the council meetings, however, serious reorganization of the entire Festival was being discussed. It was suggested that the administration should be divided into five sections – artistic, business, theatre and box office, finance, and illuminations.[33] Walsh would naturally be head of the artistic section, with Eugene McCarthy dealing with the business aspect.[34] This reorganization came in the wake of Walsh's threatened resignation and may have been a direct result of it. Now he was responsible solely for the artistic aspects of the Festival. This was a telling indication that the Wexford Festival was becoming more professional in outlook. The golden amateur period was destined to end, as the days of amateur production became more difficult to sustain; the involvement of the RÉLO was already in place, and now Walsh had made it clear that he could not personally oversee the smooth running of all aspects of the Festival.

Bord Fáilte had guaranteed the 1958 Festival up to a maximum of £2,000[35] and the Arts Council had provided a guarantee against loss of up to £430,[36] but the Festival council had failed to negotiate with the Gulbenkian

Trust for the 1958 season.[37] Nevertheless Alfred Beit had advised Walsh to continue negotiations for future years.[38] Beit was becoming increasingly involved in council affairs and he offered to donate money towards the cost of re-upholstering seats in the theatre.[39] Meanwhile Walsh had just returned from Milan where he had sought and auditioned singers.[40]

Walsh's genuine love of opera and his dedication to the Festival could never be disputed, but the task of presenting opera was becoming more difficult, as he himself intimated at a council meeting in January 1959. He pointed to the added competition of the newly established Dublin Festival that would inevitably affect his own enterprise.[41] In the absence of any solid proposals, it was suggested that the 1959 Festival be postponed. Yet the council was aware that they would lose out drastically if they allowed the Dublin Festival to become established in the absence of a Wexford Festival; indeed if Wexford might not be able to recover its past support at all in the future. As reported in the minutes of the council meeting:

> [it was] understood that Dr Walsh would not be willing to act as Director for another Festival without the Dressing Rooms. To which Dr Walsh said that it was not his willingness in this matter but the fact that it would be impossible to get artists to come and work under the conditions as in the past[42] ... At this stage Dr Walsh suggested that if the Members could not see their way to be responsible for the provision of the money, it would be well to consider winding up the Festival now on a high note.[43]

This feeling was also evident in a letter to his wife-to-be, Ninette Hant, a week later, when he disclosed that the financial situation was becoming too difficult to rectify. Walsh had met Ninette on a cruise, and they were married in February 1960. Ninette's daughter, Victoria, was to play a central role in her new stepfather's life. Aside from Festival considerations, it was a difficult time personally for Walsh and, not surprisingly, he became dejected with the amount of work and fund-raising that was expected of him. He wrote:

> This year a further £3,000 was needed for dressing room and back stage accommodation. I saw our bank manager who said, 'If you can get guarantees for £2,000 I will advance you the extra £1,000.' David Price and I agreed to guarantee to raise £500 each which we can by doing a certain amount of work ...There the matter stuck with the remainder sitting on the fence and

waiting for me as on many occasions heretofore, saying alright I'll find the remaining £800. The meeting on tomorrow night is to discuss the motion 'That the Wexford Festival should be discontinued' – it will be if I don't agree to take over the responsibility. But after eight years I have become sick and tired of finding money.

I will have to decide tomorrow night either to let the Festival end, or to accept the burden of carrying it on. On the other hand, I may be wrong about what will transpire tonight, and maybe they will find the money – I don't know.[44]

As Walsh had inferred, the dire financial situation had, yet again, the potential to put an end to the Wexford Festival.

It was at this time too that Walsh retired from general practice and took up the full-time appointment of Anaesthetist at the Wexford County Hospital.

A letter from Mackenzie to Walsh in February 1959 indicated that, in the interest of the financial well-being of the festival, Mackenzie had suggested his own retirement, citing old age. This would leave the position open for Alfred Beit. Beit was, at this stage, vice-president of the Festival. Moran Caplat of Glyndebourne has claimed that it was he who had encouraged Beit to become involved in the Festival. They spoke while at Wexford (Caplat does not remember the exact year) and Caplat outlined to Beit the significance of the Wexford Festival.[45] The very fact that Mackenzie was considering retirement from his position as president of the Festival council suggested that the financial situation had deteriorated rapidly.

I say again what I have already said: if you think that in view of the finance you ought to make Sir Alfred Beit President you are to let me know and I'll make it quite easy by resigning on score of old age.[46]

Beit was obviously in a strong financial situation and his potential for assisting the Festival could not be ignored. When considering Mackenzie's immense value to the Festival from the very beginning, the situation which the Festival council found itself in was all the more poignant. Walsh had described Mackenzie as 'the first person who made me realise – and I was then just 39 – that all I ever dreamed about, was possible, and for that I will always love him'.[47]

Walsh was becoming increasingly infuriated with the financial situation that faced the Festival. Although the council was in contact with Bord Fáilte regarding the possibility of receiving an interest-free loan, Walsh had set the council a deadline, before which time he expected them to have a number of solutions to the financial problem.[48] His deadline was 9 January 1959 and he refused to budge on this. It was an unfortunate situation, considering that the Festival was in danger of folding simply because it was an amateur, middle-class venture. This had been its very charm from the beginning. Walsh had decided, not for the first time, that his position as artistic director was being compromised, as he was expected to deal with the business side of the Festival as well as the artistic side.

It was surprising then, that on 11 February Walsh presented himself at a council meeting only to declare that he was willing to run the Festival in 1959 despite all he had said before and despite the lack of dressing rooms. He did suggest, however, that he would not be free to give as much time to the organization of the Festival as he had in previous years. The council members also agreed that the burden of financing the Festival should not rest with him. He was busy enough in any case with the artistic direction as the artists were proving difficult to obtain. Walsh subsequently took a trip to London to interview various agents.[49]

The situation seemed to be in a somewhat healthier state with the confirmation from Bord Fáilte that the Minister for Finance had agreed a loan of £3,500 to Loc Garmain Enterprises Ltd. This money was to be utilized in building dressing rooms and in the general renovation of the Theatre Royal.[50] The Gulbenkian Foundation had also guaranteed that the sum of £5,000 would be available for the renovation of the building.[51] The funding was invaluable, and for the first time the council considered the possibility of making the public aware that there might not be a Festival the following year, in order to gauge the local interest in keeping the Festival going. After all, the feeling was that if the local people were disinterested, there was little hope of expecting 'outsiders' to contribute.[52]

The fact that money was needed was obvious, even in media circles, but most believed it was for the improvement and extension of the Festival, not for its survival. The cultural significance of the Festival was always stressed in the reports. The *Wexford People*, in October 1959, printed part of a sermon by Fr M.J. O'Neill, at the church of the Immaculate Conception, Rowe Street, Wexford. O'Neill spoke of the Wexford Festival, not only as a means of entertainment, but also as a means of educating the public in the appreciation of higher and more finely developed forms of music and the arts.[53]

> While we are justly proud of our own national culture, [the Festival] was humble enough to learn from the great masters of other nations. They had as their honoured guests some of the most eminent artistes of Europe. The very high standard of their artistic performances should be an incentive to them all to raise their own cultural standards and make them more worthy of the Irish Catholic Nation. A nation might very rightly be judged by its culture. They could, therefore, realise how important it was that they should, on the one hand, foster and support all that was genuinely artistic and beautiful, and, on the other hand, should reject and despise all that was vulgar and degrading ...[54]

Why Fr O'Neill used the Wexford Festival as a symbol of Catholic nationality was unclear, yet his desire to stress the Festival's Irishness and more directly its community spirit was prominent.

'Here you have something which was created by local effort and was continued by local effort,' stated M.J. O'Driscoll, director general of Bord Fáilte, guest speaker at the inaugural night of the 1959 Wexford Festival, – 'a festival which from being a matter of pride for the town of Wexford, has become something of which the country is proud, and something which is establishing abroad the good name of our people and our country.' [55] In front of an audience that included prestigious figures such as An Tánaiste, Seán MacEntee, the Italian ambassador and Prince and Princess Carraciolo, Verdi's *Aroldo* was performed on four nights of the season. The second work, the opera *La Gazza Ladra* by Rossini, occupied an equally important position in the Theatre Royal that year.[56]

The prestige of the Festival was augmented this year by the presence of the BBC Symphony Orchestra at the Abbey Cinema. Help from Glyndebourne for the 1959 season was recorded in the *Irish Times* in October of the same year. While praising the local chorus and their participation in the success of the Festival, the paper reported that:

> inevitably there have to be a few professional leaders engaged from Glyndebourne, who give added confidence to the chorus. Though some of these will always be necessary, it is the Wexford people themselves who really are the chorus, who earn the praise, whom every conductor extols.

39 Giorgio Tadeo, Janet Baker, Nicola Monti, Mariella Adani, Elizabeth Bainbridge and the cast in *La Gazza Ladra*, 1959

40 Mariella Adalia and Paolo Pedani in *La Gazza Ladra*, 1959

A combination of private initiative, public aid and British help had thus produced a spectacular effect at Wexford, ensuring, as the *Irish Times* put it, that the town was at last 'on the musical map of the world'.[57]

On the musical map of the world

The first indication that the Festival would perhaps be taking a different route in the future was Walsh's admission in October 1959 that the Festival had 'grown up' and

should be in a position to look forward three years ahead. It was now considered that certain changes in the Festival would have to be made, but these would not alter the original character of the Wexford Festival.[1]

There was no Opera Festival in 1960. It was decided in January of that year that it would be necessary to have entire renovation carried out on the theatre before the next Festival and this could not be done by October.[2] The council had managed to produce nine consecutive years of opera, but at this stage it was forced again to consider the permanency of its venture. Its meetings continued regularly, and matters were discussed with the same enthusiasm in the hope that the lapse of opera for one year would not result in permanent disbandment.

The transition from an amateur event to a professional one was subtly introduced by Beit, as his part in the work of the Festival council became increasingly authoritative. A confidential memo sent from Beit to Walsh set about trying to improve the situation in order to ensure the festival's continued success. The council had no choice but to heed him. Beginning with an overview of the financial situation, Beit indicated that the council now had £8,500 for the purpose of building dressing rooms (artists had often changed into costume in their hotel rooms because of lack of changing facilities at the theatre) and enlarging and redecorating the Theatre Royal. Beit suggested that a further £6,000 would be needed to complete the task. He suggested this be sought, not by appealing to the public, but by targeting large business enterprises in Ireland and then a select number of individuals who would be

41 Sir Compton Mackenzie and his wife arriving at the theatre in horse-drawn carriage
42 Sir Compton Mackenzie and TJW

willing to help. At the same time Beit questioned the very suitability of the Theatre Royal as the primary centre for the opera performances. He displayed his distaste for the theatre itself, commenting that 'the more I see of the Theatre Royal, the less I like it'. He complained that the noise of operatic singers in full flow in the tiny space was something little short of 'deafening'. Beit noted also that some of the singers had made complaints of this nature to the *Sunday Times* and to the *Financial Times*;[3] this was bad publicity for the Festival. It was important for Wexford to satisfy its cast, and the Festival was obviously reliant on its international entourage of singers.

Beit turned his attention then specifically to the Abbey Cinema, which he felt should be used for productions during the Festival. He offered to enquire about the availability of the building, not knowing whom it belonged to. He suggested that the Festival council should either enter into a contract to rent the Abbey for perhaps a period of a fortnight each year for five years, including some time for rehearsals. Other rehearsals, he added, could be held at the Theatre Royal, presuming that it was the property of the Festival. He mentioned that if any work needed to be done to the Abbey Cinema, dressing room extensions or orchestra pit, the Gulbenkian Foundation and the Irish Tourist Board would surely agree to use their grant and loan respectively on the Abbey Cinema instead. He added that the economic situation should improve due to the increased number of seats available at the Abbey.

Beit recognized that, with the recent conclusion of the 1959 season, the bank overdraft would probably be in the region of £5,000. However, he first-ly dealt with the problem of meeting all future running costs. According to him, the Tourist Board had agreed to provide £2,000 for each Festival for the next three years and it was supposed that the Arts Council would not renege on its grant of approximately £400. A press report had suggested that the Tourist Board grant would be provided on a £1 to £1 basis and Beit was keen to investigate whether this was true or whether an unconditional grant of £2,000 was being offered.

Most importantly, Beit himself agreed to anonymously guarantee up to £1,000 a year for the next three years, but the guarantee was conditional. Firstly, Wexford town (the Chamber of Commerce, the town council and private guar-antors) had to guarantee a similar amount. Secondly, Beit requested that the council no longer engage the Radio Éireann Light Orchestra. He also demand-ed that an executive committee of the Festival council should be formed, which would be responsible to the council itself and would plan all details of the Festival in the future. The demands made by this prestigious outsider to the group were indeed stringent, but Walsh was in no position to bargain.

Beit expanded his issues, particularly with regard to the retention of the Radio Éireann Light Orchestra in future years by saying:

> The second condition regarding the orchestra may be controversial but in my opinion is essential if the Festival is to maintain its reputation, let alone increase it. I have heard enough to be able to state that conductors of the cal-ibre we engaged this year will be reluctant or may even refuse to appear again with an orchestra of such exceptionally low quality. If, therefore, a new one is to be found I see only two alternatives. The first and the most obvious is that a new approach be made, possibly by a deputation, to obtain approxi-mately 30 of the best players from the Radio Éireann [Symphony] orchestra itself. They are not heavily engaged at the particular season we want them and a new approach based on the money to be spent, and the improvements which will result, should be worth trying. Failing this an English Chamber Orchestra, such as the Boyd Neel or the Goldsborough, might be engaged.

Relations between the public enterprise and the private, amateur organization were on the verge of breaking down again, this time due to the demands of Beit, who had appeared on the scene to ensure the Festival's permanency.

The final condition, which Beit had touched on in his memo, had the potential to cause great distress within the ranks of the Festival council. The suggested creation of an executive committee implied that the Festival council itself could not cope with rising financial problems. According to Beit, the committee should consist of some six or seven persons, among whom Walsh and Beit himself would take priority seating. Two or three more from the original council, those 'who take a real interest in the Festival', would be asked to join this committee. In addition, other individuals, not at that time members of the Festival council, would be asked to join. One addition to the committee, suggested by Beit, but not obviously publicized, was Moran Caplat, as representative of the Glyndebourne Opera Festival for the purpose of maintaining 'the useful liaison that has been established between the two centres' (the link was beneficial and no one acknowledged this more than Walsh himself). The executive committee would essentially plan each Festival, the engagement of its singers, conductors, producers, designers and its orchestra. As Beit pointed out in his memo, probably to the distaste of those already serving on the Festival council and certainly to Walsh, the committee would:

> largely confirm the work which Dr Walsh himself undertakes, but in view of the growing size, cost and importance of the Festival and the additional financial burden borne by a wider circle of people or institutions it should have a final say in all matters of artistic policy.

Beit concluded his memo by dealing with the immediate overdraft incurred by the Festival just ended. Believing that it was not feasible to expect the public 'to make gifts of money to pay off the debts of the past', Beit suggested that a reduction in the overdraft could gradually be brought about over a period of years by organized events such as bazaars, lotteries and dances. Of course, the exact intentions of the committee in this area would not be publicized; merely the public would be made aware that such organised enterprises and events would be for the benefit of the Wexford Festival. In this way, they could see their money being utilized in present and future festivals.[4]

Beit's memo was confidential for obvious reasons, but Walsh distanced himself from it.[5] The public at large was oblivious to the disarray in the ranks; to them the Festival was apparently under complete control. Following Beit's stern indication that money urgently needed to be guaranteed to ensure a successful Festival in the future, Raymond Corish, auctioneer, valuer and insurance broker, named, in a letter to Walsh, those council members who were willing to guarantee the sum of £750 for 1960, 1961 and 1962.[6] But opera was an expensive pastime and this gesture was not in itself sufficient. As Walsh commented:

> Opera *must* be grandiose. The simple small-scale production may work occasionally as a novelty, but in the end it loses out on concept.[7]

Walsh informed his council members what had transpired between himself and Beit. He disclosed that Beit and his allies, including Lord Donoughmore, were willing to form a trust in order to ensure the continuance of the Festival. They would underwrite the present debt of approximately £2,500 and would provide £1,000 each year for the next three years towards the cost of running the Festival. The moves which Beit was insisting upon were definite steps towards professionalization. Walsh also noted that a second trust would be formed to deal with the artistic and business affairs of the Festival, and although the Festival council in its present form would remain in operation, the newly-formed trust would reserve the right to make final decisions on any given matter. He mentioned that he and McCarthy would join the trust with a guarantee of £200 each against the Festival's overdraft, while assuring the council members that all would have the opportunity to join, provided that they were willing to also guarantee £200 against the overdraft in addition to paying £100 each year for the next three years. Walsh also stipulated that the artistic standards of the Festival must be improved.[8]

Beit's involvement with the Festival increased when, in early 1960, he offered to lend the necessary money in excess of the Gulbenkian grant, in order that work on the theatre could begin as soon as possible.[9]

By 1961, it was certain that a Festival would be held that year, but as James O'Connor, press officer to the Festival pointed out, the Irish were 'creatures of habit' and after a year of operatic lapse, ticket sales were very poor in 1961.[10] This was to be the first Festival undertaken without the co-operation

43 Alain Vanzo, Andrea Guiot and Jean Borthayre in *Mireille*, 1961
44 Lino Puglisi in *Ernani*, 1961

of the professional Radio Éireann Light Orchestra. There was no discussion in the council minutes as to why Walsh had decided to engage the Liverpool orchestra in place of the RÉLO.

Beit's growing influence must be duly noted in this instance. His criticism of the Radio Éireann Light Orchestra at Wexford obviously did not go unheeded, and the very fact that he stipulated that all the criteria in his memo be met before he would agree to act as guarantor for the Festival, served to heighten suspicions that he was now at the head of the organization at Wexford.

It had been decided as early as March 1961 that the Liverpool Philharmonic Orchestra and the Wexford Festival chorus would accompany the four performances of each opera.[11] The operas performed this year were Verdi's *Ernani* and Charles Gounod's *Mireille*. Peter Ebert returned to produce *Ernani*, conducted by Bryan Balkwill, another Glyndebourne man, and designed by Reginald Woolley. Gounod's work was produced by Anthony Besch, conducted by Michael Moores, a new addition to Wexford, and designed by Osbert Lancaster.[12] The tenth Wexford Festival lasted from 24 September to 1 October 1961.[13]

In a magazine article of November 1961, Marese Murphy tried to outline the reasons for the fall-off in ticket sales in the first year following the renovation of the theatre:

Possibly due to the change of date – a month earlier than usual – or, perhaps, to the lapsed year, or the almost simultaneous incidence of similar events in Dublin and Cork, this was not the gayest of Wexford Festivals until the latter half of the week. Throughout, however, it was the most artistically successful to date and, with the impeccable co-operation of the Royal Liverpool Philharmonic Orchestra, the operas achieved a higher all-round standard than in any other year of my experience.[14]

Schemes were discussed immediately to combat the problem of falling ticket sales. This problem was perhaps unforeseen by the council members whose main priority was to ensure that sufficient funding would be available to allow the Festival to go ahead.

It appeared that Walsh had taken ill during the immediate Festival preparations and that Moran Caplat was contacted to suggest a replacement for him. However, Walsh was able to continue as artistic director for 1961 but the experience served as a reminder to the council that Walsh played a huge part in the Festival preparations and that replacing him would be no easy task.[15]

The total cost of the 1961 Festival, including the working expenses of 1960, was estimated at £16,600. A deficit of £3,770 was recorded after the consideration of grants and guarantees and it was concluded that this deficit could only be regulated by increased membership and admission charges.[16] It was an ongoing concern that financial support was not forthcoming from the town itself. Walsh was of the opinion that members of the council were in a position to do more to help the Festival, considering the value of the Festival to the locality. Particularly with regard to the illuminations of the town which added to the overall ambience of the Festival, Walsh sought to encourage volunteers from the council to deal with this task.

> I think some other Members of the Council who are business men may realise the value of the Festival to the Town, especially since Wexford as a Tourist centre has begun to be stressed. The value of a £16,000 to £17,000 promotion lasting eight days plus the attendant publicity must be of considerable value from a business point of view.[17]

Beit played his part by paying for advertisements in three of the Dublin morning papers, the *Cork Examiner* and the *Belfast Telegraph* at the end of August 1961, and in the *Kerryman* and the *Limerick Leader*. The cost of these advertisements amounted to £136. Beit did not think it proper for him to be compelled to pay his £125 guarantee in addition to this sum, so he did not do so. He made it known that all the trustees of the Festival had already agreed to guarantee the amount of £125, thus bringing in the sum of £875.[18] Beit further suggested that the method of arranging a Guarantee Fund, of the sort devised by both the Dublin Grand Opera Society and the Dublin Theatre Festival, would have worked very nicely at Wexford, had Walsh and his committee employed the method.

> On reflection, a mistake we probably made was in not arranging for a Guarantee Fund some time ago to cover possible losses. Having myself been a guarantor of both these for some years I have found that they have never yet asked for the full amount. Since our accounts were based on the assumption, which you now think is faulty, that the theatre would be booked out, we must in future have some guarantee fund of this nature.[19]

As well as becoming chairman of the executive council for the Festival, Beit had become the financial mentor at Wexford, a post at which he excelled, and it was not surprising that Walsh handed over this particular burden without much regret. Money remained devastatingly important to the successful continuance of the Festival. Wexford, unlike Glyndebourne, lacked, in the first decade of its existence, a rich patron to privately fund the amateur venture. Now, in Beit, they had one.

Beit's continued dominance of Council affairs left little room for discussion as the original Festival council realized in the wake of the 1961 Festival. The gross deficit was estimated at £8,500 and it was generally agreed that local guarantors had reached their limit. At this stage, even, two guarantors of £50 each had aired their discontent at having no say in the choice of programme for the Festival each year. They pointed out that if they were to continue paying this sum annually, they should have a small say in the running of the Festival.[20] Again the professionalization of the Festival was becoming evident, with criticism arising from the fact that an executive council had been constituted and the original team were left with very little power to affect policy changes. The complaint was noted at a council meeting and the views of certain council members were duly aired:

> There was no function for the Council any more except to provide voluntary

workers and they felt that this was evident during the past year. While they were not objecting that the Trust should run the Festival and make major decisions, since they were financially responsible, and in any event they were made aware of this when the Trust was formed, they were at the same time left to understand that they would have some say in certain matters but instead they were just told that the decisions had been made and that was all. Also more often than not they were not aware of what was happening …[21]

This feeling continued into the new season and saw the steady dissolution of the old Festival council in the place of the new executive council.[22] The preparations for the 1962 Festival witnessed a marked change in artistic policy. Walsh had stipulated in earlier years that it was his desire to produce little-known operas at Wexford, hence increasing the sense of uniqueness at what was being achieved. But for the first time, Walsh set out before the Festival council, at Beit's request, the proposed plan for the 1962 Festival, which included the presentation of two operas, one unusual and one popular. It was unanimously agreed by the council that it was a good idea to combine the popular with the unique, probably because the ticket sales had proved so slow the previous year. Inevitably, it would contradict Walsh's designated plan to keep the Festival exclusive in its productions, but at this point, in order to ensure its continuance, all options had to be explored. Walsh was evidently in agreement with the production of a popular opera at this stage.

Films and lectures as usual were produced as fringe events, and the Festival took on a new title in 1962, the 'Wexford Festival Opera'. Perhaps the subtle title change was an attempt to focus on the importance of opera rather than the actual Festival and its fringe events. It was also agreed by the council members that the Festival would have to be produced for £9,000 – that all possible grants and funds had been extended to their limits.

The hiring of the Liverpool Philharmonic Orchestra in the place of the Radio Éireann Light Orchestra had served its purpose well, and the Council realized in 1962 that the Radio Éireann Symphony Orchestra would be available for the Festival, for a fee considerably less than that of the Liverpool Philharmonic.[23] The Wexford Festival council, particularly Walsh who dealt directly with Radio Éireann, had taken a substantial risk by choosing to employ the Liverpool Orchestra over Ireland's national orchestra, but Wexford benefited from its no-tolerance tactic at this point. Beit had initiated this shift, but the standard of the RÉLO had consistently fallen short of

45 Mirella Freni in *I Puritani*, 1962
46 Mirella Freni and Paddy Fitzpatrick, 1962

the expectations of Walsh who aimed to produce opera to the highest standard possible. Incidentally, it transpired that even the first desk players from the Radio Éireann Symphony Orchestra were available for the Festival in 1962 at an inclusive fee of £1,700.[24]

The artistic direction of the operas, which was, in effect, Walsh's responsibility, was discussed more frequently than ever at the council meetings. Walsh felt his position compromised as Beit strayed from his financial direction, to propose specific operatic productions. In a letter to the council that was read out in his absence, Beit had stated that

> while I agreed to your suggestion that we should put on one popular opera I personally could not agree in any circumstances that we should put on a hackneyed opera such as *Traviata, Rigoletto, Trovatore, Aida, Lucia di Lammermoor, La Bohème, Madame Butterfly, Tosca, Cav.*[sic] and *Pag.*[sic] and the like.

He went so far as to suggest that *Simone Boccanegra* would be an excellent choice.[25] It must be taken into account, however, that Beit had donated £500 to the Festival and had guaranteed a further £500.[26] His private funding was absolutely essential to the Festival's successful continuance.

It was again a telling sign that Walsh was far from satisfied with the direction and financial instability of the Festival, when in January of 1962, he reasserted that he would not remain on the council as artistic director unless Bord Fáilte's grant was assured and the financial liability of the theatre reconstruction was resolved.[27] It was not the first time that the council members had been faced with the possibility of replacing Walsh with a professional artistic director. Walsh's main grievance had been that he felt they left the financial burden for him to resolve, presuming that he would find a solution each year – and he did. His threatened resignation was really the only strong card that he could play, for the notion of finding and then paying a professional artistic director had potential to put a permanent end to opera in Wexford.

By this stage, the old council had practically disbanded, with the executive council functioning in its place. Many of the same members remained but those on the new council was now more financially involved with the Festival's progression. Walsh had to point out in January 1962, however, that matters discussed by the Council should remain confidential. He had met a 'traveller from Dublin' in Wexford who was able to relate to him in full detail, the points discussed at an earlier meeting. This was obviously not a satisfactory manner of conducting business, and it was agreed that in future the subject matter of council meetings would not be disclosed.[28]

It was becoming increasingly difficult to encourage voluntary workers to dedicate time to the Festival. The local chorus was voluntary but was augmented considerably by paid singers from Glyndebourne.[29] Backstage workers, an integral part in Festival proceedings, were all volunteers. The importance of voluntary work to the survival of the Festival was stressed by Walsh, who stated that only the officially appointed staff could be paid.[30]

As chairman of the executive council, Beit outlined the position regarding a Festival for 1962. He explained to the council that there was a moral obligation to run a Festival in view of the commitments to the Gulbenkian Foundation and to Bord Fáilte Éireann in respect of their grant and loan to the theatre. He explained that if the Festival was to fold, the executive council would have to return practically £700 that had been subscribed to the theatre by the same parties. If this were done, the outstanding liabilities on the theatre would create a serious problem.

With this in mind, it was decided that the Festival should go ahead in 1962.[31] Council members who were paying subscriptions continuously requested the privilege of having some small say in the progression of events, particularly with regard to the operas chosen. Beit, too, had considerable say in Festival affairs. He had extensive opera knowledge, partly due to the fact that he was a travelled man, and this would inevitably have given him the opportunity to experience opera elsewhere.[32] By 1962 then, Walsh found himself again in the position of being compelled to discuss his artistic direction at the council meetings. An example of this was recorded in the minutes of one such meeting on 10 April 1962.

> Dr Walsh referred to *The Lily of Killarney* and said that 1962 was the centenary of the opera. However there would be difficulties – the orchestral parts would be out of print although possibly the BBC might have them, the libretto was very bad and would have to be re-written … An Irish character tenor and possibly Veronica Dunne would have to be kept strictly to the budget. With regard to the Italian opera, Dr Walsh *asked for* possible alternatives so that he could fit in artists etc. *It was decided* that the first choice would be *I Masnadieri* by Verdi, second choice would be *Duca d'Alba* by Donizetti, third would be *Favorita*, fourth *Linda de Chamonix* and fifth *Puritani*. Dr Walsh was to set about getting singers as soon as possible, and then *report back* to the Executive Council.[33]

Walsh must surely have noted this decisive shift away from his total control of artistic decision-making, to communal artistic proposals being put forward by an executive council. It was no wonder that the notion of resigning was never far from his mind.

Promotion of the 1962 Festival was seen as a key element for the success of the event. Beit had communicated with members of the Dublin Festival and both he, as representative of the Wexford Festival Opera, and the Dublin Festival put forward suggestions to Bord Fáilte to improve the advertising of their respective festivals in the British press. They also inquired about the possibility of obtaining a public relations officer to promote those festivals in Great Britain.[34] The crux of the matter seemed to be that, coupled with a lack of money, there was a lack of interest. With the reduction in membership fees, it was hoped that there would be a decided increase in membership, but this had not materialized.[35]

47 Ugo Trauma in *Ernani*, 1962
48 Nicola Monti, Bernadette Greevy, Paolo Pedani and Veronica Dunne in *L'Amico Fritz*, 1962

The Festival began on 21 October with Mascagni's *L'Amico Fritz*,[36] accompanied by the Radio Éireann Symphony Orchestra and the Wexford Festival Chorus[37] whose local members had lessened dramatically since 1951. The season finished on 28 October with Bellini's *I Puritani*[38] and the council launched immediately into affairs for the next Festival. Mirella Freni sang the part of Elvira in the production, and her participation was significant. Both she and her agent were satisfied that the experience she would gain at Wexford would benefit her career abroad.

Walsh delivered an ultimatum in November 1962. He stated that if certain conditions were not met, he would not be prepared to remain as artistic director with the Festival. He insisted that the financial budget be in place by 1 January 1963 (this was a condition that he had constantly sought, but which the council had never achieved). He also stressed that the opera policy should be decided by the council by the same date. He was prepared to put on two operas and two films for the week only, the choice of operas being decided by the council as long as they were in Italian, French or German.[39]

At this point, Walsh's authority was threatened by Beit as chairman, who decided that policy statements should not be issued in this way. This was the

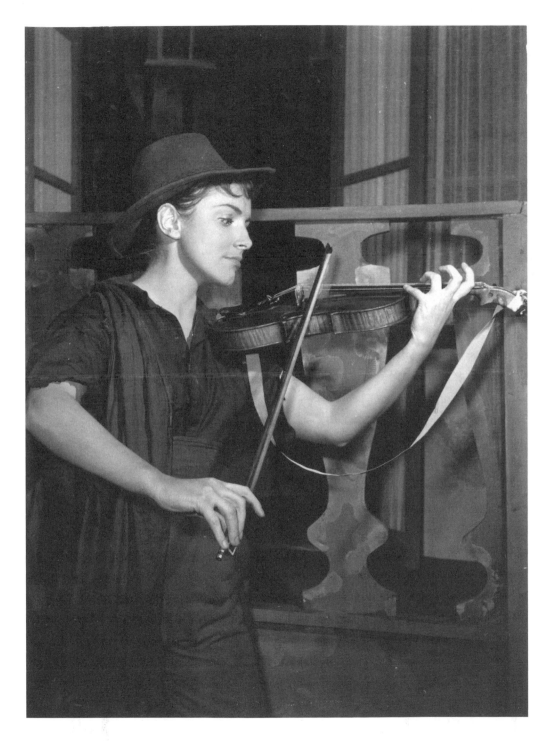

49   Bernadette Greevy in *L'Amico Fritz*, 1962

first recorded disagreement between Beit and Walsh, and Beit went on to give his policy proposals for the 1963 Festival. He favoured two operas, *four* films and one or two symphony concerts.[40] Walsh was opposed to Beit's suggestions for a number of reasons. He pointed out that opera selection was an extremely difficult process. The restriction of language affected, in some cases, the availability of singers. Covent Garden had failed to release any singers to perform at Wexford and continued to turn down all requests to do so. Russian and Bulgarian operas presented distinct language barriers to the chorus. Walsh also noted that two symphony concerts would pose enormous rehearsal difficulties.[41] But Beit's financial aid was absolutely essential and no one was more aware of this fact than Walsh. Walsh had lost the total control and authority that he had possessed since the inception of the Festival.

In an attempt to make the town of Wexford more aware and involved in the progression of the Festival, the Senior Chamber of Commerce had held a special meeting on 12 August, to meet with council members of the Festival. The Senior Chamber pledged full support for the Festival and its members, while airing some criticisms. Beit, for the most part, agreed with the Chamber's points. It was reported that:

> One member of Senior Chamber of Commerce stated that he felt that the atmosphere had been destroyed by the fact that the singers did not perform in the hotels after the opera. This was fully discussed by the Festival Council members. The Chairman, Sir Alfred Beit, stated that he was very much in sympathy with this view. He felt that our Festival was not a Salzburg or a Munich, and that we had drifted from the fun in the old days. Several members expressed the opinion that it would be good for the festival to try and bring back the old atmosphere … A member of the Senior Chamber stated that he felt that the public should know more about the Festival.

It was ironic that Beit should be in agreement with the Festival returning to the 'fun in the old days', as he had not been part of the Festival council at that stage. Indeed, he had had no direct connection with the Festival at that time. He was, however, named among the list of subscribers in 1956. It was true that Walsh had put a stop to singers entertaining guests at their hotels, as he felt it would strain their voices and their performances might suffer in consequence. It was even written into each singer's contract that it was forbidden for them to sing outside the Theatre Royal without the permission of Walsh

50 Alfonz Bartha and Birgit Nordin in *Don Pasquale*, 1963

himself. Walsh indicated to the Senior Chamber and to Beit, however, that he would be willing to grant permission to singers in certain instances, to sing at their will, but those who did so without his permission would be fined.[42]

The 1963 Festival witnessed for the first time the production of three operas in one season – Donizetti's *Don Pasquale*, Ponchielli's *La Gioconda* and Balfe's *The Siege of Rochelle*.[43] Walsh's original idea was to engage Irish singers to sing for this Irish composer's opera, but he found it impossible to do so. He wrote to Gerard Victory, the Director of Music of Radio Éireann, to air his discontent:

> it was impossible to get a cast of Irish singers, the reason for this being that some of our best Irish singers were tied up with Sadler's Wells, and some were simply not interested. In the circumstances, I decided where good Irish

artists were not available, to engage English artists, who were more than pleased to sing this opera.[44]

So, along with the engagement of Glyndebourne singers for the chorus, it was easier to entice English singers to sing at Wexford than it was to get Irish artists. Of course, many artists could not justify singing at Wexford for the fees that Wexford was prepared to pay.

In the aftermath of the Festival, Beit congratulated all involved, stating that the Festival had been 'a considerable artistic and social success'. Bookings had increased once again and it was noted that there was a general revival in interest for the Festival in 1963. Financially, however, it was an unfortunate consequence that all guaranteed sums of money had to be utilized in full.[45]

> I started the Festival when I was younger and much more enthusiastic. I continue it now because we have a good theatre and an excellent organisation but more especially perhaps because I love opera more than ever,

Walsh told the *Irish Independent* in July 1963.[46] Walsh was indeed the last of the great amateurs, and this was becoming disappointingly clear as the Festivals were produced year after year, with a progressively professional outlook. It was inevitable of course that Walsh would lose his grip on the affairs at Wexford, because the more renowned and public the Festival became, the more it required this professional approach. This would never have happened at Glyndebourne in John Christie's time, incidentally, because Christie was funding the venture himself – a luxury which Walsh could not have afforded. Christie had handed over the running of his opera festival to a professional team and he allowed them to carry out their work without interference. But Walsh was the artistic director, a position that was pivotal to the production of an opera festival.

The difference between the aristocratic and the middle-class venture became strikingly clear at this point. Beit was perhaps the rich patron of Wexford but, realistically, the extent to which the Festival relied on its grants from Bord Fáilte Éireann and the Arts Council ensured that Beit would never assume complete authority over the Festival. At the same time, however, his involvement indicated that the difference between Christie's amateur festival and Walsh's amateur one was really a matter of class distinction and not nationality. Both countries were capable of extracting outstanding results from amateur beginnings, differing only on the matter of adequate funding.

Walsh made a statement again in November 1963 to the effect that he was quite unsure if he would remain as artistic director for the following season. It is difficult to decipher exactly what Walsh's reasons were for doing so, but evidence points to the fact that he did not enjoy the position of taking orders about how to direct his own venture. The minutes taken at a council meeting in November 1963 indicated that his suggested resignation was greeted with little surprise:

> Dr Walsh explained that, as already mentioned, there was a 50/50 chance of his not being available next year to act as artistic director. He said that he would be quite prepared to give as much help as he could as a council member, but pointed out that he did not consider it practical for anybody to act as director for a certain period, and then leave, as the artistic director had a responsibility both *for* the artists and to the artists. He also mentioned that he did not consider that a change in the Festival policy at this stage would be a bad thing. The chairman said that he thought it would be extremely difficult to replace Dr Walsh either from Wexford or elsewhere in Ireland and he said he thought it would be a good plan to write to George Christie of Glyndebourne [son of John Christie] to ask about the possibility of engaging a professional artistic director with their assistance. It was finally agreed, after discussion, that the Chairman should do this and that the matter should then be considered further.

Peter Ebert was the suggested replacement for Walsh, but it was thought that he would be too expensive.[47] Walsh had implied that a 'change of policy' might be necessary in future but he did not suggest what this new policy should be. Perhaps he wanted the Festival to change utterly following his resignation as artistic director, so that his private and amateur policies could be easily distinguished from the air of professionalism that was beginning to surround the Festival.

No decision was reached by Walsh regarding his future with the Festival, and by December 1963, he concluded that it would be impossible to produce operas of 'the established standard' within their budget of £8,000. He added that he personally did not wish to be involved in directing 'second-rate productions'. He again alluded to the fact that some group of people might wish to take over the Festival and run it in a different way. It is uncertain whether

51   Joe Breen and his 'opera taxi'

he had a specific group of people in mind when he put this suggestion to the council. In any case, Beit agreed that the Festival council in its present form did not wish to lower the standard of operatic productions to satisfy budgetary figures; he suggested therefore that the Council should resign as a body, if no other solution were found.[48]

By 27 December, it was decided that the Festival should return to its original title of 'Wexford Festival of Music and the Arts',[49] but this was a premature decision, as on 5 February 1964, a unanimous vote by the executive council concluded that, because of inadequate funding, there should be no Festival in 1964.[50]

5

Walsh and Wexford, Anthony and Cleopatra, bacon and eggs

The coming to an end of Tom Walsh's era at Wexford marked a significant turning point for the whole make-up of the Festival. The *Irish Times* reported in 1964 that 'if there is one man who is irreplac[e]able in the Irish musical world, that man is Tom Walsh'. This was certainly a true reflection of Walsh's worth to the Wexford Opera Festival, and the executive council was more than aware of this. No one would deny that he had ruled with an autocratic hand – or that that had not been absolutely essential. As Tony Grey pointed out in his article written eight years after the inaugural Festival,

> perhaps Dr Walsh has been a bit autocratic in his handling of the operatic material of the festival, but if he has, again it has paid off. Too many festivals fall by the wayside because the organisers cannot agree among themselves.
>
> You know the old definition of a camel – a horse designed by a committee. There is none of that sort of indecision and compromise at Wexford. The pattern of the Festival has been firmly set, and Dr Walsh and the committee are not going to depart from it to chase after shadows.[1]

But the entire organisation had changed dramatically, and had been forced to do so by the crippling debts, not least those due to the renovation of the Theatre. Although a decision had been taken there would be no Festival in 1964, the executive council continued to explore avenues to make a season possible after all.

The press became aware of the fact that Walsh was unhappy with the Festival council's policies and was considering withdrawing his support for this year's proposed Festival. Walsh told the *Irish Independent* in February of 1964:

> I wrote to the members concerned, saying that I realised that certain mem-

bers wished to have a change of policy and that I thought that they should have it. I said that if the next Festival was better than the twelve which went before, then they were right; if it was not, then I was right. It was what might be termed a friendly disagreement.

'My job', he added 'was that of artistic director. I felt that when the policy was changed I was not directing.' Walsh implied that these policy changes of the Wexford council had nothing to do with the financial difficulties that the Festival continued to face. 'If we ran it for a hundred years we would still be without money', he vehemently declared.

The ambiguity surrounding Walsh's proposed departure was heightened by conflicting reports to the national newspapers, including reports by Walsh himself. This notion that the council wished to change policy against Walsh's will was not apparent in the minutes of the executive council meetings, and it was indeed out of character for Walsh to discuss council policies at such an early stage with the press. While Walsh was saying one thing, James O'Connor, public relations officer for the Festival, was saying the opposite: in the same *Independent* article O'Connor reaffirmed that there was no dispute between Walsh and the Festival council: 'the Council have at all times supported Dr Walsh in maintaining the tremendously high standard for which the Wexford Festival is now famous'.[2]

Walsh, on the other hand, was reported in the *Evening Standard* the following day, as having declared that:

> If I am to be an artistic director of the Festival I must have full powers. Should there be a lowering of standards because of a change of policy, then I would be held responsible for that falling-off in standards … I can see the right of the Council to take a decision to alter policy. If I cannot agree with that policy, then I have the right to withdraw as artistic director.

Although both had reported that there was no animosity between the sides, O'Connor subsequently disclosed that the council had not intended to lower the standards of the Festival, as was reported by Walsh. But what Walsh had said was entirely correct. The Festival would inevitably be forced to take a different direction in the future due to both financial problems and the increasingly difficult task of engaging suitable singers. Walsh had discussed on various occasions the possibility of his resignation, but both parties knew how important his role was with the Festival. When he no longer found himself in control of artistic direction, but instead having to confer with an executive council, Walsh realized that his position had dramatically changed. This inevitably lessened his incentive to remain. As he stated in his *Evening Standard* interview, he understood the right of the council to change the policy of the Festival.[3] He understood, because the entire process towards the professionalization of a now internationally acclaimed Festival was inevitable. The 'amateur' venture could not survive without funding. Walsh could not provide this, and was ultimately tired of seeking money year after year from various sources, including his own pocket.

The press had reported *ad nauseum* on the proposed ending of an era of opera at Wexford, when the 1964 season still hung in the balance. Sectors of the public were particularly incensed about the idea that the Wexford Festival Opera might be no more. A letter to the *Irish Times* in February of 1964 aired these views:

> So the great Wexford Festival is now no more! The merchant princes have discovered that their short excursion into 'culture' is less rewarding than the more prosaic commerce. Must everything in this little country be judged and valued on its monetary return? Among our small but fabulously wealthy merchants is there not one who could be influenced by something other than the profit motive? When I think over the early years of the Wexford Festival – with the first nights, the mink stoles, the long cigars and the midnight parties – what hypocrisy it all was! The merchants and their glamorous ladies were there only to see and be seen – not a genuine lover of the arts among the lot. Goodbye Wexford. For a few short years you had us fooled. Get back to your trade and commerce and build up those big bank balances with the consolation that, one day, your graveyards will hold some of the wealthiest merchants in the country.[4]

At the last moment Guinness stepped in with an offer of sponsorship for three years, securing the 1964 Festival and saving the Festival as a whole from this type of criticism. It could not have come at a better time for the Festival or indeed for Guinness, who were making concerted efforts to become involved at grass roots level with ventures that they sponsored. It was actually in 1957 that Guinness first took an interest in the Wexford Festival Opera, donating a cheque for £100 towards the liquidation of the Festival debt. It was a novel idea for Guinness to send their front man, Guy Jackson, to converse with Walsh on how the sponsorship scheme would work to the advantage of both parties.[5] The Wexford Festival Opera could not have continued into 1964 without the financial help of Guinness, as the decision to disband had already been reached by the executive council. For Walsh, too, it was a significant event, because it ensured that he would remain with the Festival at least until 1966. Walsh's alliance with Guinness essentially placed the authority over Festival proceedings back into his hands.

Messrs A. Guinness Son & Co., as represented by Guy Jackson, contacted the Wexford Festival council in March 1964 to inform them that the company was prepared to make a gift of £2,500 each year for three years, on condition that the 1964 Festival was 'a success artistically and financially'. The terms of the agreement were straightforward. Guinness requested that the 'old level and standard of the Festival' be maintained and that Guinness should receive publicity in 'a dignified way'. The objective of Guinness was naturally the promotion of their products but it was also stipulated that they were extremely anxious to ensure the continuance of the Wexford Festival Opera. They required no say in the choice of operatic productions. Interestingly, the contract stated that:

> it is essential that the Director and Council agree on all these points and that the Festival will carry on as usual under the control of Dr Walsh as Director, and Council combined.

And so Walsh made the vital decision to accept this offer, given that the financial burden of the Festival had been eased considerably.

It was a strong indication that Walsh had assumed control again when an agreement was drawn up between himself and the executive council for his successful continuance as artistic director. It was stipulated that he be appointed Director of Wexford Festival Opera for a period of three years and that the Festival would be renamed the 'Wexford Festival'. Walsh was also to be appointed manager of the Theatre Royal for three years, with the responsibility of theatre maintenance. Press releases for the Festival would in future be released by Walsh to the public relations officer, James O'Connor, and all operatic publications were to be prepared by Walsh. It was the task of the Council to draw up the budget allowance for the operas, and Walsh was requested not to exceed this amount.[6]

52 Karolo Agai and Franco Ventriglia in *Lucia di Lammermoor*, 1964
53 The cast in *Il Conte Ory*, 1964

For the 1964 season, Walsh himself devised *Corno di Bassetto*, an entertainment based on the musical criticism of Bernard Shaw. Singers for this included Bernadette Greevy, Franco Ventriglia and Jeannie Reddin. Walsh's own brother, John Walsh, had a spoken part.[7] Also performed the same year were Donizetti's *Lucia di Lammermoor*, Rossini's *Il Conte Ory* and *Much Ado about Nothing* by Charles Stanford.[8]

Having informed the press that he was not willing to accept any lowering of standards by the council for the coming Festival, Walsh again explained to the council that he would not have as much time to devote to the Festival in 1965, compared to previous years. He therefore requested the assistance of a personal secretary and permission to make Festival calls from outside the Festival office. These calls would naturally be recorded for payment.[9] It was clear at this stage that Walsh continued his retreat from the frontal position he had held with the Festival. Interestingly, after the intervention of Guinness, financial matters no longer monopolized the agenda at council meetings.

Walsh appeared to be searching for a new challenge, and on 2 June he reported to the council that he had been in contact with the Northern Ireland Arts Council, who had requested that the Wexford Festival perform two operas in Belfast in October 1966. The idea was agreed in principle, but discussion on the matter was deferred[10] and the venture never reached fruition.

Walsh informed Beit in June 1965 that he would retire after the 1966 season, concluding that:

> the Festival, which for many years has taken up all my spare time I now find, perhaps, due to the fact that I have less time to spare, is completely monopolising my life, and so I must withdraw when our three year agreement ends … I naturally will miss the Festival very much as it has been so much a part of my life for so many years.[11]

The executive council was notified of this on 9 August 1965, but it was hardly a surprise to anyone present at the meeting.[12]

Despite grievances aired by Walsh, the Executive Council denied that there were any discrepancies in the ranks. The 1965 season successfully produced Massenet's *Don Quichotte*, Verdi's *La Traviata* and Mozart's *La Finta Giardiniera*.[13] Three generations of the Ebert family took part in the production and design of this year's Festival. Carl Ebert, Peter's father, had made a

54 Birgit Nordin and Federico Davia in *La Finta Giardiniera*, 1965
55 Birgit Nordin, Ugo Benelli and Stephania Malagu in *La Finta Giardiniera*, 1965

huge impression on audiences at the Glyndebourne Opera Festival with his operatic productions, and it served Wexford well that he agreed to produce opera at the Wexford Festival.

A memorandum from Walsh to Guy Jackson in December 1965, however, indicated that Walsh now had more respect for the Guinness contingent than he did for his own council. In this confidential document, intended to discuss the future of the Festival, Walsh began by saying that he had 'little enthusiasm' for another Festival year that would compare to the 1965 season. He made reference to the fact that the financial situation of the Festival would be a serious one again in 1966, believing that the Festival owed the bank between £2,300 and £2,500 *unsecured*. With regard to the 1967 Festival season and subsequent years, Walsh emphatically declared that he 'would not be happy to continue acting as Director of Wexford Festival Opera under the Festival council as presently constituted, though I should be very content to be responsible to Guinness'.[14]

56 Carl Ebert and Ivana Mixova, *Don Quichotte*, 1965
57 TJW and the cast in *La Finta Giardiniera*, 1965

On 8 January 1966, Alfred Beit wrote to Walsh to clear up an issue that had been discussed between Walsh and Guy Jackson. Beit was incensed at the fact that Walsh had indicated to Jackson his disagreement with the Festival council's decision to incorporate only two operas in the 1966 Festival instead of the regular three. Beit was of the opinion that Walsh had agreed to concur with the wishes of the council.[15] Jackson told Beit that the opera which Walsh had wanted to include was Johann Strauss' operetta *Wienerblut*. Beit was obviously uncomfortable about the fact that Walsh had turned to Jackson with his proposed policy rather than to Beit himself, and he continued:

> I am surprised that you raised this matter with him since we had a long and free discussion on the subject at our meeting on 30 December last. Several members of the council participated in this discussion and one or two were in favour of a third opera at the beginning. However, I thought I had convinced the council that for financial reasons and also because we were going to get the orchestra one day late it would be better to stick to the two main operas. Your opinion was asked and in my clear recollection you stated that you would fall in with the wishes of the majority, and consequently the decision only to do two operas was taken. You never said a word about the Strauss operetta.[16]

Beit went on to say that even Walsh himself had been in agreement that the chorus could not undertake three operas, if a chorus was required for *Wienerblut* at all. Beit again stressed that an extra opera for the coming season would put a more financial strain on the make-up of the Festival, bearing in mind that full opera prices could not be charged for tickets to see 'lesser works' such as operettas, or works where 'full blown opera singers' were not engaged.[17]

Beit had sent a copy of his letter to Guy Jackson, and two days later Walsh replied to him, hastily correcting his many errors, as Walsh saw it. Firstly Walsh explained his reasons for not mentioning the production of *Wienerblut* as the third opera for 1966 at the last council meeting. He declared that he

> realised that the feeling of the Council was entirely against the third opera and I had no wish to be out-voted twelve to one. The decision to do two operas only was not taken either because the Orchestra was coming a day late, or because I fell in with the wishes of the majority, but because the Council decided it.[18]

This clearly went to the heart of Walsh's grievances with the presently constituted executive council. He was annoyed at his loss of complete control over
policy-making. He explained further that *Wienerblut* would incorporate a very
short chorus. Although Beit had accused Walsh of agreeing that three operas
in one season was too much for the chorus to undertake, Walsh denied this,
citing that they had mounted three with chorus in 1963. Walsh ended his discussion with Beit by emphatically concluding:

> I do not think that the financial problem should be added to the many oth-
> ers that I have to solve, but I am satisfied that it could be solved.[19]

Walsh was astute enough to realize that if he could work under the aegis
of the Guinness group, rather than as part of the Festival council, money and
financial considerations should no longer be a contentious issue. He was
clearly uneasy about the notion that his Festival had come under the increasing influence of a rich, individual patron. Beit and Walsh conflicted on a
number of issues regarding Festival policy.

The minutes of the early July 1966 meetings were taken up with discussions about the future of the Festival. A replacement for Walsh was the most
significant issue. There were no viable solutions at this stage, for the Festival's
budget would not stretch to employing a really first-class artistic director to
replace him. Beit was in the chair and did not take kindly to the idea of having to discuss this issue at this stage. Guinness and Bord Fáilte were involved
in the discussion, in an attempt to ascertain whether or not they would be prepared to pay for the engagement of a professional artistic director. Both parties declined to comment at this point.

Walsh was at the forefront of the discussion regarding his replacement,
but, ultimately, it would depend on the financial situation of the Festival.
Peter Ebert's name was put forward again. He had served as producer for
many seasons at Wexford. As Walsh then divulged,

> there was the question of prestige and there really was nothing to offer a
> Producer of repute who would consider coming to Wexford ... The qualities
> required were a knowledge of singers and an administrative ability ...[20]

No decision was reached at this point, however, as the most pressing issue was
the oncoming 1966 Festival.

Walsh continued with his duties as artistic director and in April 1966 travelled to Paris to find singers for the new productions.[21] The council's decision to present only two operas this year ensured that there was no place for Walsh's proposed Strauss operetta. Instead, Daniel Auber's *Fra Diavolo* and Donizetti's *Lucrezia Borgia* were presented at the Theatre Royal.[22] The costumes for *Lucrezia Borgia* were obtained from Covent Garden and those for *Fra Diavolo* from Paris.[23]

The future of the Festival was still in doubt. On 17 August, a special meeting of the Wexford members of the executive council was held in White's Hotel to discuss the dilemma of Walsh's imminent departure. Walsh had asked to be excused from this meeting. Des Ffrench, chairman of the meeting, opened the discussion by reading a letter that he had received from a council member, indicating that it would be more desirable for the Festival to 'end on a high note' in 1966, 'rather than to continue on a lower level until we fade out unmissed and unmourned'.

The question was posed whether or not the donors and guarantors who were listed for the 1966 Festival would continue in their support if the Festival came under new direction and chairmanship. It was generally assumed that support would still be forthcoming if such changes were implemented. It was also stipulated that the unsecured debt of £1,700 would have to be taken care of before a new council was put in place.

A very significant question was posed by John Small, council member and owner of Whites Hotel, at the meeting – 'Does Wexford want to continue the Festival?' This was promptly put to a vote at the council meeting. One council member indicated that he did not wish for the Festival to continue without Walsh as its artistic director. David Price stated that he 'was not prepared to go back to "square one"', but added that he 'would support the continuance of the Festival if the standard was maintained'. James O'Connor was indecisive about how he wished the council to proceed. Having indicated that he was 'disappointed' to hear the reservations of Price, whom he considered to be a key figure associated with the Festival council, he went on to say that he could not reach a decision at this point because he was unsure as to what the Council would become involved in. Tom Keatley reiterated the point that there was an urgent need to resolve the problem of accumulated debt.

Not all the council members were pessimistic about the future of the Festival, however. John Small, for example,

58 Nigel Douglas and Alberta Valentini in *Fra Diavolo*, 1966
59 Antonio Boyer and Anna Reynolds in *Fra Diavolo*, 1966

said that he was extremely sad to hear the despondency of the foregoing Members of the Council. First of all he said he would like to declare his commercial interest in the Festival. He added, however, that the town of Wexford needed the Festival, which as an institution of 15 years standing had brought great prestige to the town quite apart from the commercial side, and that without the Festival Wexford would fade off the map. He would give his all-out support to continue the Festival.

The chairman, Des Ffrench, then spoke on behalf of Sean Scallan, who agreed to support the Festival in the future. The chairman's own outlook was quite pessimistic, however.

The chairman said that he was one of the original tribe at the instigation of the Festival in 1951 and his feeling was that the Festival had come to the end of the road [even] without the resignation of Dr Walsh. He felt that costs had risen to such an extent that the maintenance of the alleged high standard would be impossible in any event. He felt that Wexford was too small to support the kind of Festival with which it had made its name, and for which all credit must go to Dr Walsh.

The meeting ended with the realization that unless the council could raise substantial extra funding for the employment of an artistic director and to pay any remaining debt, the future of the Festival was again in doubt. It was also noted that the citizens and firms of Wexford would have to be prepared to contribute substantially to the maintenance of the Festival.[24]

A sub-committee was formed to investigate how much money could be obtained through a local Wexford appeal. On 23 September, it was reported at an executive council meeting that an appeal had proved quite successful and the sub-committee had managed to obtain promises of £1,250.[25] On 10 October, an urgent meeting was held at the Guinness headquarters in Dublin with representatives present from Guinness, Bord Fáilte, RTÉ and the Wexford Festival executive council. The points that were agreed upon were critical for the continuation of the Festival. Significantly, RTÉ was expected to reduce the cost of providing the orchestra for productions from £2,400 to £1,500. Guinness agreed to renew their donation of £2,500 for the next three years and also agreed to provide £250 annually for a party. Although the Arts Council was not represented at the meeting, it was expected that they would contribute £1,000 towards costs. The final stipulation that was laid down at the meeting was that 'the existing high standard of Wexford Festival, set by Dr Walsh, must be maintained'.[26]

The professionalization of the Wexford Festival was highlighted in the number of executive committees, sub-committees and special committees that were springing from the original Festival council. In November, another level of the executive council, the Opera Management Committee, was set up to oversee the appointment of an artistic director. Beit was naturally part of this subcommittee. An advertisement for the position was placed in the *Irish Times*, the *Irish Independent*, the *Irish Press*, the *Daily Telegraph*, the *Times* and *Opera* magazine. A stipulation for appointment was that the suitable candidate would have 'two-thirds musical qualifications and one-third business qualifications'.

It was obvious that, with the transition from amateur to professional values, the council would continue to play an integral part in policy-making, much to

60 Virginia Gordoni and Ayhen
Baran in *Lucrezia Borgia*, 1966

Walsh's disgust. It would not have been an exaggeration to say that, where opera was concerned, Walsh knew best. His first priority was the operatic production at Wexford and although Beit was also a knowledgeable man in the field of opera, his motives were largely linked with financial viability where policy-making was concerned. Walsh's reign was coming to an end after his three-year contract with Guinness concluded and with it threatened the end of Compton Mackenzie's very personal presidential working arrangement with the Festival. In May 1967, Mackenzie had written to Walsh to explain that

> between ourselves, I think I ought to make this a farewell Presidential occasion and hand over to Alfred Beit. It will never be the same for me without you.[27]

This handover had been suggested by Mackenzie when Beit first appeared on the Wexford scene, but Walsh obviously managed to convince him to reconsider.[28] It must be noted too that all the voluntary backstage workers, including Seamus O'Dwyer, agreed to resign with Walsh, although in the event, some were persuaded to reconsider.[29] This was a massive indication that Walsh was hugely respected and his insight as founder and as artistic director of the Wexford Festival was duly noted.

Walsh had agreed to remain on the executive council for the foreseeable future and he got assurance from Mackenzie that he would also stay on as president. Walsh was incidentally absent from a meeting on 7 November 1966 when the future of the Festival was yet again considered. This time the discussion was largely taken up with Walsh's resignation and the uncertainty of the Festival as a result. The chairman read a letter from Michael O'Mahony, a subscriber to the Festival, urging the council to engage a paid administrator to ease the burden of Walsh's former post, so that he could be persuaded to remain with the Festival as artistic director. Many of the council members were in agreement with this request and all seemed to be of the opinion that Walsh should be offered £1,500 to employ an assistant, so that he personally could 'run the Festival as he so wished'. It was even suggested that the executive council should be divided into four committees, the first of these being a Wexford Festival Opera Committee, under the chairmanship of Walsh himself, who would be free to choose his own committee. Five applications had incidentally been made for the position of artistic director, but it was generally felt that Walsh should be approached in the first instance. As the council reported:

> it was also agreed that without Dr Walsh it would be almost impossible to maintain his high standard, since the Festival had revolved around him alone since its inception.[30]

The point that was being overlooked was the fact that Walsh was aware of the strains and compromises of administering and directing a Festival and there was no hope of diverging from the professional steps that the Festival had already taken. In 1977, he cited his reasons for retiring as artistic director from the Wexford Festival Opera.

> I recognised that there were other reasons. I would be retiring at the age of 55 – time to leave the strenuous job which directing the Festival had become, but still time to find another role in the opera world. When I resigned, I had no clear idea what I wanted to do. Vaguely I thought about writing, vaguely I thought perhaps I could retire temporarily and later return to the Festival.

In retrospect I realise now that I had grown tired and that what I really needed was a sabbatical period away from the Festival, just to think.[31]

Describing it fondly as 'the Festival for the man who is tired of festivals',
Desmond Shawe-Taylor indicated in an article in the *Sunday Times* in 1967
that the spirit and atmosphere of Wexford could be retained for the future.

True, it arrives at the fag end of the year, when the travel-stained journalist
may be forgiven if he hankers after a few nights at home with a good book
and an autumn fire and a stack of not the very latest records. What, cross the
sea and sand down through Wicklow to hear a couple of forgotten operas in
a converted cinema! It sounds mad.

Once there, however, the magic works. Nor is it all a confidence trick
made up of Irish geniality, festoons of coloured lights along the narrow
streets, and non-existent licensing hours. Wexford can offer a novel and genuine musical experience: the fun of exploration, the chance of encountering,
in surroundings so intimate and pleasant, a fine new singer from Italy or
Ireland, France or America, in one of those operas that our grandfathers
loved and that we have always wanted to hear.[32]

But Walsh had constituted an integral part of the make-up of the Festival,
particularly considering the fact that the entire idea for a Festival originated
with him.

Walsh and Wexford, Anthony and Cleopatra, Napoleon and Josephine, bacon
and eggs, these things just went together and that was the end of it,

wrote Brian Quinn in *Hibernia* in 1967.[33]

Press criticism, on a relatively small scale, of Walsh's ability to work as part
of a team, particularly from Fanny Feehan, appeared also in the *Hibernia*
magazine.[34] Walsh retorted:

On behalf of many hundreds of voluntary workers, several now dead, who
over sixteen years gave so generously of their time and effort to the Wexford
Festival and their loyalty to me, I challenge Miss Fanny Feehan's 'doubt' that
I 'could have secured the team-work which Ricky Shannon and Brian Dickie
have in recent years ...'[35]

But Feehan was determined not to let Walsh have the final say, and conclud-ed her personal attack by reporting that she 'shall continue to have doubts about co-operation in the early days … Dr Walsh's loyalty to his old friends is admirable and only to be expected.'[36] Feehan had praised Walsh at length in her article, but the comment about non-cooperation had hit him hard. She softened her criticism, however, by stating that

> Walsh infuriated many people, but I don't think there is an artistic director anywhere in the world worth a damn who does not do so. If they didn't have that extra amount of arrogance they couldn't get on with the job any more than a nice, easy-going man can get the best out of an orchestra. Walsh fought many battles, and his most successful was in preventing this marvel-lous festival from being run as a souped-up Fleadh Ceoil. A lesser man would have been swamped by those who can never see beyond the end of their immediate bank over-draft[37]

Even Brian Dickie, who was to become Walsh's successor, recognized Walsh's unique musical ability and intense knowledge of his subject:

> Dr T.J. Walsh … probably knows more about the history of opera in Ireland and Irish opera than anyone else alive.[38]

Perhaps the most significant story appeared in a newspaper, the *Free Press*, (a cutting of which Walsh kept), quite possibly written by a friend of Walsh's. Some articles that he kept in his files were anonymous letters to the editors of various newspapers, to which he had added names of those he believed to have written them. The article implied that Walsh was in a way ousted from his position with the Festival, partly by those who believed they knew best and partly by the inevitable professionalisation of the venture. The story took the form of an old-type children's story and is worth relaying in full.

THE DWARFS WITHOUT SNOW WHITE

> Once upon a time in a land far away there were seven little dwarfs, none of whom at that time had even heard of Snow White (or any other detergent) for that matter, and the names of the seven were Grumpy, Dopey, Sleepy, Sneezy, Happy, Bashful and Doc.

At one time the seven little dwarfs decided to hold an annual celebration and to organise and arrange that celebration the six, by unanimous choice, selected Doc [Walsh]; for you can see by their very names, which were appropriate, that only Doc had any qualifications.

Under Doc's guidance, the annual celebration became a great success and in time the celebration became known all over Fairyland. However, one year all the dwarfs, with the exception of Doc of course, decided Doc was getting a bit old for the job, and decided to appoint a successor to him.

Later they heard of Dick Whittington [Brian Dickie] who was making a wonderful name for himself, and so they appointed him.

Now Dick proved such a success at the job that he won applause from all the folk of fairyland and the six little dwarfs were very pleased with him and got on such friendly terms with Dick that they put a pet name on him.

About that time the six dwarfs became the owners of a wonderful mirror which could foretell the future and could also speak. It was known as the Flattering Mirror, for each day the six little dwarfs would individually and secretly go to the mirror and say: 'Mirror, mirror, on the wall, which of us is best of all?' And the mirror would reply: 'You dear Dopey (or whoever it might be), are the best; you're a better man than all the rest.'

Having made such a grand success of his first year, Dick was invited back again to organise the merriment and fun. The next year, when he was busily arranging all the events, the six little dwarfs came to him and said, 'We have appointed six others to help you next year.'

Now Dick didn't know what to say, because he thought he was doing very well on his own, but as the statement of the dwarfs implied that he would be appointed again next year he decided that it would be best to be discreet.

'Why should six be selected to help me?' he asked.

'We thought it was a good idea, said the six vaguely. Dick could do nothing but agree, but the next year there were seven organising the fun and merriment and a strange thing happened: the Magic Mirror never spoke again. It did not know what to say anymore.[39]

The implication of the story was clear enough. The magic of the original Wexford Festival had been extinguished. Needless to say, fingers were crossed for the future.

6

The professional amateurs

The rift between Walsh and the executive council was becoming more apparent as the 1967 Festival began its seasonal plans. Walsh had refused to return to council meetings until certain conditions laid down by him were met. Ffrench had had a meeting with Walsh in the Theatre Royal and an inventory of the furniture that Walsh owned was recorded. At an executive council meeting in January 1967, it was agreed that tapes of performances should be presented to Walsh. Copies of these tapes could be made at the council's expense. It was further agreed at the meeting that Colonel Price would approach Walsh in an attempt to encourage him to resume his position as an integral part of the executive council.

The appointment of Brian Dickie as artistic director of the Wexford Opera Festival marked a decisive shift from the amateur charm that the Festival had under Walsh. Walter Legge had accepted the position but had to withdraw after falling ill. Dickie's salary was set at £1,200 plus foreign travel expenses of £200 and £100 to cover domestic travel. The link between Glyndebourne and Wexford became more apparent than ever during Dickie's term as artistic director. His associations with Glyndebourne were well known, and as early as February he suggested that the Glyndebourne contract form should be adapted to suit Wexford. Further, Glyndebourne now offered Wexford its 'members mailing list' which ran to 4,000 names. Discussion at this meeting also centred on the possibility of a visit of a BBC camera team to the Festival.[1]

Meanwhile the relationship between the executive council and its previous artistic director had reached its lowest point. In a letter to the chairman in June 1967, Walsh made his feelings clear:

> I should be obliged if you would tender my resignation as a member of the Wexford Festival council at your next council meeting. As I am writing I should also like to suggest that it would be better that council members did

61   The cast of *Otello*, 1967

not discuss either Wexford Festival Opera or Belfast Opera with me in future on social occasions.[2]

Walsh was incensed by the fact that he had been asked by the council to return the keys of the office to the executive council and two files that had been removed from the office. Furthermore, the chairman had undertaken to ask Walsh to return all property belonging to the council that was in the possession of Walsh at his home.[3] Walsh was by this stage becoming more involved with the Ulster Opera, and for its 1967 season he was its Honorary Opera Adviser.

But surprisingly, by 16 August Walsh had again withdrawn his resignation from the council. The council were relieved that cordial relations had been restored.[4] Walsh did not want to jeopardize the success of the forthcoming Festival.

Two operas were performed in 1967 – Rossini's *Otello* and Charles Gounod's *Roméo et Juliette*. Albert Rosen conducted the RTÉ Symphony Orchestra for the performances of *Otello*, and David Lloyd-Jones, conducting for the first time in Wexford, conducted *Roméo et Juliette*. The Festival performances began on 21 October and continued until 29 October. The *Sunday Independent* reported that Compton Mackenzie had expressed his desire to 'keep the Festival intimate' and he added that he 'wouldn't like to see the Festival become too expanded and thus become perhaps a financial burden'.[5] There was indeed a recurring concern that the Festival was moving away from the intimacy of its early days.

It was not long before Walsh again aired his discontent to the executive council and explained his reasons for withdrawing his resignation from the council in August. In a letter that was read by the chairman at an executive council meeting on 3 November 1967, he stipulated that he did not wish for any plaque or 'demonstration of appreciation' to be considered for him (he had read in the local paper that this was under consideration at the time).[6] Walsh went on to say that

> when we have arranged affairs in the Theatre next December I intend to resign from the Council. My reason for allowing my name to remain among the list of members this first year of my retirement was to keep private the fact that a serious rift exists between us, which had it become known to the Press could, I believe, have done the Festival harm. The absence of my name from the list of members in future years, will, I feel, pass unnoticed.

Walsh had never been so infuriated. He added:

> Finally, may I suggest that the ending of the pretence that I still have any interest in or connection with the Wexford Festival will save us both a considerable amount of pointless correspondence.[7]

The 'affairs in the Theatre' that Walsh alluded to most likely referred to the various items that Walsh believed to be his, but that still remained in the Theatre Royal.

On 23 January 1968, Walsh's letter of resignation was finally accepted by the executive council. He had again listed reasons for his decision to resign, this time his main reason being,

> the defamatory remarks made by Mr Dickie to the Press during the 1967 Festival concerning [Walsh's work] as Director of the Festival and the fact that the Council had condoned these remarks by making no protest whatsoever.[8]

But Walsh's grievances had been aired even before the 1967 Festival, and it would appear that Dickie's comments about Walsh were enough to ensure that he would proceed with his resignation.

Walsh's departure passed as an unmarked event, as he had indicated he would prefer, but his resignation would undoubtedly have repercussions for the successful future of the Festival. Its founder no longer wished to be associated with the enterprise, a fact that was not made known publicly for fear that it would cause decline in the Festival's popularity.

In addition to the disruption involved inemploying a new artistic director for the first time, it was noted at an executive council meeting in March 1968 that, aside from hotel contributions in the locality, Wexford local financial support remained poor. It was agreed that letters should be sent out to individuals to encourage them to make a contribution towards the pending 1968 Festival.[9] It was also decided to raise the price of seats and membership subscriptions.

The growing concern about financial uncertainty was compounded in June 1968 when an article appeared in the *Irish Times*, indicating that 'Organisers of Festivals need more help'. The report went on to comment how festivals, the Wexford Festival in particular, had a positive influence on its surrounding county:

> Tourism officials have for a considerable time recognised that festivals are an ideal way of extending the tourism season in any given area, and also that they are responsible for bringing local people together, hopefully – in harmony … Festivals which can be cited as outstanding successes are the Wexford Opera Festival and the Kilkenny Beer Festival, both of which are rated among the best of their kind in Europe.[10]

The 'outstanding success' of the Wexford Festival was reflected in a critically acclaimed season in 1968. With performances of Mozart's *La Clemenza di Tito*,

Bizet's *La Jolie Fille de Perth* and Rossini's *L'equivoco stravagante* the season extended from 25 October to 3 November. The Taoiseach, Jack Lynch, was reported in the *Evening Press* as saying that 'Wexford is Tops' and that

> the Festival was clearly in the class that had gained its international reputation. Its prestige was in no small measure due to a special quality of thoroughness which was typical of all good Wexford products including their hurling teams.[11]

When evaluating the success of the 1968 Festival, Brian Dickie's commitment to Wexford came into question. The then chairman of the executive council, Des Ffrench, had decided to write to Dickie to enquire as to why he had spent so little time in Wexford and why there was an apparent lack of control of stage staff. Dickie had aired his own grievances previously, and these were put before the council in January. Dickie replied that he could not guarantee that the figures next year would not also exceed the budget as long as he was presented with what he described as a 'shoe-string budget'.[12] The council had made it clear to Dickie that he must keep to the budget that had been put in place. In Walsh's time, Walsh himself would have set about finding the extra money required for the maintenance of performance standards. Dickie, as a professional employee of the Wexford Festival, however, felt no need to concern himself with such financial matters.

The increased reliance on help from Glyndebourne was apparent again in early 1969 when the Glyndebourne Festival requested that the Wexford council increase the amount paid to Glyndebourne in administration costs by £50 per annum. The Wexford Festival council had no option but to agree.[13] Relations with Glyndebourne had always been amiable and were of huge importance for the successful continuation of opera at Wexford.

By May 1969, tentative discussions had begun about the 1970 season. Sean Scallan was particularly concerned, due to the fact that all contracts between the Wexford Festival and its sponsors ceased at the end of the 1969 Festival. An additional £4,000 was necessary if the Festival was to continue. It was agreed that the acquisition of another sponsor was desirable and the council decided to discuss the matter with Guy Jackson of Guinness following a press conference that was due to take place in Dublin.[14]

The Guinness conference proved to be very successful from the Wexford Festival's point of view. The executive council was represented at the conference by Brian Dickie, Bernard Doyle, John Small and the chairman, Des Ffrench. Guy Jackson represented Arthur Guinness, T. O'Gorman was present on behalf of Bord Fáilte, Mervyn Wall represented the Arts Council, and Gerard Victory was present from RTÉ. There was unanimous agreement that the Wexford Festival should continue and that, in order to make this possible, sponsors of the Festival would increase their subsidies. The grip that the executive council had enjoyed on the Festival was beginning to weaken, however, and this was evident with the growing strength of the sponsors with regard to the Festival. It was inevitable that the sponsors would eventually want to become involved in policy-making, to ensure that the Festival did not lapse. The situation had been similar to that which transpired when Beit joined the Festival council. Beit had not been prepared to hand money over to a council with which he was not involved. Luckily, when the future of the Festival was threatened in mid-1969, the Festival's sponsors agreed to increase their subsidies. But this came with a price. Both Mervyn Wall of the Arts Council and Gerard Victory of RTÉ suggested that the Wexford Festival should do modern opera in English.[15]

In the end, Haydn's *L'infedeltà Delusa* and Verdi's *Luisa Miller* were performed in 1969. Bernadette Greevy was part of the cast in *Luisa Miller*, but the newspaper reports were far from kind. An *Evening Press* reviewer commented:

> On the whole I am afraid, this has been a most disappointing festival. It has taken almost 20 years to build up the highly international reputation of Wexford Opera, and I think the time has come for those in charge of the festival to consider very seriously whether these standards are being maintained. For this year at any rate they are not.[16]

The Festival executive council correctly pointed out that 'the Irish critics had given us very adverse notices but on the other hand the English papers had been more favourable'.[17]

Looking ahead to the following year, it was agreed that the main production in 1970 'must be excellent'.[18] Press criticism in 1969 stemmed from Irish dissatisfaction with Wexford's apparent growing reliance on Glyndebourne support. The Festival council, however, was satisfied that this was not the case:

> Regarding the press criticism of the growing influence of Glyndebourne, Mr

Dickie informed the Council that he had done a random check on the number and, with the exception of the technical staff, there were less people employed now who had Glyndebourne connections than there had been before 1967.[19]

The financial strain on council affairs had not eased by the time the 1970 Festival was about to begin. £4,000 was needed to supplement the increased costs of the artists, the conductors and the producers. At an executive council meeting in September 1970, Dickie aired some of his views about how to meet rising costs. First of all, he pointed out that an extra £8,000 was needed – £4,000 to cover rising costs of 1970 and £4,000 for the following year. He suggested that the Wexford Festival should produce only two operas in 1971 and that the price of seats should be increased. He argued that more money could be collected locally by voluntary efforts. This last suggestion must have particularly aggravated council members who had been making concerted efforts each year to raise money for the Festival. The entire discussion was then turned back on Dickie and he was criticized for his inability to stay within the allotted budget for the pending 1971 season.

> It was pointed out to him [Dickie] that at the moment the problem was where we would get the money for this year. Mr Scallan stressed the fact that the Budget had been drawn up in November [1970] and that Mr Dickie had said that he was quite happy with it. Since that date he and the secretary had amended it frequently according as events warranted it. They had had no indication until late July that the fees would go so far astray. Mr Lambert felt that it was just a farce for the committee to waste [its] time drawing up a budget when no attention was paid to it ...[20]

The council was in agreement that money needed to be found to ensure that the forthcoming Festival was not sub-standard.

On the eve of the 1970 Festival (with its double bill of Rossini's *L'inganno Felice* and Donizetti's *Giovedi Grasso*, Delibes' *Lakmé* and Britten's *Albert Herring*), the *Enniscorthy Echo* was positive about the overseas support, even if local support was less impressive. It reported that 'overseas bookings have trebled'; and,

> When asked to comment on the slowness of Wexford bookings [a festival

62 Ugo Benelli, 1970

spokesman] replied, 'I think our people are inclined to leave it to the last minute. However, this is Wexford's own festival and it is a festival of far greater prestige than any other in this country and many in Europe. I would be sorry to see any festival audience with a minority of Wexford people in it. With a steady stream of bookings daily from outside, our concern is that when Wexford people go to book them they may not be there.'[21]

It became apparent in early 1971 that a large Festival was planned in Ulster and that it would include operatic performances. The Wexford Festival executive council acted quickly to contact the Arts Council of Northern Ireland to enquire as to when this Ulster Festival was being planned. It would most definitely have impinged upon a successful audience at Wexford had the dates of the Festivals coincided. Christopher Fitz-Simon of the executive council added that he had heard what he deemed to be a 'most unusual complaint' in Bord Fáilte – 'that the Festival was attracting too many overseas visitors and that maybe we would lose our Irishness'.[22] This was a recurring observation in media circles and the executive council no doubt feared that this type of publicity would affect its efforts to gain financial support locally.

Brian Dickie was quoted in the *Cork Examiner* in May 1971 as saying that there was a 'resistance to change' at Wexford:

Brian Dickie said that it was no secret that there was a resistance to change at Wexford … Mr Dickie was referring to the practice of producing two little-known operas coupled with a third wider-known one. This policy was a good one and one which he still believed to be the right one for Wexford.[23]

As had become the norm, three operas were indeed performed in 1971; Bizet's *Les Pêcheurs de Perles*, Puccini's *La Rondine* and Mozart's *Il re pastore*. The Festival lasted for ten nights, from 21 October to 31 October. The critics were satisfied with the standard that had been achieved, commenting that 'opera succeeds with zest and conviction'[24] at Wexford. It was further noted that 'Wexford is not so much a festival as a way of life. What other festival is so incongruous and so intimate, so friendly and so fantastical?'[25]

Harold Rosenthal, editor of *Opera* magazine, kindly contributed an article to the newspaper *Hibernia* to coincide with the Festival. Interestingly, he divulged that he

> fail[ed] to discern any real shape or artistic purpose in the way the Festival is planned. But then perhaps that is the peculiar charm of Wexford, which appeals to so many of its regular visitors, and which I find so baffling.[26]

Anthony Lewis of the *New York Times* described the sheer experience of the Festival.

> The romantic quality that we outsiders find so attractive in the Irish, the ability to escape one way or another from the hard world of fact, is gloriously illustrated by the opera Festival.[27]

Dickie's dedication had again come under scrutiny in June 1971, however. Beit was the first to pose the question whether or not Dickie was devoting enough 'time, drive and energy' to his work at Wexford. Des Ffrench felt that 'Dickie's first allegiance was to Glyndebourne'. Beit was further concerned because few 'exciting new discoveries' had been made in recent years with regard to singers.[28] It was unfair to compare Dickie to the local doctor whom he had replaced, but the fact that a professional artistic director had been appointed clearly did not rest easy with the council. It would take time for the council members to learn the new director's ways.

There was a general feeling among the council members that there was perhaps too little work being done between meetings. The intentions of the group were clear, yet the group was relatively large in size and decisions were becoming more difficult to reach. Of course, the problem was obvious – the

63   The chorus in *La Rondine*, 1971

council lacked the leadership of Walsh. As instigator of the Festival, Walsh had been the dominant figure at council meetings and the most valued member in decision-making. It was decided in November 1971, then, that a sub-group of five members of the executive council should be elected with the power to make quick and decisive decisions on behalf of the council.[29] This, it was felt, would ensure that the council could in future work more efficiently. The growing professionalism of the organization demanded this type of efficiency.

The question of chairman of the executive council was another important matter that coud impinge on the effectiveness of the council as a working body. It was proposed that Sean Scallan be re-elected as chairman. Scallan himself had some reservations about this; he believed that the term of office should only last for one year and that more council members should be given the opportunity to act as chairperson for a period of time. According to Scallan, if more council members were involved,

> it would overcome (1) the lack of overall knowledge of the workings of the Festival amongst the council members and (2) that if the chairman stays too long in office he is likely to part on bad terms with the council.[30]

Scallan's final comment was surely a reminder for the council members present that relations with Walsh was particularly tense since his departure from Festival affairs. It was noted, however, that the sponsors of the Festival would not be satisfied to see a new chairman appointed every year.[31] This point again highlighted the control that the Festival's sponsors now had over policy.

It was further proposed that at least two deputy chairmen should be appointed to assist the chairman and to learn, from a practical point of view, how best to carry on the position in the future. This method would ensure continuity for the Wexford Festival. Beit suggested retiring as vice-chairman but was persuaded to retain the position 'as his help and guidance were of great assistance'.[32]

It became apparent in 1972 that Derek Bailey from London Weekend Television had spent some time in Wexford and had expressed an interest in preparing a feature on the Festival.[33] The publicity was invaluable yet it doubtless fuelled the argument that the Festival was attracting foreign visitors rather than Irish opera lovers. A discussion took place on the problems of the acoustics in the Theatre Royal – a solution to which was urgent if London

64 Jack Lynch and Mayor Jim Jenkins, 1970s

Weekend Television were going to publicize opera at Wexford.[34] Talks continued in 1972 about the importance of the Festival looking 'to the future' rather than taking one Festival at a time.[35] Dickie's comments on the Festival were again captured in print and what he had to say certainly had a positive effect on the critical acclaim of the Festival.

> What does the festival do for Wexford? Mr D.[Dickie] sees it in terms of a cosy family hobby in which everybody co-operates to produce something enjoyable, something that improves the quality of life for the local people. That is the important part of it.[36]

The 1972 opera season began with von Weber's *Oberon* and also produced Bellini's *Il Pirata* and Janáček's *Katá Kabanová*. Following this season, advertisements appeared in English and Irish newspapers and *Opera* magazine for a new artistic director.[37] This change would mark a further turning point in the Festival's history.

Probably one of the most poignant events in the history of the Festival was the announcement of the death of Sir Compton Mackenzie in 1972. As Walsh had written to Mackenzie's third wife on the death of her husband, the Festival was completely indebted to the man:

> Monty's influence on my life has been enormous – as his influence was on so many lives. Not alone in the twenty odd years before when I was searching like so many other young men for a broader and fuller life he gave it to me through the pages of *The Gramophone* and through many of his novels which told me much about the world before I had discovered those things for myself.
>
> I need not go into what he did for Wexford and the Festival except to say that had it not his tremendous prestige and backing in the beginning it never would have happened. It exists today as one of the many lost causes in which he believed, but which because he believed in them somehow took root and flourished.[38]

Mackenzie's death marked the end of the old guard at Wexford. He had threatened to leave before when Walsh resigned but had been persuaded to retain his position. He was the remaining link to the memories of the how the Festival had come about. The presidential position was now vacant for the first time since the inception of the Festival.

Mackenzie was the first man to understand the financial burden of events such as opera festivals and had commented to Walsh in the beginning about how the Edinburgh Festival had similar financial concerns. Things had not changed by 1973, and financing the next season was again the burning issue. The Governor of the Bank of Ireland was approached to lend financial support. Interestingly, one of the questions he put to the Festival council was what kind of support was available from local firms. It was further decided to approach the Government and to notify them of the future plans of the Festival.[39]

By February 1973, applications had been received for the position of artistic director, although interestingly not one of the applicants was Irish.[40] It was unanimously agreed at an executive council meeting that Thomson Smillie be appointed. His contract would initially be for one year, to be extended to a two-yearly contract. Smillie had worked as a public relations officer for Scottish Opera. According to the chairman of the executive council, Sean Scallan, 'he has been in Wexford and is aware of our *special situation*'. The

Council was generally satisfied with the high standard of applications that they had received for the position.[41] This was a positive sign that Wexford had managed to retain its international standing on the opera scene.

The growing professionalism of the executive council was again apparent with the establishment of a fringe group, the Wexford Festival Development Council. This was set up to look at the future of the Festival. Clearly the work of the existing executive council centred on the daily organization of affairs, and policies for the future were not being explored to their full potential. The first decision taken by the council was to agree a sum of £300 to send John Boyle, a council member, on a fundraising trip to America. It was evident from this action that the future of the Festival was heavily reliant on outside and foreign help. This increased professionalism could further be seen in the discussion that took place regarding the safekeeping of the minutes book and also the press cuttings that were housed in the theatre.[42] This had never arisen as an issue before. It was agreed thereafter that this material would be stored in a fireproof location.[43] Up to such time, as a safe was built, the material would be stored in the bank. It seemed that, suddenly, the executive council had begun to take notice of the importance of the whole enterprise and of the archiving of its history.

A further discussion at this meeting concluded with the agreement that 'Wexford Festival policy regarding opera selection was "no policy".'[44] The executive council was obviously reiterating the point that it wished to maintain complete control over the operas that were performed at Wexford. Yet publicity and press relations were not in the hands of the executive council, a fact that became obvious at a meeting that took place between the major publicity agents involved, in March 1973. Bord Fáilte and Guinness were among the bodies that were represented at the meeting; the publicity aims of each body were discussed and 'a policy of full information exchange between the various groups was determined upon for future festivals'.[45]

The financial situation seemed somewhat healthier in June of 1973 with the agreement of Guinness to provide an extra £1,500 for the Festival. Bord Fáilte agreed to provide £1,400 and the Arts Council promised an additional £1,000. Discussions were ongoing about the possibility of approaching the Government for a direct contribution towards running costs.[46] Matters had come to a head in November when it was suggested that 'a direct attack should be made on the Government for funds'.[47]

In July 1973, the chairman of the executive council approached Walsh to ask him if he would agree to become the next president of the Wexford Festival, but he declined the offer.[48] He clearly had no desire to have any further part in Festival proceedings. The 1973 Festival which produced Glinka's *Ivan Susanin*, Prokofiev's *The Gambler* and Donizetti's *L'ajo nell'imbarazzo* was another remarkable success. Journalists were fully supportive of its high standards, and this served as invaluable publicity for the healthy state of the Festival. The *Sunday Times* reported of the 'constant charms' of Wexford:

> So much for Wexford's initial attraction. Once he is there, the visitor's curiosity gives way to admiration at the general standard of performance and artistic involvement which extends to every facet of the productions. Moreover, one is almost certain to be hearing, also for the first time, some vocal talent soon likely to be heard elsewhere, in grander houses. So Wexford draws the talent-scouts as well.[49]

The Minister for Labour, Michael O'Leary, too, was kind in his words on Wexford's contribution:

> O'Leary said that the excellent standard of the Festival was attested by its record over the years and this standard he believed, was much higher than in other important opera centres in Europe, if not in the world. He hoped that elsewhere in the country opera companies might emulate what was done in Wexford.[50]

It was not only the Irish newspapers that praised the 1973 Festival; the *Glasgow Herald* reported that 'it could happen only in Ireland' and went on to observe that:

> the Irish are noted for being contradictory – or is it that they have a logic of their own that escapes others? ... To some extent the festival's opera reflects the same attitude, since the Theatre Royal, where the performances take place, is the sort of building that no-one in his right senses would dream of using as an opera house.[51]

By December 1973, the Wexford Festival Development Council, formed in September 1972, drew up a report to highlight causes for concern. First, there was raised in the report was the theatre itself, an aging building that was

65 Backstage crew
66 The chorus preparing to go on stage
67 The cast getting ready to go on stage

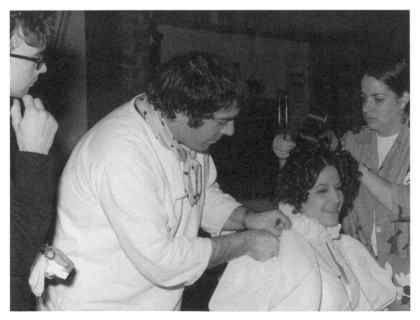

densely surrounded by other property which would naturally prevent any type of major expansion to the building. Recent improvements and repairs had been carried out, but it was an ongoing process to keep the theatre in a useable condition.

As usual, money matters took up much of the report. It was pointed out that any money that was accumulated was being used to repair the Theatre and to maintain operatic standards. This left little scope for expansion or improvement. In some ways the council felt that they had reached a type of 'plateau', and where they should aspire to go next was unclear:

> The Festival Council is conscious of a continuing responsibility to the town and county in which it exists. It would like to contribute more to the life of the area and the nation than simply two weeks of opera – however internationally acclaimed – and mollify the eternal if misguided criticism that the essential steep prices create an elitist and exclusive entertainment monopoly for the enjoyment of a few.[52]

It was a promising sign for the future, that the Development Council had realized that the Festival must continue to progress; there was no question about standing still. The report also took note of the general environment in which the Festival was trying to survive and improve. According to the report, Wexford was

> exceptionally well placed for the future. Accepting that the troubles in the North are going to pass in the next few years and that we have now entered the Common Market, the importance of the town as a communications centre with Europe and England cannot really be over-emphasised. New links are being established with the Continent and it is obviously confidently expected that Rosslare will build itself into the most important gateway to Ireland after Dublin itself. Industrial and commercial interests press for the expansion of the port's facilities and it is noticeable, when the majority of our English friends have for a time abandoned us, that the visitors from the Continent are in fact increasing in numbers.[53]

The Development Council had recognized the need to promote the Festival as a cultural catalyst that could draw visitors to the town. The tourist industry in the region would benefit as a result.

Proposals put forward by the Development Council centred on the possibility of extending the Theatre Royal or constructing a new building to house fringe Festival activities. An earlier suggestion of transferring the entire operatic proceedings to a new theatre was met with stern opposition. It was not disputed, however, that the theatre was in need of modernization. The expansion and updating of the theatre would naturally require less financial assistance than building a new theatre. This was a huge consideration for the Wexford Festival executive council and also for the development council. No decision was reached about how to proceed; the report was presented to the executive council for consideration.

Thomson Smillie now entered the scene as Wexford's artistic director. He was born in Glasgow in 1942 and studied at Glasgow University, where he was president of the opera club. In March 1966, he began full-time employment with Scottish Opera as publicity officer, a position he held until his move to Wexford.

Following the tremendous loss of Compton Mackenzie, Lauder Greenway came in as President in 1974. Greenway, an American, had already given much help and support to the Festival. He had been Chairman of the Metropolitan Opera in New York from 1956 to 1970 and had valuable musical connections all over the world. His kindness and generosity to the Wexford Festival was noted on many occasions. Taking up his position at Wexford, he declared that:

> I feel like a 'Johnny come lately' American that the Wexford Festival is something so much to be treasured, the world should know of the honour it is to be invited to take a serious part in these October festivities ...[54]

7

Not so much a festival as a way of life

It was apparent by early 1974 that the executive council was aware of the magnitude of the annual cultural event, when it was decided that the history of the Festival should be written. It stipulated that 'the history of the Festival should be written in a convivial style rather than exposing the many ups and downs it has seen'.[1] The council recognized that in order to generate enthusiasm for the Festival which might translate into sponsorship, it was important not to emphasize its difficulties, financial and other, thus far.

In making a subvention in June 1974, the Arts Council reiterated that it was more than satisfied with the standard of each Festival and that it wanted to see its successful continuation.[2] The chairman of the executive council, Scallan, reiterated that 'the Festival must expand and diversify if it is to maintain its present status and support'.[3]

The *New Ross Standard*, although complimentary of Wexford's cultural enterprise, noted that local support was particularly poor by 1974. In the year that produced Mayr's *Medea in Corinto*, Massenet's *Thaïs* and Cornelius' *Der Barbier von Bagdad*, Tony O'Brien reported how 'live music is dead in Wexford'.

> Wexford is known throughout Britain and Ireland and indeed the world as a centre of art and culture. This comes about principally (or solely depending on your point of view) through the presentation each year of the Wexford Festival Opera. This annual Festival is a grandiose auspicious affair which appears to mean a lot to the world of opera but other than being the reason for extended drinking hours it holds little or no interest for those of other music persuasions, particularly the young. Yet this is the only major music event in Wexford's social calendar.[4]

There were a number of disgruntled members on the council by 1975, all, however, with the same grievances. The chairman read out letters that he had

68   Richard McKee in *Der Barbier von Bagdad*, 1974
69   Jill Gomez in *Thaïs*, 1974

received, airing discontent. In his letter, Seán Mitten expressed his dissatisfaction with 'the artistic trends of the Festival'. Ted Collins mirrored this concern, noting also that he was discontented with 'the current artistic standards of the Festival.' Marie Fane, upon offering her resignation to the council, mentioned what was by now becoming a common concern – that she was also dissatisfied with the artistic development of the Festival. This outpouring of discontent was a positive sign that the executive council members were active in their attempt to ensure that the Festival progressed and maintained its high international standards. To aggravate an already tense situation, however, it was reported that an application to the Taoiseach for financial support had not been successful.[5]

The 1975 season remarkably delivered well in terms of high standard of opera. Between 22 October and 2 November, performances took place of Lalo's *Le Roi d'Ys*, Cavalli's *Eritrea* and Rossini's *La Pietra del Paragone*. The press noted how Wexford took on a 'Festival face' at this time of the year and how private sponsors had ensured its successful continuance to date:

> The festival has had its good and lean years. Many times its survival has been in doubt and that it has been able to build up an immunity to the viruses that have killed so many other artistic endeavours is due in large measure to frequent expensive injections paid for by powerful friends.[6]

70 Sandra Browne in *La Pietra del Paragone*, 1975
71 Ian Caddy in *La Pietra del Paragone*, 1975

In an attempt to show that opera was not an essentially 'Anglo-Saxon' hobby, Nicholas Furlong wrote of student interest that had been aroused in the Festival:

> The rare opera lovers which we find coming annually to Wexford do not belong to a decaying Anglo-Saxon or old ascendancy remnant. Nor are they aged. Over a hundred students were involved in our half-price offer and a like number worked like demons backstage, front of house and all over the town in dozens of events as volunteers.[7]

New ways of obtaining further financial support was of vital importance for the continuation of the Festival, and offering these half-price tickets to students was one way of increasing ticket sales. Local fundraising, coupled with fundraising in America, did little to alleviate the large debt that had been accumulated. Barbara Wallace, chairman of fundraising, intimated that she felt that more council members should share the responsibility of raising these much-needed funds, rather than leaving the task to a select few.[8] This was a contentious issue that Walsh had raised many times in the first decade of the Festival. He felt that the fundraising responsibilities had rested with him alone. He had remarked on various occasions how he had hated this responsibility.

Again the changing dynamics of the Festival were noted, especially difficulty in obtaining voluntary workers.[9] From the start, the availability of these volunteers had been a feature of the Festival's distinct private and amateur nature. The suggestion now that more of these workers would have to be paid for their services marked the changing of the Festival to a public, professional organization.

Even the newspaper articles of 1976 looked back with fondness to the early days of the Festival and tried to link the old school with the new. Rodney Milnes reported how he believed that those involved in running the Festival in its present form had not changed its direction, but had successfully continued it in Walsh's mould:

> President Ó Dálaigh's last official act before resignation [as President of Ireland] was to open the twenty-fifth Wexford Festival Opera ... The whole issue of neglected masterpieces is fairly bogus: an opera is worth performing or it is not. The only way to find out is to perform it and this Wexford has been doing since those heady days when Dr Tom Walsh started to explore *bel canto*

long before anyone else and his successors have maintained both his enterprise and his canny way with casting. Around fifteen good operas have found their way back into the repertory from beginnings at Wexford, and dozens of singers, conductors, designers and producers have cut their teeth there.[10]

The *Wexford People* made the point that many of those who had been involved from its inception were still integral to the make-up of the Festival in its present form.

The folk that operate the Festival in the Theatre Royal are seasoned campaigners, many wearing the coveted badge of 25 years' service and as such have weathered upsets and catastrophes like the Rosslare lifeboat crew have tasted saltwater.[11]

Although with the absence of Walsh and Mackenzie from Festival affairs, a new guard had emerged.

The year 1976 saw the production of Verdi's *Giovanna d'Arco*, Nicolai's *The Merry Wives of Windsor* and Britten's *The Turn of the Screw* and the season was reportedly as successful as ever.

It was perhaps a sign that the council had failed to remain in control of the financial situation when the decision was taken in 1977 to employ a professional fundraiser. Ian Fox accepted the position and agreed to work towards a target of £300,000 to be used primarily for capital expenditure and also for running costs.[12] This decision left the council free to concentrate on productions for 1977. Barbara Wallace, Chairman of Fundraising, took an alarmist approach in the 1977 Festival programme book, in an article entitled "Will You Let Wexford Die?" She outlined the continuous problems that the theatre building faced, including the age-old problem of lack of space backstage. Dressing-room plans for the development of the Theatre Royal were being put in place. A sum of £350,000 was put forward as the target amount to be collected to ensure the future survival and development of the Festival. This work was due to commence after the 1978 season. This was Richard Jefferies' first year as chairman of the council, a position he retained until 1979.

In 1977, Massenet's *Hérodiade*, Gluck's *Orfeo ed Euridice* and Cimarosa's *Il Maestro di Cappella* were produced. As a way of ensuring local involvement in the Festival, the Wexford Children's Choir took part in *Hérodiade*. To add to the national participation, members of the Irish Ballet Company under its artistic director, Joan Denise Moriarty, performed in Gluck's *Orfeo ed Euridice*. Moriarty had participated in the very first opera that took place at Wexford, Balfe's *Rose of Castile,* and it was fitting that she should return with the Irish Ballet Company in 1977.

Wexford's artistic director, Thomson Smillie, told the *Sunday Independent* that Wexford had done remarkably well in ensuring that it could attract talented artists within a limited budget year after year:

> Our policy in Wexford is to engage young opera talents, for Wexford just would not be able to afford the top commodity. I think we have done very well on the small resources at our disposal.[13]

This was Alfred Beit's first year as president of Wexford Festival, Lauder Greenway having been forced to retire through illness. In his opening address, Beit commented on the incessant financial turmoil of the Festival.

> The financial position of the performing arts in Ireland is even more critical than it is in other western European countries and the United States. Countries such as Great Britain, France and Germany are in the happy position of being able to enjoy enormous grants from their respective Governments; even so most of them want more. In America no such money is available but its place is taken by lavish private benefactors and by charitable or educational trusts.
>
> In England some of the principal banks and business houses have made valuable contributions to the performing arts over and above Government subsidies through similar Trusts which they have set up.
>
> Ireland probably has only about one-twentieth of the population of some of these western European countries but how happy we would be if we could get anything like one-twentieth of the subsidies they enjoy. This is not to disparage the invaluable help given over the years by the Irish Tourist Board, the Arts Council, Guinness and other sponsors, but there is a limit to the amount these can give and many more sponsors are needed.
>
> Unfortunately the type of Trust referred to above simply does not exist in Ireland, at any rate as far as the Arts are concerned, so we struggle on year after year with ever present inflation, a declining pound, and an uncertain future. Even so I hope we continue to give pleasure.[14]

By August 1978, the potential for further funding of the Festival was a distinct possibility. Barbara Wallace reported at a council meeting that negotiations had begun with Heinz Food Company. Allied Irish Banks had agreed to give £5,000. Beit was responsible for contact being made with the Lombard and Ulster Bank.[15]

Smillie went on a promotional tour of the United States to publicize the 1978 opera season. There was no doubt that the executive council was willing to try any promotional activity to ensure that tickets would be sold for the coming season. Eugene d'Albert's *Tiefland* was a feature of this year's Festival, along with Haydn's *Il Mondo della Luna* and Smetana's *The Two Widows*.

At this point, having raised £150,000 of the proposed £350,000 needed for the theatre renovations, Wallace thanked the new Friends of the Festival who had lent their valuable support at this time. Further, she made special mention to local people and companies in the Wexford area, noting that 'this is another tribute to local involvement in the Festival'.[16] She was acutely aware that it was vital to maintain the support of local businesses and individuals to ensure the Festival's success and she paid tribute to the major contributors to this fund – the Arts Council, the Bank of Ireland and Allied Irish Banks.

As the 1979 season approached, the Festival benefited greatly from the volume of publicity that it received from the very beginning of the year. Television and radio programmes produced reports on the Festival, and newspapers carried stories that provided valuable early publicity. It was estimated that the publicity had saved the Festival Council £150,000 in advertising expenses.[17]

Another matter had arisen in early 1979 to cause further concern over funding. Concerns over the legal status of the Festival as a profit-making organization were becoming apparent. Barbara Wallace, who had brought this concern to the attention of the executive council, stressed that the council 'must be *seen* to be using the money raised.' To this end, she was keen to start work on the Theatre as soon as possible.[18]

It was the Arts Council that came to the rescue of the Festival in 1979. In May of that year, it intimated that unless it was satisfied with the long term plans of the Festival, it could not guarantee to financially support it for the next three years. However, following a specific subvention in its budget, the Arts Council could now provide a grant of £25,000 to go towards current debt and a further £25,000 to be used specifically to strengthen the theatre development programme. It was stipulated however that the funding would be provided only on condition that the Festival would incur no further debt

72 Sesto Bruscantini, David Beavan and Gianni Socci in *Crispino e la Comare*, 1979
73 Alvaro Malta in *L'Amore dei Tre Re*, 1979

through production costs. The total amount to be awarded by the Arts Council had naturally exceeded the executive council's expectations; nevertheless the executive council was adamant that each member must remain as pro-active as ever in identifying funding for the future.[19]

The artistic directors were also inclined to speak out about the current state of affairs at Wexford. On 6 November 1979, music critic Charles Acton made a public plea for financial aid on behalf of the Festival, and reported the views of the then artistic director, Thomson Smillie, as well as the incoming director, Adrian Slack:

> If anyone in a position to write a cheque for £22,500 would do so within the next week or so, the Wexford Festival could be saved a continuing expenditure and could actually be given an income–producing asset, and a load could be taken off their communal minds ... To return, however, to fees, Thomson Smillie, when asked how he would spend extra money if he had it he replied, without hesitation 'on more expensive singers'. Adrian Slack seemed to have a more perceptive attitude. He denied that he would spend any extra money

he got on singers because already singers were willing to come to Wexford for about a quarter of their going fee and paying more to other singers would only 'destabilise' the entire operation.[20]

Adrian Slack had been Director of Productions at the State Opera of South Australia. Having completed an apprenticeship at the London Opera Centre and Sadler's Wells Opera, he joined Glyndebourne Opera. Slack remained with the Wexford Festival Opera for three seasons.

The 1979 Festival produced Montemezzi's *L'Amore dei Tre Re*, Spontini's *La Vestale* and Luigi and Federico Ricci's *Crispino e la Comare*. The Wexford Children's Choir again took part in Montemezzi's creation. At the end of the Festival, it was brought to the attention of the council that Slack was not satisfied with the short-term policy of the Festival. Permission for the engagement of artists was generally granted less than a year before they were due to perform, but this was often too late to book many of the artists that Slack would require. He stipulated that ideally he would rather be in a position to employ artists two or three years in advance. This request marked a further step on the road to professionalization.[21]

In the Festival programme book of 1979, Albert Lennon, the consultant architect to the Theatre Royal, gave an update on work that was being carried out to the theatre. He noted his amazement at the backstage conditions:

Visitors to the Festival over the years may occasionally have remarked the somewhat shoddy appearance of the Auditorium, seating etc. However when the curtain goes up this is quickly lost in the elegance and often sheer brilliance of the many fine sets which have graced the stage over the past twenty-eight years, not to mention the quality of the stars, Orchestras and Choruses which enthralled us. What they will not have realised, is the appalling backstage conditions which produced such beauty. There was literally no sets workshop, except already undersized stage, a props workshop which doubled as a canteen, dressing rooms hardly fit for Rugby players, an attic wardrobe reminiscent of Hong Kong sweat shops, and sub-standard toilet accommodation. One watched with wonderment this magical use of such a small stage, but if familiar with the backstage conditions this wonderment must turn to awe. A debt is owed to the many Professional stars, on and off stage, and indeed to the 'Professional Amateurs' who have produced such beauty from such an impossible base.[22]

He went on to make his justification for spending in excess of £300,000 to renovate this theatre rather than building a new one. Although the building was old, it was structurally sound. If a new building was planned, it was very possible that the costs would spiral out of control. He concluded by saying that 'whatever its shortcomings, and it will still have many, Wexford's Theatre Royal has and, we hope will retain, that indefinable and unrepeatable thing we call "character".'

The matter of the 'Irishness' of the Festival surfaced once more. It was decided that for the 1980 Festival,

> where possible Irish people should be employed, Irish goods should be used and sets should be made in Ireland, provided the highest standards could be maintained, and costs would not be increased.[23]

This again was a sign of the times and was a sign of a renewed awareness about the potential of the Festival to give employment to young Irish musicians. Slack was notified that he should abide by this preliminary policy for the 1980 season.

Financial problems again threatened to mar the continuation of the Festival in 1980. RTÉ was at the centre of the discontent when an invoice received from them for the 1979 Festival amounted to £16,892. Budget estimates had presumed that RTÉ's fee would be £9,500. Concerns arising from the grave financial situation prompted a discussion on RTÉ's involvement in the Festival. Only once before had the future of the orchestra's involvement been questioned, and this was during Walsh's time as artistic director. At this stage, it was intimated that the Ulster Orchestra would charge a more reasonable rate for its services. Ian Fox was wary of the discontinuation of the RTÉ Symphony Orchestra as the main orchestral body of the Festival, pointing out that any hostility between RTÉ and Wexford might cause difficulty with the future of RTÉ recordings; still, he was more than willing to work with the Ulster Orchestra in place of the RTÉ Symphony Orchestra.[24]

Further difficulties arose with the decrease in the Arts Council grant for the 1980 season. It was stipulated at a Festival council meeting in March of 1980 that there would be substantial cutbacks in Government aid for the Arts. The Arts Council said that they would continue to provide 'a minimum grant' to all major festivals; the amount provided in 1980 would be £46,000, instead of an estimated £50,000 that had been calculated in the budget figures. The executive council made clear however, that it 'must not lose sight of [its] Artistic standards but must try to balance artistic standards with financial constraints'.[25]

This renewed concern about artistic standards must surely have been linked with beginning of Jim Golden's term as chairman of the council. Golden had worked with the Festival for many years and watched the Festival progress to the stage it was now at. Not only was he aware that artistic standards had to be maintained; he knew what the costs associated with this could be. Fundraising, then, was one of the main items on the agenda of each Festival council meeting. Local fundraising was proving particularly difficult, even though many small businesses and local people had expressed an interest in lending their support. The problems with fundraising, at a local and national level, were a direct result of the worldwide recession.[26] In the United States the fundraising situation was reported to be 'promising', although no money had yet been received for 1980. To compound concerns about the future difficulty of maintaining a high standard of opera at Wexford, Bank of Ireland had turned down an application for an interest-free loan of £40,000.[27]

The newspapers were full of articles relating to the acute financial difficulties and the sponsorship that had been promised thus far. According to Brian Quinn, a reporter;

> The Irish America Fund under the auspices of Dr A.J.F. O'Reilly came to the rescue [of the Festival]. There is acute disappointment that so far the festival has got only £10,000 from the National Lottery. Some £80,000 must be still found for the building and there is 30,000 outstanding for this year's festival. But as Mrs Wallace put it: 'We still believe in miracles in Wexford.'[28]

The Festival produced another three critically acclaimed operas in 1980 despite the financial strain. Giacomo Puccini's *Edgar* was presented;, Handel's *Orlando* was performed on four nights, and Carlisle Floyd's *Of Mice and Men* was the third choice for the season. *Edgar* was accompanied by the RTÉ Symphony Orchestra and the reliable Wexford Festival Chorus, and the Bride Street Boys Choir took part, constituting local participation in the Festival proceedings,

The growing professionalism by now expected from the executive council was again apparent when the council experienced a further reshuffle to leave each member of the 14-body group with a specific responsibility. Marion Creely was named as the Arts Council observer on the council.[29]

Press acclaim for the achievements of the Wexford Festival Opera was substantial again in 1981. Performances of Wolf-Ferrari's *I Gioielle della Madonna*, Mozart's *Zaïde* and Verdi's *Un Giorno di Regno* were enjoyed. Kenneth Loveland, in the *South Wales Argus*, praised the success and uniqueness of the Wexford annual event:

> Wexford is the festival you just have to love. There is the picturesque town itself, a unique atmosphere of tradition and spontaneous welcome and a sense of community involvement rivalled by only a few similar dates, including Fishguard, just opposite on our side of the water.[30]

Following what was agreed to have been a very successful Festival, the executive council received much correspondence praising the standard of performance. The chairman read aloud a letter from the mayor of Wexford, 'thanking him for a most enjoyable Festival.' Mark Hely-Hutchinson, director of Guinness Ireland Limited, had also contacted the council to express the enjoyment he had experienced during the 1981 Festival. The Director of Music at RTÉ, Gerard Victory, too, voiced his congratulations on the success of the annual venture. However, his praise was followed by the sobering account of RTÉ's plans 'to recoup the total direct costs in connection with the orchestra on a rising scale over the next four years' (up to 1981, Wexford had been responsible for only fifty per cent of the direct costs). This delivered yet another financial blow. Following a discussion at an executive council meeting in December, it was suggested that the council request that RTÉ postpone the proposed increase for 1982 as the budget for the season had already been put in place. RTÉ could open discussions regarding an increase for subsequent festivals.[31]

In December 1981, the Wexford Festival executive council received a very interesting offer. An individual, who wished to remain anonymous, offered to donate the sum of £31,000 'if certain conditions were met'. The first condition was that the opera *Medeé* by Luigi Cherubini should be presented during its 1983 season. The second condition was that Helen Lawrence should be selected for the leading role. The council agreed immediately that the artistic director should decide on the artistic merits of both opera and singer and that the financial offer should not be the deciding factor. The offer was indeed a fascinating one as it posed a difficult dilemma for the executive council. The money of course was badly needed but perhaps not at the expense of relinquishing control over operatic standards and performance choices at Wexford. Discussions were opened with Elaine Padmore, artistic director, on the issue.[32] The offer was eventually declined, perhaps strengthening the notion that the executive council was now responsible for a professional enterprise and could not afford to let the standard of opera deteriorate as a result of an innovative funding opportunity.[33]

Elaine Padmore had joined Wexford Festival Opera for the 1982 season. She had studied music at Birmingham University, where she occupied leading roles in university opera productions. She lectured in opera at the Royal Academy of Music and on the radio. Before taking up her position at Wexford, Padmore had become a full-time radio producer, in charge of planning and producing opera broadcasts. She was to have a hugely successful career at Wexford, lasting thirteen years.

In preparation for the 1982 Festival, Barbara Wallace, in her final report as chair of fundraising, set out the points that needed to be stressed so that individuals and businesses alike could identify the very significance of the Festival for the town of Wexford:

> Wexford Festival, in a very positive way, creates a good impression of Ireland abroad thereby helping to counteract the bad publicity generated by Northern Ireland news. The fostering of good music in particular, Opera, the opportunity which this affords to young Irish artists and the educational aspects for the Wexford community, both young and old, with offshoots such as the Arts Centre, School of Music, Wexford Singers all justify supporting the Opera Festival.[34]

But, in a sense, Wallace was preaching to the converted and the difficult task would be the communication of these ideas throughout the town.

The professional contract between the Festival council and RTÉ remained unclear as could be seen from a letter sent by John Kinsella of RTÉ, questioning dates of the 1983 Festival and future Festivals. The letter implied that RTÉ was less than enthusiastic about any future arrangement with the Wexford Festival Opera.[35] Although the executive council had discussed on occasion the possibility of employing a different orchestra at a lower cost, in reality much of Wexford's success had depended on a good working relationship with RTÉ. Suspicions about RTÉ's desire to break with Wexford were compounded in October 1982 when Ian Fox intimated that, due to cutbacks in RTÉ, the RTÉ Symphony Orchestra might not be available for the 1983 season.[36] The orchestra, however, played as usual for the 1982 season of Alfano's *Sakùntala*, Haydn's *Arianna a Naxos* and *L'Isola Disabitata* and Massenet's *Grisélidis*.

An unusual situation arose early in 1983 concerning Elaine Padmore. Up to this point, the artistic director had been assigned virtually complete control over the choice of operas. However, because of differences between Padmore's choice of operas and the executive council's, a decision was taken that, for future festivals, the artistic director would no longer have complete control over opera choice.[37] The following report emerged in January of 1983:

> It is the principal responsibility of the artistic director to choose and mount successfully the Festival's operas and recitals. This is to be achieved in association with the Repertory committee. The council expects that the committee will contribute to the discussions concerning the selection of the operas and recitals. In the unlikely event of a real disagreement the committee can make a separate report and the matter will be resolved by council.[38]

The age-old complaint that the Wexford Festival Opera had lost its appeal of earlier days resurfaced, not for the first time, in February 1983. The Repertory committee reportedly had long discussions about the possibility of re-introducing 'a few more late night events and a bit of "sparkle" back in the Festival'.[39] The early tradition of opera singers singing in the Wexford pubs after performances had been stamped out by Walsh himself in the early days, for fear that the singers might strain their voices. This late-night entertainment, it was felt, might interfere with performances in the Theatre Royal.

The issue of renewing the early excitement of the Festival was picked up by more than one newspaper, and, as the *Enniscorthy Echo* reported,

> At the first meeting of the Council in 1983 an enthusiastic Council gave considerable thought and discussion to ways and means of injecting new vitality into the event ... A most welcome note of strong local co-operation was introduced when it was reported that many local people ... have decided to raise modest amounts to help the Festival's financial problems.[40]

It was enough to offer hope for the future of the Festival and yet evasive enough not to identify any of the areas that this 'modest' financial aid might come from. At least the issue of the discontinuance of the RTÉ Symphony Orchestra's role as an integral part of the Festival seemed to have subsided, as they once again took part in Wexford's operatic treats – Marschner's *Hans Heiling*, Wolf-Ferrari's *La Vedova Scaltra* and Donizetti's *Linda di Chamounix*. This year's Festival lasted from 20 to 31 October.

In the wake of a successful Festival, not surprisingly, the budget was again the main item on the agenda at the beginning of 1984. It was noted that the financial outlook for the country as a whole was bleak, and this was reflected in the increased difficulties that the executive council was experiencing in its quest for funds. The council also realised that 1984 would see significant expenditure cuts throughout the industry and commerce sectors. The fee for the employment of the RTÉ Symphony Orchestra had risen – an added expense that the Festival council could not afford. Padmore made reference to the fact that the Festival could not sustain its current standard of performance within the proposed budget, especially with the added pressure of media and television interest in the Festival.[41]

Amidst the financial worry which never seemed to go away, the 1984 Festival opened with a flourish and, despite the bad weather, a large crowd turned out to witness the opening of the Festival by Pat Kenny, who was beginning to make a name for himself in RTÉ.[42] The opera crowd was treated to Massenet's *Le Jongleur de Notre Dame*, Cimarosa's *Le Astuzie Femminili* and Smetana's *The Kiss*. The press was full of praise for the 1984 season. Charles Acton in the *Irish Times* recalled:

> 'This is Wexford as it used to be' was a sentence that I heard there [in Wexford] often this year, which nostalgia being what it is, means that it is better than it ever was, habitually that is. That, fundamentally, is the highest praise that can be given to Elaine Padmore, the artistic director, since it reflects people's views of the three operas and their presentation as well as the general pattern of the festival. The council carry the can (and its chairman, Jim Golden, was one of the many who expressed that quotation) but it is the artistic director, who makes the plans.[43]

Not only could the Wexford Festival Opera be distinguished for its operatic performances; there was a distinctive Festival feel throughout the town which could only be attributed to the fringe events. Perhaps the most important aspect of these was the fact that they instilled a feeling of local participation in the Opera Festival. Although most local Wexford people did not attend the actual opera performances, the streets were thronged daily with people admiring decorated shop windows and attending various art exhibitions. It was no surprise therefore that the executive council took special note of the state of these annual fringe events.

In January 1985, a letter from Medb Ruane, Visual Arts Officer of the Arts Council, was read out to the executive council, commenting on the standard of the exhibitions that were held in Wexford in recent years. The chairman had requested this report from the Arts Council as a means of gaining advice on how to raise the current standard. There had been a reported drop in standard of fringe events, including exhibitions, the reason cited being a lack of suitable venues and a lack of finance.[44] An added concern was the fact that the Arts Centre in Wexford had recently adopted a policy of promoting the performing arts during the Festival. It was apparent that a 'world-class exhibition' might be available for the 1985 Festival if a suitable venue was identified. But the large costs associated with exhibiting for the short duration of the Festival meant that it was not worthwhile for many artists to exhibit their work during the Festival.

Meanwhile, RTÉ continued to provide its Symphony Orchestra for operatic performances, and the 1985 season saw the production of Catalani's *La Wally*, Handel's *Ariodante* and Weill's *The Rise and Fall of the City of Mahagonny*. The *Enniscorthy Guardian* reinforced the point that the support of Guinness was imperative to the continuation of the Festival; moreover, the Government did not seem to be supporting the Festival as it should be:

> Indeed without the support of Ireland's leading brewery, there would be no festival, [Jim Golden] said … He called for tax deductability status for the festival under the terms of the 1984 Finance Act. Since the Government cannot adequately fund the arts in Ireland, it could make it easier for events such as the Wexford Festival to help itself by providing the tax status.[45]

Again it was an indication of the increased professionalism of the Festival that the press continued to carry stories about how it was being annually funded and supported.

∞ 8 ∞

Walsh's final farewell

The 1986 preliminary council meetings opened with a report from the chairman that 'a serious financial problem' was predicted for 1986. To add to this, Padmore requested an increase of £14,000 for the season.[1] It was amidst this tumultuous period that the chairmanship of the executive council passed to Barbara Wallace.

The worst was yet to come: in February of 1986 a letter was circulated to the council members from Patricia Quinn, Music and Opera Officer of the Arts Council, indicating that the Arts Council had taken a decision to suspend its grant aid to the Festival in 1986. Quinn attended the meeting where she pointed out that the Arts Council had only taken the final decision in February and that the Festival council had been notified as soon as possible. Quinn requested that they keep the Arts Council informed of their plans for the 1987 season, although funds could not be guaranteed.[2]

The executive council was naturally incensed by the by the Arts Council decision, which left the deficit for 1986 at £101,250. Immediately, fundraising, local and national was discussed with a proposed target of £120,000.[3] Quinn was faced with a very angry council, who had prepared some questions for her. They wanted to know first of all where the money received by the Arts Council for 1985 and 1986 had gone, requesting to see a list of those who were supported. They demanded to know who the members of the Arts Council were; what organisations they were representing; whether any members were political appointees; and whether any organisation received more money this year than it had in the past. The session ended with the sarcastic question as to whether the 'Arts Council [is] saving some of the money for administration or to buy guns?'

This matter could not come to a satisfactory conclusion for the Festival council but they were adamant that they would have their say. The situation was a grave one for the Festival's future, if indeed it had any future at all. 'I am very surprised that the [Arts] council members who would not support

74 Pauline Tinsley and Daniela Bechly in *Königskinder*, 1986

[Wexford] have not resigned because it is obvious to the whole country that the members of the Arts Council are not capable of making a reasonable and logical decision', one council member declared disdainfully:

> It is obvious that there is no use in requesting anything from the Arts Council and they are of no further use to this country and as a matter of fact they would be a hindrance … As we see things tonight there is no hope of mounting a festival for 1986.[4]

This indeed was a difficult period for the new chairman, Wallace, who had pioneered the fundraising cause with great energy up to this point.

Immediately a document entitled 'Save the Wexford Festival' appeared and formed part of the national and local fundraising initiative that was ongoing to maintain the Opera Festival.[5] Ted Howlin reported that Tom Walsh had agreed to give two lectures on the Festival, one in Wexford and a second one in the Royal Hospital, Kilmainham, Dublin. The aim of the lectures was to publicize the Festival, and the Arts Council undoubtedly understood the significance of Walsh presenting these lectures. Jim Golden was instrumental in encouraging Walsh to participate in Festival affairs at this stage. Walsh's significance as the founder of the Festival had never been forgotten.

The decision was taken at the beginning of March to go ahead with the Festival in 1986, as artists had already been contracted. On 2 April, Wallace reported at a meeting that the Arts Council had agreed to support Wexford with £30,000 for the running and upkeep of the theatre in 1986.[6] A letter from Ivan Yates, TD, expressed further concern regarding the state of funding from 1986 onwards for Wexford's Festival Opera:

> [Yates] suggested that a meeting should take place between all public representatives in Wexford to brief them on why Wexford Festival Opera is good for tourism, the local economy and its national contribution to the Arts. They can then, in turn, make representation to have Wexford Festival included in the Book of Estimates for 1987.[7]

The dire financial situation that had unfolded before the executive council had one positive effect on proceedings. Innovative ideas for the improvement of the annual event were discussed at length. This uncovered many viable options for the successful progress of the Festival into the future. In May 1986, Wallace reported on 'a major new plan to strengthen the financial base of the Festival.' The introduction of 101 new seats in the extension of the theatre was discussed which would benefit box office income. The cost of such an extension was debated among council members, although all appeared to see this as one realistic solution to a deteriorating financial situation. According to the chairman, 'this expansion would give Wexford Festival something to sell to new sponsors in 1987'.

> Another development would be Opera for Children in which a company would go to the schools and rehearse with the children to put on an Opera; Scholarships and bursaries for Irish singers to observe and attend classes dur-

ing the Festival; Summer school for teaching of Production techniques, stage management, [and] lighting.[8]

Wallace astutely pointed out that if correct policies were put forward for these initiatives, the Department of Education or even the Arts Council might, in the future, provide some money for their successful implementation.

By 27 August, the crisis was over. Wallace reported that the 1986 Festival would now safely proceed as planned because 100 per cent seat occupancy was now expected.[9] The Festival opened with Humperdinck's *Königskinder*, accompanied by the RTÉ Symphony Orchestra and the Wexford Festival chorus, under chorus master Ian Reid. Rossini's *Tancredi* followed on 23 October and was performed with the aid of the Wexford Festival male chorus. Ambroise Thomas' creation, *Mignon*, was the final selection for the season. The press realized how fortunate the town was, this year in particular, that the Festival had survived into its thirty-fifth year.

> The 35th Wexford Festival got underway this week having overcome the financial problems which had earlier threatened to sink the event without trace. For weeks during the spring it looked as if there would never be a 35th Wexford Festival but the determination which has helped it through so many crises in the past, saw it through what was possibly its most serious problem ever.[10]

The professionalization of the Wexford Festival reached new heights with the decision taken by the Festival's executive council to appoint a chief executive to run the Festival. Sean Scallan inferred that the need for the creation of such a position had arisen out of the realization that the executive council, as presently constituted, was 'too weak'.[11] Wallace deduced,

> Wexford Festival was now in a good position to raise money and that professional help was now needed for the business which was in 1987 in excess of a half a million pounds. It was no longer possible to raise this amount on a voluntary basis.[12]

The 1987 Festival was indeed another successful event, with the productions of Bellini's *La Straniera* and Giordano's *La Cena delle Beffe*. The third choice for 1987 was *Cendrillon*, a fairytale in four acts by Jules Massenet. Members of the Dublin City Ballet participated in this novel piece.

75   Peter Lightfoot and the chorus in *The Devil and Kate*, 1988

In the aftermath of the Festival, Wallace reported to the council that the Festival had reached 'an all-time high.' This, she added, was a new concept for the Opera Festival that had struggled, albeit successfully, to overcome a myriad of difficulties since its inception. The continued success of the Festival, however, was heavily dependent on the availability of the orchestra; on being viable financially; and on selling the extra seats.[13] The participation of the RTÉ Symphony Orchestra was never assured from one year to the next, and this was a significant concern for the executive council. Wallace, however, was satisfied with the progress that had been made, particularly since she had taken up her role as chairman. This could be seen in a letter she wrote to Alfred Beit following the 1987 Festival She told him of her delight in negotiating a £30,000 grant from the Irish National Lottery for work on the theatre, and a further £13,000 from the Arts Council for the 1987 season. A successful application had also been made to Bord Fáilte for £10,000 to put towards theatre costs. Further, Guinness had renewed its contract for a further three years at £35,000 a year. 'I hope to present a four-year plan to Festival Council sometime early in the New Year,' she said, 'showing all the exciting things which we hope to try to do, not least improving the standard even more'.[14]

To further emphasize the notion that the Wexford Opera Festival was instrumental in the promotion of the county, John Small requested permission to employ John O'Hagan to conduct a study on the 'Economic and Social Impact of the Wexford Festival on a Local and National Level.' The cost of the proposed report was £4,000. Professor O'Hagan was due to visit Wexford in April to carry out a preliminary examination of Festival proceedings.[15]

Jerome Hynes joined Wexford Festival Opera as its new managing director. The justification for his appointment was due to the experience he had acquired as general manager with the Druid Theatre Company. He had been responsible for the successful management of that company during a time of significant growth, aiding its transformation from a small regional company to a significant national company, whose reputation was steadily growing, due to its tours in the United Kingdom, the United States and Australia. With his appointment came another significant shift towards professionalism.

The 1988 Festival witnessed an ambitious programme. The Festival opened with Dvořák's *The Devil and Kate*, and was followed by Mercadante's *Elisa e Claudio*. There was a double bill again this year with Gazzaniga's *Don Giovanni Tenorio* and Busoni's *Turandot*. The Wexford Festival Chorus and the RTÉ Symphony Orchestra played their respective vital parts as usual.

Tom Walsh died after the 1988 Festival. A poignant obituary appeared in the *Times* on 14 November 1988, written by Bernard Levin. Levin, who religiously attended the Wexford Festival, and had dedicated the final chapter of his 1981 book *Conducted Tour* to the Wexford Festival Opera, describing it as one of his favourite festivals. It was fitting that he should write about Walsh's legacy:

> We laid Tom Walsh in the earth on Friday, under a glorious Indian-summer sun, in the Barntown cemetery outside the town; that way he can sleep amid the soft green hills of his native County Wexford which he loved so much.

After the requiem mass in his home church, the cortège formed up; we filled the street from side to side and end to end. Solemn robed figures walked immediately behind the hearse; easily mistaken for members of the Guild of Mastersingers, they turned out to be the entire borough council, in full fig.

The town band wasn't there; perhaps it had been wrongly thought insufficiently reverent for such an occasion. The Taoiseach, though, had sent a telegram. The flowers, piled up, made an Everest of beauty and farewell; the church was heady with their scents. We sang 'Abide with Me', and meant it …

Well, your man had done a lot for the place, starting by being born there, in 1911 (he missed his 77th birthday by a fortnight). He qualified as a doctor at Dublin University in 1944; he practised in the town from 1944 to 1955; from 1955 to 1977 he was the anaesthetist for the Wexford County Hospital. In 1951 he founded the Wexford Opera Festival, and was its director until 1966 …

His worth and achievements were recognised; the University of Dublin made him first an hon. MA, then a Doctor of Philosophy, then and Doctor of Literature. He was an hon. fellow of the Faculty of Anaesthetists of Ireland, a fellow of the Royal Historical Society, a Knight of Malta, a freeman of Wexford (well I should think so). He wrote a series of scholarly books on the history of opera; he was twice married and widowed; he is survived by his daughter and sister …

Tom died smiling. At least, I assume he did; he was certainly smiling when I saw him in Wexford Hospital a few days before the end. As a doctor, he could not deceive himself about his condition, and his colleagues did not try to bluff him. But there were no solemn farewells; solemn farewells were not much in his line, except, to be sure, operatic ones.

Wexford know him as 'Doctor Tom', and would call him nothing else. I often wish I had been living in Wexford at the time; I would have loved to watch the scene as he went about the town telling people of his plan, while the news went much faster about the town that Doctor Tom had gone mad. For consider: Wexford in 1951 was not only a quiet place, unheard of outside Ireland and hardly heard of even inside; it was also savagely poor. The Theatre hadn't been used as such for a century (some say two); moreover it would hold only 400 people, and anyway it was now a furniture repository.

The very Muses wrung their hands and wept at so forlorn a hope, but they didn't know Doctor Tom; the iron-clad principles of rectitude and honour that guarded his life were translated into an irresistible inclination to see his dream realised. The Wexford Opera Festival, with the weeping Muses

76 TJW receiving the Freedom of Wexford
77 TJW with wife, Ninette and daughter, Victoria, on receiving his doctorate, 1972

engaged for the Chorus as a token of forgiveness, opened its doors on time; that was 37 years ago, and they haven't shut yet…

He sought no fame, no fortune. He had got hold of the notion that he was on earth to tend the sick and spread the love of music, and he pursued both vocations with great diligence and no fuss. It pleased him, as it pleased all of us, that over the years Wexford had become noticeably better off; his festival brought a good deal of money into the town…

We returned, en masse, to the hospital, to see him for the last time.

He fought on for another week; death would not have dared approach his bedside until the 1988 festival was over. Last Tuesday afternoon, he fell asleep, and in sleep he left us. We who knew him will keep his memory bright, forever in his debt for the joy and friendship he and his festival have given us. We are even more blessed by having known and loved a man of such goodness, wisdom, generosity and laughter. Doubt not that he feasts in Heaven this night, with Mozart on one side of him and Hippocrates on the other, and a glass of good red wine in his good right hand.[16]

The local *Guardian* wrote of a man who would be remembered in Wexford for what he had brought to the town, trying in some way to explain why he had not been an integral part of the Festival for some years now.

After the 1966 Festival which had a very 'Walshish' programme, Dr Tom … had a disagreement with the festival board. He was replaced by an Englishman, Brian Dickie, who was later to become General Administrator at Glyndebourne. Walsh was not pleased with the change in the festival which artistically he had managed to run almost single-handedly right down to the editing of the programme in which his own face never appeared. For some time he went back only reluctantly to the theatre where once he attended every performance.

But Dickie continued the policy of Wexford much in the Walsh mould, as does the current festival director Elaine Padmore, in going for little known operas cast with singers on their way up.

The Wexford wounds had healed and he came back to the festival he had created although usually avoiding first nights. The door of his house, five minutes walk from the Theatre Royal, was ever open both to singers and the critics whom he realised had helped turn Wexford into an international affair.[17]

78   TJW on receiving his doctorate, 1972

A minute's silence was observed at the meeting of the Wexford Festival council in his memory. Wallace, as chairman, spoke about his contribution, stating:

> Wexford Festival was deeply indebted to Dr Walsh. His courage and vision as a founding member was instrumental in taking the Festival and making it truly international. His deep interest in the future of the Festival was evident from his ideas for its development, right up to his death.[18]

Somehow this did not even seem sufficient.

9

We still believe in miracles at Wexford

O ne year after the idea for an economic study was discussed, the O'Hagan Report was officially launched in Wexford and Dublin. Albert Reynolds, Minister for Finance, had attended its launch in Dublin, where he 'praised the Festival for its excellent efforts and agreed to bring the report to the attention of the Taoiseach'.

As stipulated at a council meeting in September 1989, the findings of the report would be used in the pursuit of more state-aid sponsorship, while all the time conveying the Festival's worth for Wexford.[1]

Marschner's *Der Templer und die Jüdin* was the first choice for the 1989 season. Mozart's *Mitridate, Re de Ponto* was performed for five of the festival nights, and Serge Prokofiev's *The Duenna* (Betrothal in a monastery) was also put on.

Despite the perceived stability of the Festival as it moved towards its fortieth year, below the surface, particularly at the executive council level, the situation was somewhat different. The feeling of uncertainty at this time can be seen in a document circulated to the council in September 1989 by Mairéad Furlong, a council member. It proposed a seminar on 'Strategy for the Wexford Festival council into the year 2000'. The document was, for the most part, optimistic about the future of the Festival, as Furlong declared:

> it is indeed possible to be optimistic about the Wexford Festival and beyond the year 2000 but it seems to me that the Wexford Festival Council should seek to promote and stimulate further public and institutional interest in its future. Now that Professor O'Hagan's report has been published, it must surely stimulate national and local interest and concern for the future of the Wexford Festival.[2]

Questions were put forward as topics in need of serious and immediate discussion. First of all, there was the matter of artistic policy: the question was posed whether the Festival's policy should not take a different route in the future. (As Walsh himself had admitted, opera policy could never remain static: it must continuously evolve). There was even suggestion that the Wexford Festival could exchange performances with other continental opera houses, or that a twentieth-century opera could be commissioned. The document ended by addressing the fundamental question; 'what is the position today of council members and how do they wish to see the role of the council in future?'[3]

As Wallace neared the end of her chairmanship, she philosophically addressed its members in March 1989:

> May I leave you with a thought? To remain as we are, we must change. We cannot stand still; if we try to stand still we will lose ground. Let us display the same courage and determination as did the founders. Let us hand the Wexford Festival Opera over to our successors as we were 'handed it', strong and vibrant.[4]

It was ironic that she should put the phrase 'handed it' in inverted commas, as there was nothing smooth about the move from Walsh's reign to the more professional hands of an executive council. With the engagement of a managing director at Wexford, the role of the executive council had inevitably changed. Council members found themselves in the uneasy position of having less power over decisions than before. But a managing director was badly needed to bring the Festival forward to a new phase of professionalism. The most ironic thing of all was that what the executive council now strived for, was the one thing that the council had left behind with Walsh – the presence of one obvious leader. Without realizing it, they were now seeking a return to the Walsh 'martinet' days.

Sean Scallan's views highlighted this changing pace of professionalism.

> I would suggest to you that, in the interests of peace and harmony and the future of the Festival we should have good communications from the officers to the Council, including the full and exact financial position, so that we may get total co-operation from everybody. Admittedly we were given figures and breakdowns this time which we have not had before. Nevertheless, it is many years since I saw the morale of the Festival Council so low.[5]

It is remarkable that the Wexford Festival Opera managed to continue its role of producing critically acclaimed performances year after year. This proved that there was one clear goal – to produce opera to the highest possible standard. In 1990, Barbara Wallace summed up the changes that had come about since the inception of the Festival and, in a document brought forward for discussion at a council meeting, she outlined why the existing structure of the Wexford Festival Opera needed to be examined: the Council now had reached a membership of between 25 and 30, and was obviously too large to deal sufficiently with urgent matters.

Wallace's document centred on the issue of change. 'My concern', she said, 'about the structure of the Wexford Festival Opera, about which I have made no secret, has intensified since taking up my position as chairman.' Although she had intended to give most of her energies to building up the voluntary work force, in structure and in spirit, she had been deflected from this by the urgent needs of the theatre building and the extension of operatic programmes. She also made reference to the fact that it was the general assumption of those outside the Festival council that there was 'an inability to accept new ideas or blood'. She was keen to dispel this notion and essentially welcomed change to the council as presently constituted while also welcoming new ideas. She set out what she felt were the important points to consider in an attempt to move forward from the summit that the Festival had reached. She began by saying that:

> perhaps we should examine what and who is needed to run the Wexford Festival as opposed to trying to make what we have fit, or to try to effect change for change's sake. I suggest that this should be the basis for a discussion by the Council.
>
> My reason for suggesting a holocaust leaving only YOU was not in an effort to be dramatic but simply to try to get everyone to be objective, and to stop thinking in terms of how change might affect any one of us who are involved at present.

She reinforced her statement by saying that she believed the structure of the Festival to be, by and large, a good one, but that was no reason for not exploring possibilities for the future advancement of opera at Wexford. She highlighted the importance of the chairman's role, the role of the managing director and the role of the artistic director: none of these should rule with a dictatorial hand. Moreover, 'sponsors and the wealthy much-travelled opera lovers' should be targeted, those 'who by their example and in their conversations assist in marketing and fundraising efforts'. It was obvious that she had Alfred Beit in mind when she made this particular point, as Beit had truly been Wexford's wealthy patron.

The work of the volunteers at Wexford and the importance of their continued presence at the Festival was never far from Wallace's mind. Her document relayed just how important the voluntary workers were to Wexford:

> Wexford Festival's success is due in no small measure to the atmosphere in the town. This is partly due to the goodwill and influence of the voluntary workforce. I believe that it is not just important but it is essential that local voluntary workers know, understand and are willing to run as many departments of the total Festival as is possible. It has been proven that they are capable once they are trained. That is why I have frequently exhorted the heads of departments to nominate a deputy to bring on stream new people in their areas, not just because of the financial implications but to ensure continuity of local knowledge and to avoid having the existing people overburdened as the Festival extended. These might work for short periods on a regular basis, e.g., there are many, many people in Wexford who are willing, able and anxious to be involved at this level.[6]

As the critics reported, any tension that existed in the council over the maintenance of high standards of the Festival, was not reflected in the successful 1990 season. The newly named National Symphony Orchestra and the Wexford School of Ballet and Modern Dance played an integral part of Leoncavallo's *Zazà*. The Wexford Festival chorus and the Loch Garman (Wexford) Silver Band took part in Maw's *The Rising of the Moon*. And Boieldieu's *La Dame Blanche* was performed, again with the aid of the Wexford Festival chorus, conducted by Emmanuel Joel.

It must have come as a relief to the Festival council when the 1991 Festival was reported as being 'one of the easiest to date'.[7] It was no easy task trying to maintain a professional standard of opera year after year in a very uncertain environment. Financing each consecutive year was an onerous task and Wallace had worked extremely hard to ease the financial burden. But the theatre was in constant need of renovation and the sum needed to ensure that it would remain a suitable venue was significant. In June 1991 a special meeting of the members of the council was held to specifically deal with the issue of the Theatre Royal. As Wallace pointed out, phase one would involve moving the location of the box office and providing a new cloakroom. Funding for these improvements was forthcoming from Guinness, and a private donor who had promised £50,000. An application was also put forward for an EEC Structural Funds subsidy. These proposed funds would need to come in before the work could commence. Plans were already in place to move offices to a new location in 21 High Street, beside the Theatre Royal. The Arts Council was reportedly concerned at this stage about the viability of such enhancements and requested the proposed cost of such extensive work.[8]

Wallace also pointed out that although the current operating procedures had served the Festival well to this point, the structure was in need of review to ensure that the correct path was followed in the future. She appealed to all council members to join in the discussion to find the best way forward. Further, she commented that the number of voluntary staff had waned significantly, yet she correctly surmised that they were not only a source of free labour but also the Festival's link to the Wexford community.[9]

The 1991 Festival season extended from 24 October to 10 November. Donizetti's *Assedio di Calais* was performed on the opening night, followed by Gluck's *La Recontre Imprévue* and Goetz's *Der Widerspenstigen Zähmung*. All operas were very well received.

Wallace's time as chairman of the council was coming to a close and she presented the group with a report in March 1992. It consisted of recommendations for the future about how the Festival could strengthen relationships, its image and its fundraising position. She noted that relations with RTÉ, that had on many occasions been strained, had improved considerably. She recognized RTÉ's contribution to the Festival from the very start and hoped that RTÉ was aware of this appreciation. Relations with Guinness, although also at times fragile, were in a healthy state indeed by 1992. She emphasised the importance of showing gratitude for support received from the Wexford community, both commercial and individual: this support was seen as key to a successful future. The Arts Council had had an uneasy relationship with the Festival council since the decision not to make the 1986 grant available; nevertheless Wallace knew the importance of appeasing the Arts Council.

By now the Wexford Festival Opera was an extremely professional body. Its finance officer, Paul Hennessy, provided the council with a report on Corporate Affairs and Statutory Compliance in August 1992. The report took note of the legal entities that Wexford Festival Opera consisted of: Wexford Festival Trust; Wexford Festival Ltd; Loc Garmain Enterprises Ltd; Wexford Festival Trust (UK); and the American Friends of Wexford Festival Inc. Hennessy set out the professional obligations of the enterprise – to ensure that Wexford Festival Opera complied at all times with statutory and legislative requirements relating to its corporate affairs; and to put in place a corporate structure appropriate to the needs of the organization.[10]

The Wexford Festival went on to buy No. 32 High Street, a property across the road from the Theatre Royal. The council had then managed to secure an agreement with the occupants of No. 25, next door to the theatre, to swap the properties. A subsidy from Guinness was going some way towards meeting these costs but a rather telling note also appeared in the 1992 Festival programme book.

> As many patrons will be aware we have plans to develop and improve the Theatre Royal so as to better serve both audiences and artists. The model on display in the foyer represents our ultimate goal in terms of the development of front of house but is dependent on our securing certain properties and, most importantly, raising the funds. We do hope to complete this development in phases and would hope to begin Phase One in 1993.
>
> Any members of our audience who feel that they, or someone they know, could assist us in this development should contact our Managing Director, Jerome Hynes who would also be happy to provide further details concerning our plans for development. We would be grateful for any donations patrons may wish to make towards this development.[11]

Mascagni's *Il Piccolo Marat* opened the Festival this year. The National Symphony Orchestra was conducted by Albert Rosen. Storace's *Gli Equivoci* was performed on six nights also and the Festival closed with an acclaimed performance of Marschner's *Der Vampyr*.

Sir Alfred Beit now notified the Festival council that he wished to step down as president at the end of the 1992 season. Having served on the council since 1957, as chairman from 1962 and 1966, and then president thereafter, it was no surprise that Beit bowed out. His departure was significant because he had left an indelible mark on the fortune of the Festival: he was its first rich patron.

Sir Anthony O'Reilly accepted the role of president following Beit's depar-

79 Christopher Trakas and Gary Harger in *Gli Equivoci*, 1992
80 Louise Malone and Ann Bosley (Festival office) with Luigi Ferrari

ture. As chief executive officer of H. J. Heinz Company, one of the world's leading food processors, O'Reilly was an impressive asset to Wexford's cause. He has remained active in many cultural and charitable organizations and holds the position of chairman of the Ireland Funds of the United States, Canada, Great Britain, Australia, France, Germany, New Zealand, Japan and South Africa. The ability of the Ireland Funds organization to raise money to support programmes that encourage peace, reconciliation and constructive change throughout Ireland must continue to give the Wexford Festival council a great deal of encouragement.

1993 witnessed another smooth process towards the season's productions. With a new chairman, John O'Connor, and following the departure of Alfred Beit, it was a relief that events progressed at a manageable pace. Tchaikovsky's *Cherevichki* opened the 1993 season. This well-received work was followed by Paisiello's *Il Barbiere di Siviglia* and Hérold's *Zampa*.

Sir Alfred Beit died in 1994. His extraordinary interest for and knowledge in all forms of art and culture was noted by the Festival council as they paid tribute to the man whose help and financial support was inestimable. His presence in Wexford was unique, and the amount of energy he bestowed on

81   John O'Connor, Jerome Hynes and Ted Howlin

the Festival was such that it truly would not have survived without him; and it was a tribute to him that it should survive after him.

There was a further shift in the future direction of the Festival with the appointment of a new artistic director, Luigi Ferrari. Elaine Padmore directed her last opera at Wexford in 1994. She held a special place in the history of the Festival, serving in her role for thirteen years. Only Walsh himself directed for a longer period. A fitting tribute was paid to the talented director:

> Wexford's standing, both nationally and internationally, has never been higher. The numbers of foreign visitors who now visit us and the massive media coverage the Festival receives bear witness to this. Under Elaine's aegis it has become a truly International Festival.

82 Linda Molloy (festival office) and Vladimir Matorin, 1995
83 Daniela Barcellona, 1996

We are richer for her years with us and we are in her debt. Traditionally after the final performance of the Festival 'Auld Lang Syne' is sung. In 1994 the words 'should old acquaintance be forgot' will have a very special meaning. Elaine Padmore will certainly not be forgotten in Wexford.[12]

Padmore's final season of opera at Wexford included Rubinstein's *The Demon*, Leoncavallo's *La Bohème* and Richard Wagner's *Das Liebesverbot*. The standard of the Wexford Festival chorus continued to progress, this year under the leadership of chorus master, Gregory Rose. Padmore indeed ended her term on a high note. The success of the Festival this year was noted in the council minutes. The chairman, John O'Connor, said that in his view the season was a 'resounding success'. More voluntary workers than ever before participated, and the operatic standard was highly praised. It was further noted that 'the company spirit throughout the Festival was excellent'. Against the backdrop of such enthusiastic praise, Luigi Ferrari entered the scene in Padmore's place.

Luigi Ferrari was well known on the international opera scene when he accepted the position at Wexford. He was born in Milan in 1951 and had received degrees in both composition and musical analysis from the Verdi Conservatory in Milan. He worked as assistant to the director of the International Festival of Contemporary Music at Venice. Ferrari's musical publications include the critical edition of the opera *La Pietra Del Paragone* by Rossini; and the Italian translation of the books *Verdi* by William Weaver and *Mozart's Operas* by Edward Dent. He had also been a member of the jury at several international singing competitions in Italy and Spain and at the BBC's Cardiff *Singer of the World* competition in 1991 and 1993.[13] Ferrari's unique style was marked from the beginning, with a strong emphasis on the Italian and late Romantic operas.[14] He himself admitted that crucial policy decisions had been taken by the Festival council before he arrived at Wexford. These decisions made it possible for him to extend the repertoire of the Festival to include his own distinct choices.

The first decision that had been taken received an immense amount of press criticism. It was decided that the Festival could no longer rely on its local chorus to constitute the majority of the singers on the stage. The reason for this decision was that the local people involved in the chorus were in full-time employment in Wexford and could therefore only dedicate Saturdays to rehearsals. Further, there was the additional irritation of people dropping out in the weeks before the Festival was due to commence (sometimes they received offers to sing elsewhere and were paid for their efforts). This was becoming increasingly inadequate as the Festival became more professional in outlook. It was a reasonable solution to employ professional singers who would come to Wexford for an extended period before the Festival and who could dedicate substantial time to rehearsals. Ferrari thus employed twenty-four professional singers from the Prague Chamber Choir with their chorus master, and sixteen singers were also chosen through auditions.

Ferrari had attended the 1994 opera season in Wexford: in fact it was his first time to visit Wexford. On this visit, he had noticed that the orchestral pit was absolutely inadequate to house the number of musicians needed for many of the works that Wexford had the potential to perform. As a result, music regularly had to be reorchestrated to suit the number of musicians that could actually fit in the orchestral pit. As Ferrari attended his first Festival council meeting, he produced a drawing, sketched by himself, to highlight his proposed solution to extend the pit under the stage. The council was puzzled by his drawing that suggested the knocking down of one of the original walls under the stage and putting up a pillar in its place. The viability of the plan was nevertheless checked and subsequently the pit was extended to cater for eight extra players. As Ferrari admitted, this gave the orchestral repertoire significant scope for extension. It was not particularly unusual that Ferrari's first efforts involved trying to solve the problem of an inadequate orchestral pit, considering the fact that he had a degree in Architecture from the Milan Polytechnic.

The new artistic director was agitated by the length of rehearsal time that was available to him before the season began. He succeeded in persuading the council to arrange the extension of this rehearsal time from three weeks to four weeks, adding to the cost of festival preparations. He also persuaded the orchestra to extend its rehearsal schedule.

Ferrari's incremental triumphs allowed him to pursue an artistic policy that was distinct to the man himself. His main focus during his tenure at Wexford was threefold. First, he re-evaluated the repertoire of Eastern Europe, including Czechoslovakia and Poland. Further he explored early Italian repertoire and also the music of composers between the First and Second World Wars who did not belong to the second Viennese School.

The chairman, John O'Connor, was delighted to inform his council that the Arts Council had reconsidered its award to the Festival and had decided upon issuing the Festival with a further £40,000 of the 1994 season. This brought the total amount of grant aid to £230,000, an increase of £50,000 on the 1993 season. Jerome Hynes was congratulated for his part in securing this increase.[15]

Ferrari's first season opened on 19 October with Pacini's *Saffo*. This year also witnessed the production of Rimsky-Korsakov's *Mayskaya Noch* and Mascagni's *Iris*. The Festival council paid tribute to Ferrari for his 'extraordinary achievements' over the previous few months.[16] Ferrari's influence on Festival affairs ensured that international recognition was growing steadily for the Festival.

It was becoming increasingly obvious that the Festival council had matters well under control by 1995. This was obviously a cause of great relief to its members. As the chairman indicated in a statement to the Wexford Festival Trust, 1995 was a real turning point. On the financial side, the elimination of the working capital deficit was achieved, and for the first time in many years the balance showed a surplus on the working capital account. A policy of 'strict budgetary control' was in place and this was appropriate for an organisation with a gross budget of £1.2 million. O'Connor further intimated that the number of voluntary workers was unprecedented in 1995 – a vital factor for the successful continuation of opera in Wexford.[17]

The age-old complaint that Wexford favoured international singers over its Irish counterparts resurfaced in 1996. A report appeared in the *Wexford People* on 30 October entitled 'Quality before passport the criterion'. This statement had apparently been made by the Festival's chairman. It was a recurring criticism over the years at Wexford that foreign singers were utilized and, as the Dublin-based tenor Brian Hoey pointed out,

> there were plenty of young Irish singers well capable of playing roles in the operas and various fringe events, but were not being given the chance to do so. If an Irish director was working in Italy he would be expected to fill over half of his cast and chorus from native Italian singers. [18]

But Wexford had invested much energy into producing a world-class event and from the very early days when Walsh was artistic director, public comment, good or bad, was not allowed to affect decisions taken at Wexford. Other comments, however, were more positive about artistic decision-making, and one report carried the story that Wexford Festival Opera managed to uphold its 'cosmopolitan image' by attracting artists from fifteen different countries to perform at Wexford. [19]

Amidst these doubts about how international the Festival should be, the 1996 Festival moved ahead, extending from 17 October to 3 November. Donizetti's *Parisina* was the first opera to be performed, followed by Meyerbeer's *L'Étoile du Nord* and Fibich's *Šárka*.

Ferrari's distinct choice was again apparent in 1997 with the production of Respighi's *La Fiamma*, Dargomïzhsky's *Rusalka* and Mercadante's *Elena da Feltre*. As far as the Festival fringe events were concerned, Ferrari's revolution was with the production of opera scenes in White's Hotel. The idea was first introduced by Elaine Padmore, where operatic repertoire was reduced significantly and performed during the Festival, firstly at the Arts Centre in the town and later at the hotel. Ferrari began to use this platform as a type of training ground for potential singers and young producers. The idea was that they would come to Wexford to sing in the opera scenes event, and if they were deemed to be of high quality they could be invited back to sing in one of the actual operas at the Theatre Royal. A similar tactic was used with producers who were given the opportunity to produce the opera scenes. This gave Ferrari the opportunity to try out new talent in Wexford and for Wexford.

Another somewhat radical change that can be associated with Ferrari's term as artistic director was the renewed and exclusive emphasis on the voice.

84 Jacek Janiszewski, Elizabeth Woods and Dariusz Stachura in *Straszny Dwór*, 1999

85 Cornelia Helfricht in *Die Königin von Saba*, 1999

86 Tereza Mátlová and Cornelia Helfricht in *Die Königin von Saba*, 1999

87 Scene from *Straszny Dwór*, 1999

88 Elizabeth Woods singing in
    Simon's Place bar, 1999

Ferrari was conscious of the growing number of musical events during the Festival that were not related in any way to opera. He managed to shift the focus back to singing. After all, it was the duty of the Festival council to give singers the opportunity to make money when they arrived in Wexford by performing extra concerts. They were still agreeing to come for a fraction of the fee they could receive elsewhere. The singers were, in effect, making an investment to Wexford in the hope that their exposure there would lead to an international reputation. Subsequently, the Festival became exclusively focussed on the voice.

Ted Howlin assumed the position of chairman of the Festival in 1998. He had been involved with the Festival for many years in his capacity as box office manager. The transition therefore was a smooth one. The Festival Council continued to support the distinct flavour of Ferrari's taste, and year after year his choices of opera were acclaimed. In 1998 he put on Gomes' *Fosca* and Haas' *Šarlatán*. The length of the season did not change and Zandonai's *I Cavalieri di Ekebù* rounded off another highly successful season.

By 1999, the Arts Council grant to the Festival had reached £450,000, an amount that was welcomed by the Festival Council.[20] The 1980s had proved such a struggle financially that it was a relief to be able to deal with other matters, including strategy for the future. Ferrari had proved to be a huge success and his choice of operas continued to bring acclaim for Wexford Festival Opera.

The President of Ireland, Mary McAleese, opened the Festival in 1999. Ferrari had chosen Goldmark's *Die Königin von Saba*, Moniuszko's *Straszny Dwór* and Giordano's *Siberia*. There was a noticeable enthusiasm about the Festival this year, generated by both the council and the audiences that had attended the performances. All operas had achieved 100 per cent occupancy, with 53 of the 57 fringe events also booked out. Perhaps because of this feeling of stability, it was decided to set out a plan for Festival direction over the coming years. Howlin noted at a council meeting that a proposal had been put to the Government in the hope of securing funding and that a new body, the Wexford Festival Foundation, had been set up. This new entity would be charged with the task of identifying areas of potential private funding and using the money raised for capital development.

At the same meeting two issues arose which highlighted the Council's desire to ensure a steady progression of Festival policies and also to ensure that the regular visitors to Wexford were satisfied with these policies. The first question asked was whether or not some of the operas chosen were really worthy of production. It had been the Festival's trademark to produce little-known works, but perhaps it was inevitable that at some stage these choices should be rigorously assessed; obviously not all little-known works were worthy of production. Secondly, a question was posed concerning the quality of the productions. This epitomized the professional attitude that had by now become inherent in the Festival's policies: the standard of opera at Wexford must be continually progressive.[21]

The 2000 season saw the reintroduction of the composer Zandonai; this time the opera was *Conchita*. Tchaikovsky's *Orleanskaya deva* was performed on opening night and was followed by Adam's *Si j'étais roi*.

The fiftieth anniversary celebrations of the Festival were indeed spectacular. The fireworks scene on the opening night was more impressive than ever. The magnitude of the event did not pass unnoticed by the President of Ireland, Mary McAleese. She commended the Festival for its wonderful achievement, commenting that it 'has long since enjoyed an international reputation for excellence and this year will be no exception, providing a feast of glorious music which will be enjoyed by Irish and international visitors alike'.[22]

The operatic choices for 2001 did not disappoint. Flotow's *Alessandro Stradella* opened the season on 18 October and was followed by Dvořák's *Jakobín* and Massenet's *Sapho*. For only the second time in the Festival's history, the National Symphony Orchestra was not engaged. It was an unusual and potentially damaging decision to employ the National Philharmonic Orchestra of Belarus for this, the Festival's fiftieth anniversary. The Festival had been supported by RTÉ since its inception and the decision to move away from the country's national orchestra was no less difficult in 2001 than it had been for Walsh in 1961 when he employed the Royal Liverpool Philharmonic Orchestra.

Negotiations with Radio Teilifís Éireann had reached a stalemate over terms and conditions of the contract as well as fees. As Ferrari pointed out, the problem was not artistic but financial: the Festival council ended its lengthy relationship with RTÉ because it could no longer afford to bring the orchestra to Wexford. He further commented that the National Symphony Orchestra was essentially a symphony orchestra, not an operatic one, and as such was used to performing *on* the stage rather than *under* it. The regimented schedule of the orchestra no longer suited the needs of those trying to stage

89   Sir Anthony O'Reilly, Jerome Hynes and Ted Howlin, 2002

an opera. Ferrari recalled an occasion where he needed to switch the order of the opera rehearsal because of a set problem. When he notified RTÉ about the schedule change, he was duly told that RTÉ could only accept emergency changes. 'But this is an emergency,' Ferrari told the broadcasting station in exasperation, only to be told that fifteen days notice were needed for 'emergency changes'.[23]

In addition to these insurmountable differences between the needs of the Festival council and the stipulations of the contract drawn up by RTÉ, the cost of bringing the orchestra to Wexford for rehearsals and for performances had reached unprecedented levels. The council could not afford to pay the salaries and expenses of these players. The orchestra was travelling up and down to Dublin between rehearsals – a most inflexible arrangement.

The National Philharmonic Orchestra of Belarus was thus selected as a replacement to the National Symphony Orchestra when there was no hope of reaching an agreement with the broadcasting station. The following year fur-

ther attempts were made to reconcile the differences between the professionals in Dublin and the 'amateur professionals' in Wexford. But these attempts
failed, and once more the Belarus Orchestra returned to Wexford for the
entire period of rehearsals leading up the 2002 Festival.

In 2002, Mercadante's *Il Giuramento* was performed, along with Martinů's
Mirandolina and Auber's *Manon Lescaut.* The performances raised quite a stir
this year and, as the *Guardian* exclaimed, 'there is plenty of sex on offer at the
Wexford Festival this year. The three operas have, it would seem, been chosen for their erotic content, and weave complementary variations on the
theme of female self-assertion and masculine responses to it'.[24]
This season was a particularly joyous one following the announcement by the
Taoiseach, Bertie Ahern, that the plans for the redevelopment of the Theatre
Royal had been approved. The expected cost of the project would be in the
region of €27 million. The unforgettable image of Ted Howlin, chairman of
the Festival council, jumping for joy outside the Theatre building was enough
to evoke the sense of relief that was now felt about the future of the Festival.
Jerome Hynes explained the phases of development that could now proceed.
Firstly, the capacity of the existing theatre would be extended from 550 to 700
seats. Secondly, a plan was drawn up for the building of a second flexible theatre that would house 300 or 400 seats and an art gallery, rehearsal rooms and
bars. 'It represents a clear milestone in the development of Wexford Festival
Opera and of the arts in the region and further afield,' Hynes said with an air
of satisfaction.[25]

The 2003 Festival saw performances of Mahler's *Die Drei Pintos*,
Granados' *María del Carmen*, and Weinberger's *Svanda Dudák.* An incident
that threatened to mar the festivities this year was the presence of members
of the Musicians Union of Ireland protesting outside the Theatre Royal. The
demonstration drew attention to the fact that the Belarussian Orchestra was
still being employed at Wexford. As Hynes pointed out, however, 'the festival's new partnership underlines the international nature of the event, and
presents exciting new opportunities for both the orchestra and the Festival,
which we look forward to developing'.[26] In fact, the Festival council had tried
each year to repair the relations with its once professional allies in Dublin but
to no avail.

Ferrari's time at Wexford was nearly up and he looked back on his years
there with positive enthusiasm. His last season would be the 2004 Festival. He

90 Alexandre Swan and Maryna Vyskvorkina in *Manon Lescaut*, 2002
91 Marco Nisticò, Joanna Burton, Alexandre Swan, Maryna Vyskvorkina and Ermonela Jaho in
   Manon Lescaut, 2002

92 Massimiliano Tonsini, Simon Edwards and Tereza Mátlová in *Mirandolina*, 2002
93 Enrico Marabelli in *Mirandolina*, 2002
94 Manrico Tedeschi and Serena Farnocchia in *Il Giuramento*, 2002

was philosophical about Wexford's future. He noted that the Festival would begin to be affected by developments in the wider operatic world, where opera houses had begun to present rare operas as part of their repertoire. In essence, this was Wexford's legacy: it had led the way to show that it was possible to successfully mount little-known works that should never have been forgotten. 'Many opera houses now have one title each season which is unknown or rare, and this affects the uniqueness of a place like Wexford,' Ferrari regretfully admitted.[27]

While preparing for his final curtain, Ferrari openly admitted that the 'budget is still ridiculous'. Yet he disclosed that many prestigious artistic directors were keen to take up his position when he stepped down. This continued interest in working at Wexford Festival Opera, Ferrari deduced, was because 'despite logistical difficulties, financial and location difficulties, the prestige of the Festival is at a high point'. He noted that he had seen operas on the stage in Wexford that he never imagined he would see performed anywhere. When asked why he had chosen to take the position in the first place, without hesitating he said, 'being an artistic director is not a career but a vocation. In Wexford, all they ask you is to dream. Wexford is the only place that will allow you to realize your dreams.'[28]

Walsh had created the stage into which these dreams could be realized. Walsh had also been keenly aware of the necessity to progress with opera and not to be complacent about what had been achieved. With the advent of yet another significant turning point in the history of Wexford Festival Opera, it is as important as ever to realize this fact. As Walsh so accurately deduced;

> Opera is a business, but it is a business in its own right and must be run by people whose business is opera. When opera becomes an appendage, however important, to something else, be it a social occasion or a commercial promotion, then it is being deflected from its true artistic purpose. I am well aware that both commerce in one or other form and the social occasion are and always have been essential for the survival of opera, but one must guard that the tail is not allowed to wag the dog. To ensure that this does not happen, one must continually ask the question – what has been achieved? You see, it all boils down to a matter of results … In opera as in every other business there is either progress or regression. There can be no standing still.[29]

And the future? The Festival has survived its most testing times and it is

95   Anna María García Pérez in *Maria del Carmen*, 2003
96   Alessandro Svab, Ales Jenis and Eric Shaw in *Die Drei Pintos*, 2003

hard to imagine a situation that the Festival council would now find themselves unprepared for. The town has adopted its foreign contingent of singers
that descend upon the seaside town in the autumn of every year, and it has
remained by far the most significant event in the Wexford calendar. Ferrari
further pointed out that every effort should be made to engage a European
orchestra in future. The trend of the local contingent attending the dress
rehearsals every year has also remained an integral part of the Festival.
Perhaps the Taoiseach, Bertie Ahern, summed it up most accurately when he
said:

> In Wexford, what began fifty years ago as the humble aspiration of a small
> number of local people has grown into a world-renowned festival. In the
> world of opera, every October, Wexford becomes the shining city on the hill,
> the beacon that draws people, time and time again, from all over the world.
>
> It is the people of Wexford who founded the festival and whose continu-
> ing welcome and hospitality make it so special.
>
> Wexford Festival Opera has a proud history. I have no doubt that it also
> has a bright future. The Festival is a focal point of the Irish cultural and
> social calendar. It makes Wexford the essential meeting place for people who
> enjoy opera and enjoy life.[30]

98 Ivan Choupenitch, Tatiana
    Monogarova and Matjaz Robavs
    in *Svanda Dudák*, 2003

99 Larisa Kostyuk in *Svanda Dudák*,
    2003

100 Wexford bridge

My Wexford

HARRY WHITE (*professor of Music, University College Dublin*)

When one thinks of the perilous condition of opera in Ireland, of the sudden withdrawals of state support to non-profit making initiatives in chamber music, of the un-coordinated enterprise by which a national academy for the performing arts was on the verge of formation and then disappeared from view, one can justifiably begin to ask questions about the underlying commitment to art music in Ireland, or lack thereof, which are prompted by these reversals. In a country in which the word 'national' still signifies a positive communion and consensus of artistic enterprise (the 'National Chamber Choir', the 'National Symphony Orchestra', the 'National Concert Hall', and so on), we are enabled, I think, to judge the progress of music in Ireland by the well-being or otherwise of such institutions.

In such a moment of protracted crisis, the success of the Wexford Festival seems (and is) all the more significant. The genius of Wexford is that it is an Irish institution and an international one in varying degrees of measure. It represents to Ireland an idea of opera which, by virtue of its location, supervenes the inherent elitism often associated with opera festivals (in the same way that Bayreuth, for all its legendary difficulty of access, seems less exclusionary than Salzburg). It transcends the dictates of a commercial repertory by which so many European (and North American) houses are bound, and it conversely explores an artistic policy through which it has acquired the reputation of recovering and representing neglected works. Put plainly, the Wexford Festival has fortified an otherwise fragile presence for opera in Ireland, even as it has projected its reputation for 'obscure' repertory as a unique preoccupation in the wider domain of European opera festivals during the last half-century. It has survived.

Anyone who has been to Wexford will attest to its international credentials. Once, in 1999, I went there a few months after my first visit to Bayreuth. I expected to be dismayed by the temptations to compare, but I wasn't. I found instead that Wexford can hold its own against the Bavarian colossus, and not only because both festivals share a sense of intimacy which is difficult to understand without having visited either place, but also because the Irish festival explores a much wider repertory than even the complete works of Richard Wagner can afford. Beyond that point, comparisons make no sense. But quite apart from its international reputation, beyond the sheer lustre of its engagement with European and domestic artists alike, there is also the matter of Wexford's *vital* contribution to the well-being of music in Ireland. In a country which lacks even one permanent opera company (and here again one thinks of the disastrous withdrawal of state support to Opera Ireland), the success, the sheer appetite for survival which the Wexford Festival constantly renews, is all the more important. At the last, the Festival is expressive of a will to incorporate opera as an essential expression of music in Ireland. This commitment, which Tom Walsh himself would have cherished, emancipates Ireland from her long travails of nationalistic debate, and encourages instead the prospect of a mature engagement with that most European of artistic achievements which is opera itself.

BRYAN BALKWILL *(conductor)*

I conducted at most of the early Festivals in the 1950s and it was a pleasure working with Tom Walsh and helping him lay the foundations of the Festival. One must remember that, even in those early days, operas like *La Sonnambula*, *Ernani*, *Der Wildschütz*, *I Due Foscari* and *Martha* were comparative rarities in both Britain and Ireland so that the present policy of presenting unfamiliar pieces is a continuation of that boldness of outlook.

I am delighted with the continuing success of the Festival and particularly with the way it has earned a reputation for itself by developing this originality in its choice of programming. The individuality of the small theatre and its geographical setting favours this policy and does away with the need to compete with others on conventional repertoire and expensive singers.

I cannot think of any better way for the future except to express the hope that more really talented Irish singers can be found to sing the principal roles. Perhaps there could be more chance for good young Irish singers to be brought to Wexford during the Festival to put on one or two short lunchtime programmes of 'scenes' from more conventional operas. This would give them some outside exposure, given that some of the audience comes from overseas.

PETER EBERT (*producer*)

At its birth the Wexford Festival was driven by courage, infectious enthu-siasm and artistic integrity. The idea of opera in foreign languages came as a shock to the community, but any reservations soon melted before the sen-sual pleasure which beautiful voices give to an audience. Dr Tom Walsh and his team showed an uncanny knack in finding exceptionally talented young artists, both foreign and home-grown, for the range of little-known operas which became the hallmark of the Wexford Festival. But Wexford was never a one-horse stable. From the beginning in the 1950s, concerts, drama, exhibi-tions and films as well as Question and Answer sessions and symposia com-plemented and interacted with the opera performances. It was this compre-hensive assault on the innocent citizens which provoked astonishment to begin with and soon developed into wholehearted support. The Wexford Festival arrived just at the right time in the right place. There were other wor-thy, smaller festivals in different parts of the country doing very good work for a relatively small circle of friends and cognoscenti, but unfortunately the opera seasons in Dublin had acquired a reputation for being rather staid and tired and conventional, partly because of the rather ad hoc character of their per-formances. Wexford acquired its special atmosphere because it was exactly the right size for almost everyone to become directly involved.

And how they did! The amount of voluntary work given to the festival idea by people who had other things on their minds as well – such as earning a liv-ing – was quite extraordinary and contributed decisively to the contagious family feeling which permeated the whole town, and still does as far as one can see.

Wexford has had a long, long rise in its fortunes (disregarding the occa-sional blip, which is natural in all such ventures). Every artistic director – and the Board – will ask themselves every year whether they are enterprising enough as well as showing a sound grasp of reality. All theatre is a living being. Complacency and traditionalism inevitably lead to the death of even the most worthy companies. All artists should follow their conscience in the demanding task of interpretation, which involves putting across to a modern audience the thoughts and intentions of the creators. Today we live in a per-vasive culture of 'marketing' – in politics, the arts, food production, you name it – image creation is more important than content in so many instances. Attention-seeking and headline-grabbing performances are just as damaging for the theatre as relentless tradition-hugging. The theatre must experiment in order to live and develop. When I was working in Germany and we were attacked occasionally about a performance being too avant-garde, our music director always said; 'it is our privilege, not to say task, to make mistakes.' Possibly Wexford could afford to experiment with offering more modern works, offering 'White's Barn' type of performances to small venues in the countryside; the crossing-the-theatre-threshold-fear is still widespread among people who have never experienced a 'live' performance. But the most important thing is to preserve the special Wexford atmosphere.

VICTORIA WALSH-HAMER (*Tom Walsh's daughter*)

My late father (Dr Tom Walsh) would today be immensely proud that more than fifty years after its first performance the Wexford Festival continues to achieve significance for opera itself. It has persisted with its original policy of putting on little-known operas, some of which, gratifyingly, have been reborn. 'Collectors' of operas do particularly well at Wexford. The intimate size of the Theatre Royal too has proved an important factor because the festival was founded with that precious thing, 'the voice' at the forefront. For participators – chorus, administrative staff, stage crew, musicians, costume and scene makers, voluntary workers – it has provided an opportunity to work towards something of a high standard, something to be proud of, and each person who gives of their skills to the Festival contributes to that professionalism. The recipients – those who attend the opera, concerts, and other events gain enjoyment, artistic enrichment, and on those rare but magic occasions, sublimity.

He would be proud too that Wexford has been a springboard for artists of many disciplines. The marvellous Mirella Freni came in 1962 to sing the role of Elvira in *I Puritani* to find out whether she was ready to sing major roles in the bigger opera houses (and boy, was she ready!). The producer John Cox, on Wexford's 50th Anniversary Festival, wrote: 'I look back on my Wexford productions with ... most of all gratitude for the part it played in my transformation to a fully-fledged director'. And the conductor Vladimir Jurowski, now music director of Glyndebourne Festival Opera has charmingly acknowledged in its programme book that his 1995 debut at the Wexford Festival 'launched his international career'.

The artistic striving for excellence has been made possible by a loyal audi-

101 The quays, Wexford

ence, sponsors and philanthropists, and the people of Wexford, and a willing and enthusiastic 'home team' which together have facilitated the continuation of this jewel of an opera festival of great significance.

Wexford Festival Opera, having achieved the milestone of its Golden Jubilee, is shortly about to start another chapter with a new artistic director. As long as the original intangible essence of its heart and welcome and particular personality of Wexford, and the giving of prime importance to 'the voice' continues, Wexford will flourish. Physically too the Wexford Festival is about to enter a new phase, having now acquired land surrounding the Theatre Royal. The Board, I am sure, will make certain that in spite of whatever alterations are to be made, 'the voice', and therefore the type of singer who has been so successful at Wexford, can continue to sing sweetly.

102 The fireworks, opening night of the Festival, 2003

The Wexford Experience

LORD BRIGGS (*historian*)

I was lucky enough to get to the third Wexford Festival in 1953 and to see *Don Pasquale*. I had missed the first Festival in 1951, a year of Festival in London, and it seemed natural that the 1953 Wexford Festival had an exhibition on the side on 'Art in Industry'. From the start I was drawn to the local community as well as the Festival, and over the changing years I have developed which I call a Festival habit. There are great years that stand out as musical landmarks, but in retrospect it is the Wexford experience as a whole that not only provides a wonderful sense of continuity but pulls everything together.

Essential parts of that experience are Wexford itself and all the history that lies behind its buildings and its streets; the surrounding countryside and waterfront, along with Rosslare and New Ross, sea and river; the people of Wexford, including its hotel managers and staff and shopkeepers, warm and welcoming and from a rich variety of geographical origins; and, not least, the visitors to the Festival, even more varied in their origins, many 'regulars', some present for the first time, always fascinated by the surprise setting of a unique opera house. Bernard Levin, who wrote so well about the Wexford Festival, initiated more visitors than any other single person.

My wife, Susan, has shared my own experience, envious, however, of the fact that I got to Wexford first in 1953. Over the years we have had great hosts, among them Bryan (Lord) Moyne, who carried with him huge binoculars to watch birds as well as delicate opera glasses to watch the stage; the painter Derek Hill, a very special friend who introduced us to many people who also became friends; and Sir Anthony and Lady O'Reilly, most generous of all hosts, who have incorporated us into the family. Others who have figured in our memories have been the Beits and two Presidents of Ireland, one of them Cearbhall Ó Dálaigh, with whom I had discussed in Sussex and at his home in Ireland a new School of Celtic Studies. How successive orchestras, Celtic and non-Celtic, have chosen to play the Irish National Anthem at the Festival is always a matter of musical interest. Wexford makes you compare operas too, not only the three on show, but Wexford versions of each opera and versions everywhere else.

I have left music to the last, but, in fact, it has always come first, including opera which I have never heard except at Wexford and which has often carried with it what Elaine Padmore called 'the thrill of the new'. I shall never forget *The Turn of the Screw* at the 25th Festival in 1976 when 14-year-old James Maguire, a native of Wexford, played Miles. That was a year when I heard Puccini's religious music for the first time, his *Messa di Gloria* at the Church of the Immaculate Conception. *The Turn of the Screw* was directed by 26-year-old Adrian Slack, who between 1970 and 1973 had divided his time between my two favourite institutions providing opera in Britain – the Welsh National and Glyndebourne. The Wexford connections with Glyndebourne, of which I was a Trustee for 25 years, have always been strong – and creative. I had links too in the early years with the BBC and Radio Eireann: I have always been interested in the broadcasting of opera.

We owe an immense debt to Dr Walsh for all his enthusiastic effort and even more for his far-ranging vision back in the distant 1950s. His daughter, Victoria, is a Sussex neighbour who has stirred all my memories by producing old programmes. (To a historian like myself the advertisements are almost as interesting as the contents.) Our musical debts remain substantial. With Ted Howlin, Jerome Hynes and Luigi Ferrari we have come to expect opera at its best, opera of more than one kind, opera which will make us talk as well as listen.

Notes

CHAPTER ONE

1   Quoted in Gus Smith. *Ring up the Curtain* (Dublin, 1976) p. 29.

2   Joseph Groocock, *A General Survey of Music in the Republic of Ireland* (Dublin, 1961) p. 5.

3   Larchet, *A Plea for Music*, p. 508, in Harry White, *The Keeper's Recital* (Cork, 1998) p. 130.

4   Aural interview with Nellie Walsh, John Bowman, RTÉ 1.

5   Aural interview with Tom Walsh, John Bowman, RTÉ 1.

6   Smith, *Ring up the Curtain* (Dublin, 1976), pp 41-2.

7   Compton Mackenzie, *My Life and Times* (London, 1970).

8   Letter Mackenzie to Walsh, 21 Oct. 1950; Walsh files.

9   Smith, p. 51. It is not known where this quotation is from or how accurate it is.

10   Walsh, 'How It All Began', Wexford Arts Centre newsletter (1977). Gus Smith had indicated in his book that two hundred guineas were sought and five hundred were received – but Walsh refuted this personally in 1977.

11   Walsh, 'How It All Began', Wexford Arts Centre newsletter (1977).

12   *The Bohemian Girl* was Balfe's most acclaimed work, but *The Rose of Castile* had achieved success at Drury Lane when it was first produced on 29 Oct. 1857, Smith, p. 35.

13   Walsh, 'How It All Began', Wexford Arts Centre newsletter (1977).

14   Smith, p. 57.

15   Report on Tom Walsh, RTÉ Archive.

16   Letter Walsh to Ó hAnnracháin, 23 Feb. 1951. RTÉ Archive.

17   Smith, p. 37.

18   Letter Walsh to Ó hAnnracháin, 23 Feb. 1951.

19   Letter Ó hAnnracháin to Walsh, 3 Mar. 1951, RTÉ Archive.

20   Letter Walsh to Ó hAnnracháin, 28 Sept. 1951, RTÉ Archive.

21   Letter O'Dwyer to Ó hAnnracháin, 12 Sept. 1951, RTÉ Archive.

22   Letter Ó hAnnracháin to O'Dwyer, 14 Sept. 1951, Walsh files.

23   Letter Walsh to Ó hAnnracháin, 15 May 1951, RTÉ Archive.

24   Ibid., 3 July 1951, RTÉ Archive.

25   Letter Ó hAnnracháin to Walsh, 12 July 1951, RTÉ Archive.

26   Letter Walsh to Ó hAnnracháin, 13 July 1951, RTÉ Archive.

27   Ibid.

28   It was Walsh's singing teacher, Viani, who had founded the DOS.

29   Letter Walsh to Ó hAnnracháin, 13 July 1951, RTÉ Archive.

30   Ibid., 13 July 1951 in *The Wexford Festival – An Historical Appraisal*, 21 May 1977, Speech to the Faculty of Anaesthetists; Royal College of Surgeons in Ireland.

31   *Free Press*, 20 Oct. 1951. Also in Smith, p. 35. Dickie and Springer became acquainted at Wexford and were subsequently married.

32   Copy of agreement re. Radio Éireann orchestra, 1–4 Nov. 1951, Walsh files.

33   Memo, Ó hAnnracháin, 24 Sept. 1951, Walsh files.

34   Letter Stephenson to O'Dwyer, 25 Sept. 1951, Walsh files

35   Letter Ó hAnnracháin to O'Dwyer, 20 Sept. 1951, Walsh files.

36   Letter Dargavel Concerts Ltd. to O'Dwyer. Letter re. Programming notes, 9 Oct. 1951.

37   Letter C.E. Kelly to O'Dwyer, 23 Oct. 1951, RTÉ Archive.

38 Walsh, 'How It All Began', Wexford Arts Centre newsletter (1977)
39 Letter Perceval Graves to O'Dwyer, 13 Sept. 1951, Walsh files.
40 Moriarty founded the Cork Ballet Company.
41 Letter Moriarty to O'Dwyer, 29 Nov. 1951, Walsh files.
42 *Irish Independent*, 5 July 1963.
43 Letter Compton Mackenzie to Walsh, 21 Nov. 1951, Walsh files.
44 Letter Mackenzie to Walsh, 11 Jan. 1952, Walsh files.
45 *Evening Herald*, 15 Oct. 1951. Also in 1952 Festival programme book.
46 *Irish Independent*, 10 Nov. 1951, in 1952 Festival programme book.
47 *Sunday Times*, 28 Oct. 1951, in 1952 Festival programme book.
48 *Boston Globe*, 13 Nov. 1951, in 1952 Festival programme book.
49 1951 Festival programme book.
50 Fanny, Feehan, 'Tom Walsh: the Operatic Doctor', in *Hibernia*, 20 Oct. 1972, Walsh files.
51 Report on Walsh, RTÉ Archive.

CHAPTER TWO
1 1952 Festival Programme Book.
2 Nellie Walsh, *How Many Times Has the Festival Been in Danger?*, Photocopy, Nellie Walsh files.
3 Walsh aural interview, presented by John Bowman, RTÉ 1.
4 Smith, p. 44.
5 Elvina Ramella (soprano); Nicola Monti (tenor); Gino Vanelli (baritone); Cristiano Dallamangas (Greek bass) sang in Wexford's 1952 production of *L'Elisir d'Amore*, ibid.
6 *Echo*, 8 Nov. 1952.
7 Telephone interview with Bryan Balkwill, Jan. 2000.
8 Letter Ó hAnnracháin to Walsh, 5 Feb. 1953, RTÉ Archive.
9 Letter Walsh to Ó hAnnracháin, 25 Mar. 1953, RTÉ Archive.
10 Letter Ó hAnnracháin to Walsh, 20 Apr. 1953, RTÉ Archive.
11 Letter Walsh to Ó hAnnracháin, 2 Mar. 1953, RTÉ Archive.
12 Letter Ó hAnnracháin to Walsh, 27 Apr. 1953, RTÉ Archive.
13 Letter Walsh to Ó hAnnracháin, 28 Apr. 1953, RTÉ Archive.
14 Letter Ó hAnnracháin to Walsh, 1 May 1953, RTÉ Archive.
15 Letter Walsh to Ó hAnnracháin, 28 Apr. 1953, Walsh files. The artists who had been engaged by the end of April were Nicola Monti as Ernesto; Elvina Ramella as Norina; and Cristiano Dallamangas as Don Pasquale. Letter Walsh to Ó hAnnracháin, 28 April 1953, Walsh files.
16 Ibid., 4 May 1953, RTÉ Archive.
17 Ibid.
18 Letter Ó hAnnracháin to Walsh, 7 May 1953 and Walsh to Ó hAnnracháin, 22 May 1953, RTÉ Archive.
19 Ibid., 7 May 1953.
20 Ibid.
21 Ibid., 12 June 1953.
22 Letter Walsh to Ó hAnnracháin, 13 June 1953, RTÉ Archive.
23 Ibid., 22 June 1953: RTÉ Archive. Monti's fee was subject to Éire Income Tax and it was presumed that RÉ would accept to pay for half of his return air fare to Ireland.
24 *Irish Independent*, 1953.
25 Ibid. Sir Compton was joined on the panel for the Forum by Lord Longford, Eoin O'Mahony and Dr J. Liddy.
26 Smith, p. 51.
27 1954 Festival programme book. Nicola Monti and Marilyn Cotlow were the soloists this year. Cotlow had previously sung in a Metropolitan production of *L'Elisir d'Amore*. Smith, p. 58.
28 *Creation* (Éire), 15 Oct. 1958, Walsh files.
29 Balance sheet for 1955 expenditure account, Walsh files.
30 Balance sheet for 1955 income account – Receipts, Walsh files.
31 1955 Festival programme book.
32 Festival programme books.
33 *New York Times*, 14 Mar. 1993.
34 Ibid.
35 Kevin Collins, 'Festival is a Jewel, says Opera Expert', newspaper article (undated), Walsh files.
36 Charles Acton, 'Wexford needs to stress Irishness', newspaper article, 1 Nov. 1969, Walsh files.

37 This was due to the lack of a coherent archival system to record the history of the Festival in the early years.

38 Letter Moran Caplat to Fintan O'Connor, 3 Nov. 1955, Glyndebourne Archive.

39 Letter O'Connor to Caplat, 12 Oct. 1956, Glyndebourne Archive.

40 Ibid., 16 Jan. 1956, Glyndebourne Archive and 20 June 1956, Wexford Festival Archive.

41 Festival council minutes, 22 Aug. 1956 and 10 Oct. 1956. Wexford Festival Archive.

42 Charles Acton, 'Wexford needs to stress Irishness', newspaper article, 1. Nov. 1969, Walsh files.

43 John Mulcahy, newspaper article, 1977, Walsh files.

44 Wexford Festival minutes 1956-68, Wexford Festival Archive.

45 *RTÉ Guide*, 21 Nov. 1969.

CHAPTER THREE

1 1956 Wexford Festival programme book.

2 Letter Mackenzie to Walsh, 19 Apr. 1956, Walsh files.

3 Balance sheet, as at 7 Jan. 1957, Walsh files.

4 Letter Mackenzie to Walsh, 11 Feb. 1957, Walsh files.

5 Festival council minutes, 20 June 1956, Wexford Festival Archive.

6 Ibid., 4 July 1956.

7 Ibid., 20 June 1956.

8 Ibid., 4 July 1956.

9 Ibid., 3 Oct. 1956.

10 Ibid., 21 Nov. 1956.

11 Ibid., 22 Aug. 1956.

12 Ibid., 19 Dec. 1956.

13 It is indicated in the minutes that this subsidy had been received prior to the 1956 Festival although evidence from further minutes shows the difficulty that the Festival council encountered even into 1957 when trying to claim this subsidy for the 1956 season. By 21 Nov., the Wexford council had received a promise of £500 from the German Legation for the 1955 season but no mention was made of a subsidy for 1956. By 19 Dec. the council realised that it was highly unlikely that they would receive money from the German contingent for their 1956 Festival.

14 Festival council minutes, 3 Oct. 1956, Wexford Festival Archive.

15 Telephone interview with Terry Sheehy, Jan. 2000.

16 Moran Caplat, *From Dinghies To Divas* (London, 1985) p. 194. Significantly, the DGOS had never asked Walsh for operatic advice, although Walsh said he never expected them to.

17 *People*, 31 Oct. 1959, Walsh files.

18 Telephone interview with Terry Sheehy.

19 1957 Festival programme book. Bryan Balkwill conducted, Peter Ebert produced and Joseph Carl was the designer for both operas in this year, 1957 Festival programme book.

20 Letter O'Connor to Caplat, 12 Oct. 1956, Glyndebourne Archive.

21 Festival council minutes, 20 Feb. 1957, Wexford Festival Archive.

22 Ibid., 28 Aug. 1957.

23 Ibid., 9 Sept. 1957.

24 Letter Mackenzie to Walsh, 11 Feb. 1959, Walsh files.

25 Festival council minutes, 27 Nov. 1957, Wexford Festival Archive.

26 Smith, p. 77.

27 Ibid. Born in 1903 to an American mother, he was a Conservative who came into Parliament in 1931. Beit inherited most of his uncle's affairs in South Africa, including the trusteeship of the Beit Trust, a charity organisation for the medical and educational care in Central Africa; ibid.

28 1958 Festival programme book. Due to the illness of Frans Boerlage, the production of *I Due Foscari* was produced by Peter Ebert.

29 Festival council minutes, 19 Nov. 1958, Wexford Festival Archive.

30 *Evening Herald*, 2 July 1958.

31 1958 Festival programme book.

32 Ibid.

33 Festival council minutes, 11 Dec. 1957, Wexford Festival Archive.

34 Ibid., 11 Dec. 1957. The Artistic section covered artists, publicity, scenery, structural alterations to theatre, printing of programme; Business – payment of artists, transport, advertising, insurance, accounts, Income Tax, accommodation, grants, ordering of goods, hiring of films and return thereof; Theatre and Box Office – brochure, preparation of tickets etc., bookings, card index system,

stewarding, cleaning and decoration of theatre, seating; Finance – budget, control of finance, receiving of all cash, banking, keeping of a/c books; Illuminations – town lighting, fireworks, opening ceremony, decoration of town.

35 Ibid., 18 June 1958.

36 Ibid., 22 Oct. 1958.

37 Smith, p. 78. The Calouste Gulbenkian Foundation was operated from Lisbon but had a London office. Beit acted as Wexford's ambassador in the hope of gaining a grant from the foundation, as he had previously been acquainted with the Portuguese ambassador in London.

38 Festival council minutes, 18 June 1958, Wexford Festival Archive.

39 Ibid., 30 Apr. 1958.

40 Ibid., 12 Mar. 1958.

41 Ibid., 21 Jan. 1959.

42 This view was confirmed by another Council member, Dr Des Ffrench, who had had conversations with artists during the previous Festival to that effect.

43 Festival council minutes, 21 Jan. 1959, Wexford Festival Archive.

44 Letter Walsh to Ninette Lawson, 27 Jan. 1959, Walsh files.

45 Interview with Moran Caplat, Jan. 2000.

46 Letter Mackenzie to Walsh, 11 Feb. 1959, Walsh files.

47 Letter Walsh to Ninette Lawson, 5 Apr. 1959, Walsh files.

48 Festival council minutes, 29 Jan. 1959, Wexford Festival Archive.

49 Ibid., 11 Feb. 1959.

50 Ibid., 2 Sept. 1959.

51 Ibid., 26 Nov. 1959.

52 Ibid., 29 Sept. 1959.

53 *People*, 31 Oct. 1959.

54 Ibid.

55 'The Wexford Festival, something of which the country is proud' in *People,* 31 Oct. 1959.

56 1959 Festival programme book.

57 *Irish Times*, 31 Oct. 1959.

CHAPTER FOUR

1 *People*, 31 Oct. 1959.

2 Festival council minutes, 11 Jan. 1960, Wexford Festival Archive.

3 Memo, 'The Wexford Festival and its Future', Alfred Beit to Walsh and Colonel Price, 6 Nov. 1959, Walsh files.

4 Ibid.

5 There is no evidence to suggest that Walsh replied to this memo but his actions thereafter suggest that he took Beit's suggestions very seriously, whether he agreed with them or not. After all, he was left with little choice.

6 Letter Raymond Corish to Walsh, 19 Dec. 1959, Walsh files.

7 Marese Murphy interview with Walsh, newspaper article (undated) Walsh files.

8 Festival council minutes, 4 Dec. 1959, Wexford Festival Archive

9 Ibid., 11 Jan. 1960.

10 Interview with James O'Connor, Wexford, March 2001.

11 Festival council minutes, 1 Mar. 1961, Wexford Festival Archive.

12 1961 Festival programme book.

13 Festival council minutes, 1 Mar. 1961, Wexford Festival Archive.

14 'The Wexford Festival', by Marese Murphy, Nov. 1961, Walsh files.

15 Festival council minutes, 5 July 1961, Wexford Festival Archive.

16 Ibid., 1 Mar. 1961.

17 Ibid., 5 July 1961.

18 Letter Beit to Walsh, 23 Aug. 1961, Walsh files.

19 Ibid.

20 Festival council minutes, 20 Dec. 1961, Wexford Festival Archive.

21 Ibid., 20 Dec. 1961.

22 Ibid. (undated, but 1962).

23 Ibid., 3 Jan. 1962.

24 Ibid., 10 Jan. 1962. The Liverpool Philharmonic had been paid £2,500 in 1961.

25 Ibid., 10 Jan. 1961.

26 Ibid., 23 Aug. 1962.

27 Ibid., 10 Jan. 1962.

28 Ibid., 10 Jan. 1962.

29 Ibid., 25 Jan. 1962.

30 Ibid., 14 March 1962.

31 Ibid., 10 April 1962

32 Interview with Jim Golden (May 2000) voluntary backstage worker (Props) at Wexford Opera Festival. Later, he became chairman of the Festival council.

33   Festival council minutes, 10 Apr. 1962, Wexford Festival Archive.

34   Ibid., 29 May 1962.

35   Ibid., 2 Sept. 1962.

36   1962 Festival programme book. Bernadette Greevy and Veronica Dunne, both Irish artists, performed the Mascagni work.

37   Ibid.

38   Ibid.

39   Festival council minutes, 5 Nov. 1962, Wexford Festival Archive

40   Ibid., 28 Nov. 1962.

41   Ibid., 28 Nov. 1962.

42   Ibid., 14 Aug. 1963.

43   1963 Festival programme book.

44   Letter Walsh to Gerard Victory, 1 June 1963, Wexford Festival Archive.

45   Festival council minutes, 13 Nov. 1963, Wexford Festival Archive.

46   *Irish Independent,* 5 July 1963.

47   Festival council minutes, 13 Nov.1963, Wexford Festival Archive.

48   Ibid., 2 Dec. 1963.

49   Ibid., 27 Dec. 1963.

50   Ibid., 5 Feb. 1964.

CHAPTER FIVE

1   Tony Grey, 'Let's make an Opera Festival' – said the five mad men of Wexford, (no date) Walsh files.

2   *Irish Independent,* 21 Feb. 1964.

3   *Evening Standard,* 22 Feb.1964.

4   *Irish Times,* 24 Feb. 1964.

5   Interview with Alan Wood, East Sussex, Jan. 2000. Wood was in charge of Guinness advertising.

6   Festival council minutes, 3 March 1964, Wexford Festival Archive.

7   1964 Festival programme book.

8   Ibid.

9   Festival council minutes, 10 Mar. 1965, Wexford Festival Archive.

10   Festival council minutes, 2 June 1965, Wexford Festival Archive.

11   Letter Walsh to Beit, June 1965, Walsh files.

12   Festival council minutes, 9 Aug. 1965, Wexford Festival Archive.

13   1965 Festival programme book.

14   Confidential memorandum from Walsh to Jackson, 13 Dec. 1965, Walsh files.

15   Letter Beit to Walsh, 8 Jan. 1966, Walsh files.

16   Ibid. It is not clear what type of relationship Beit had with the Guinness group, although Alan Wood, in charge of Guinness advertising, said that Beit found the Guinness involvement hard to accept.

17   Ibid.

18   Letter Walsh to Beit, 10 Jan. 1966, Walsh files.

19   Ibid.

20   Festival council minutes, 5 July 1966, Wexford Festival Archive.

21   Ibid., 25 Apr. 1966, Wexford Festival Archive.

22   1966 Festival programme book.

23   Festival council minutes, 5 July 1966, Wexford Festival Archive.

24   Special meeting of the Wexford members of the executive council 17 Aug. 1966, Wexford Festival Archive.

25   Festival council minutes, 23 Sept. 1966, Wexford Festival Archive.

26   Ibid., 7 Nov. 1966, Wexford Festival Archive.

27   Letter Mackenzie to Walsh, 27 May 1967, Walsh files.

28   Mackenzie to Walsh, 11 Feb. 1959, Walsh files. Mackenzie actually remained president of the Festival until his death in 1972.

29   Interview with Jim Golden and interview with Nicky Cleary, voluntary workers with Festival. Also in Smith, p. 102.

30   Festival council minutes, 7 Nov. 1966, Wexford Festival Archive.

31   *The Wexford Festival – An Historical Appraisal,* 21 May 1977, Speech to the Faculty of Anaesthetists; Royal College of Surgeons in Ireland. Walsh files.

32   *Sunday Times,* 29 Oct. 1967.

33   Brian Quinn, 'Wexford without Walsh' in *Hibernia,* October 1967, Walsh files.

34   Fanny Feehan; 'Tom Walsh – The Operatic Doctor' in *Hibernia,* 20 Oct. 1972, Walsh files.

35   *Hibernia,* 17 Nov. 1972, Walsh files.

36   Ibid.

37   *Hibernia,* 20 Oct. 1972, Walsh files.

38   Letter Brian Dickie to Reverend B. Viney of Sussex, 13 Nov. 1968, Walsh files.

39   'The Dwarfs without Snow White' in *The Free Press,* 20 Sept. 1968, Walsh files.

CHAPTER SIX

1 Festival council minutes, 27 Jan. 1967, Wexford Festival Archive.
2 Ibid., 11 July 1967.
3 Ibid.
4 Ibid., 16 Aug. 1967.
5 *Sunday Independent*, 29 Oct. 1967.
6 Ibid., 3 Nov. 1967. James O'Connor had made a comment to the press regarding this. O'Connor defended his line by saying that he had stated that 'it *would* be considered', not that 'it *had* been considered'.
7 Ibid.
8 Ibid., 23 Jan. 1968.
9 Ibid., 27 March 1968.
10 *Irish Times*, 10 June 1968.
11 *Evening Press,* 26 Oct. 1968.
12 Festival council minutes, 3 Jan. 1969, Wexford Festival Archive.
13 Ibid.
14 Ibid, 14 May 1969.
15 Ibid, 26 June 1969.
16 Michael Yeats, 'Poor Standard at Wexford' in *Evening Press,* 27 Oct. 1969, Wexford Festival Archive.
17 Festival council minutes, 5 Nov. 1969, Wexford Festival Archive.
18 Ibid.
19 Ibid.
20 Ibid., 9 Sept. 1970.
21 *Enniscorthy Echo,* 10 Oct. 1970.
22 Festival council minutes, 20 Jan. 1971, Wexford Festival Archive.
23 *Cork Examiner*, 28 May 1971.
24 Robert Henderson, press cutting, Nov. 1971, Wexford Festival Archive.
25 *Country Life*, press cutting, 11 Nov. 1971.
26 *Hibernia*, 8 Nov. 1971.
27 *New York Times*, 14 Feb. 1971.
28 Festival council minutes, 9 June 1971, Wexford Festival Archive.
29 Report on meeting of local council members, 16 Nov. 1971, Wexford Festival Archive.
30 Festival council minutes, 2 Dec. 1971. Wexford Festival Archive.
31 Ibid.
32 Ibid.
33 Festival council minutes, 24 July 1972, Wexford Festival Archive.
34 Ibid., 26 Jan. 1972.
35 Ibid., 24 July 1972.
36 *Evening Herald*, 9 June 1972.
37 Festival executive council minutes, 15 Dec. 1972, Wexford Festival Archive.
38 Letter Walsh to Mackenzie's wife, 10 Dec. 1972, Walsh files. Mackenzie had been married three times and was pre-deceased by his first two wives. His latter two wives were sisters.
39 Wexford Festival development council minutes, 16 Dec. 1972, Wexford Festival Archive.
40 Festival council minutes, 2 Feb. 1973, Wexford Festival Archive.
41 Ibid., 9 April 1973.
42 Ibid.
43 Ibid., 21 Feb. 1973.
44 Ibid., 21 March 1973.
45 Publicity policy report to Wexford Festival council, Apr. 1973, Wexford Festival Archive.
46 Festival council minutes, 8 June 1973, Wexford Festival Archive.
47 Ibid., 28 Nov. 1973.
48 Ibid., 27 July 1973.
49 *Sunday Times*, 4 Nov. 1973.
50 'Irish Opera Company Needed', press cutting, 1973, Wexford Festival Archive.
51 *Glasgow Herald*, 3 Nov. 1973.
52 Wexford Festival development council report, Dec. 1973, Wexford Festival Archive.
53 Ibid.
54 1974 Wexford Festival programme book.

CHAPTER SEVEN

1 Festival council minutes, 3 Jan. 1974, Wexford Festival Archive.
2 Report on Arts Council subvention in Festival executive council minutes, 4 June 1974, Wexford Festival Archive.
3 Festival council minutes, 17 Sept. 1974, Wexford Festival Archive.
4 Tony O'Brien, 'Live Music is Dead in Wexford' in *New Ross Standard*, 7 Sept. 1974, Wexford Festival Archive.
5 Festival council minutes, 4 Feb. 1975, Wexford Festival Archive.
6 *Wexford People*, 24 Oct. 1975.
7 Nicholas Furlong, 'Wexford Festival no Anglo-Saxon Remnant' in *Irish Post*, 13 Dec. 1975, Wexford Festival Archive.
8 Festival council minutes, 30 Sept. 1976,

Wexford Festival Archive.

9   Ibid., 8 Dec. 1976, Wexford Festival Archive.

10   Rodney Milnes, 'Wexford Ho!' in *Opera*, 1976, Wexford Festival Archive.

11   *Wexford People*, 5 Nov. 1976.

12   Festival council minutes, 15 Feb. 1977, Wexford Festival Archive.

13   *Sunday Independent*, 28 Feb. 1977.

14   1977 Wexford Festival programme book.

15   Festival council minutes, 15 Aug. 1978, Wexford Festival Archive.

16   1978 Wexford Festival programme book.

17   Festival council minutes, 15 Jan. 1979, Wexford Festival Archive.

18   Ibid., 16 Jan. 1979.

19   Ibid., 15 May 1979, Wexford Festival Archive.

20   *Irish Times*, 6 Nov. 1979.

21   Festival council minutes, 15 May 1979, Wexford Festival Archive.

22   1979 Wexford Festival programme book.

23   Festival council minutes, 15 Jan. 1979, Wexford Festival Archive.

24   Ibid., 12 Feb. 1980.

25   Ibid., 11 Mar. 1980.

26   Ibid., 24 Sept. 1980.

27   Ibid., 9 Dec. 1980.

28   Brian Quinn, press cutting, 1980, Wexford Festival Archive.

29   Festival council minutes, 23 June 1981, Wexford Festival Archive.

30   Kenneth Loveland, 'Another Triumph at Wexford' in *South Wales Argus*, 30 Oct. 1981, Wexford Festival Archive.

31   Festival council minutes, 8 Dec. 1981. Wexford Festival Archive.

32   Ibid.

33   Ibid., 4 Feb. 1982.

34   Ibid.

35   Ibid., 13 July 1982.

36   Ibid., 12 Oct. 1982.

37   Ibid.

38   Repertory committee report, 4 Jan. 1983, Wexford Festival Archive.

39   Letter to Ian Fox, 7 Feb. 1983, Wexford Festival Archive.

40   *Enniscorthy Echo*, 14 Jan. 1983.

41   Festival council minutes, 16 Feb. 1984, Wexford Festival Archive.

42   Ibid., 20 Nov. 1984.

43   *Irish Times*, 2 Nov. 1984.

44   Festival council minutes, 15 Jan. 1985, Wexford Festival Archive.

45   'How Government could Help Wexford Festival', *Enniscorthy Guardian*, 5 July 1985.

CHAPTER EIGHT

1   Festival council minutes, 12 Dec. 1985, Wexford Festival Archive.

2   Ibid., 17 Feb. 1986.

3   Ibid, Finance Officer's Report.

4   Notes for Wexford Festival meeting, 17 Feb. 1986, Wexford Festival Archive. It is unclear by whom this was written but it is obvious nevertheless that tensions were extremely high at this point.

5   Festival council minutes, 3 Mar. 1986, Wexford Festival Archive.

6   Ibid., 2 Apr. 1986.

7   Ibid., 20 May 1986.

8   Ibid.

9   Festival council minutes, 27 Aug. 1986.

10   'Festival Fanfare' in the *People*, 24 Oct. 1986.

11   Festival council minutes, 1 Dec. 1987, Wexford Festival Archive.

12   Ibid., 8 Dec. 1987.

13   Ibid.

14   Letter Barbara Wallace to Beit, 21 Dec. 1987, Wexford Festival Archive.

15   Festival council minutes, 20 May 1986, Wexford Festival Archive.

16   Bernard Levin, 'Doctor Tom's Final Curtain', in the *Times* on 14 Nov. 1988. Reprinted in Ian Fox (ed.), *100 Nights at the Opera*, (Dublin, 1991) 135-7.

17   'Dr Tom Walsh – Founder of the Wexford Festival', *Guardian*, 1988, Wexford Festival Archive.

18   Festival council minutes, 10 Dec. 1989, Wexford Festival Archive.

CHAPTER NINE

1   Ibid., 18 Sept. 1989.

2   Copy of proposal for seminar; 'Strategy for the Wexford Festival Council into the year 2000', Ibid., 18 Sept. 1989.

3   Ibid.

4   Memo from Barbara Wallace, 31 Mar. 1989, Wexford Festival Archive.

5   Letter Sean Scallan to Wallace, 2 Mar. 1989, Wexford Festival Archive.

6   'Some Reasons for Examining the Existing Structure of Wexford Festival Opera', by Barbara Wallace, 1990, Wexford Festival Archive.

7   Festival council minutes, 3 Dec. 1991, Wexford Festival Archive.

8   Ibid., 11 June 1991.

9   Ibid., 3 Dec. 1991

10   Paul Hennessy, Wexford Festival Opera – Corporate affairs and statutory compliance report, Aug. 1992.

11   1992 Festival programme book.

12   1994 Festival programme book.

13   1995 Festival programme book.

14   2000 Festival programme book.

15   Festival council minutes, 28 Mar. 1994, Wexford Festival Archive.

16   Ibid., 30 Oct. 1995.

17   1996 Wexford Festival trust, the chairman's statement, Wexford Festival Archive.

18   *Wexford People*, 30 Oct. 1996.

19   *Wexford People*, 29 May 1996.

20   Festival council minutes, 23 Mar. 1999, Wexford Festival Archive.

21   Ibid., 7 Dec. 1999.

22   Message from President Mary McAleese, 2001 Festival programme book.

23   Interview with Luigi Ferrari, Feb. 2004.

24   *Guardian*, 25 Oct. 2002.

25   *Wexford People*, 13 Mar. 2002.

26   *Classical Music*, 25 Oct. 2003.

27   *Irish Times*, 14 Oct. 2003.

28   Interview with Luigi Ferrari, Feb. 2004.

29   Transcript of speech by Walsh, circa 1970, Walsh files.

30   Message from the Taoiseach, Bertie Ahern, 2001 Festival programme book.

List of Illustrations

CREDITS

1,3,4,8,9,10,11,16,18 Wexford County Library Archives.

2,13,14,15,17,21,31,52,53,58,60,70,71 Bord Fáilte Éireann archives.

Frontispiece and 5,6,7,12,20,22,24,25,29,30,33,35,36,39,40,76,77,78 TJW estate, c/o Victoria Walsh-Hamer.

19,23 *Irish Times* archives.

26,27,28,44,50,57,59,62,68,69,72,73,79 Wexford Festival Office archives.

32,34,37,38,41,42,43,45,46,47,48,49,51,54,55,56,61,63,64,65,66,67 Denis O'Connor estate, c/o Denise O'Connor-Murphy.

74,75 John Ironside photography.

80,81,82,83,88,89,102 *Echo* archives.

84,85,86,87,90,91,92,93,94,95,96,97,98,99,100,101 Derek Speirs photography.

Index of Performances

	PERFORMERS	ORCHESTRA
1951 1,2,3,4 November **The Rose of Castile** *by* Michael William Balfe	Maureen Springer (Queen Elvira) Angela O'Connor (Donna Carmen) Statia Keyes (Duchess of Calatrava) James G. Cuthbert (Don Pedro) James Browne (Don Florio) Michael Hanlon (Don Sallust) Nellie Walsh (Louisa) Seamus Roche (Pablo) Brendan Nolan (Don Alvaro) Murray Dickie (Manuel)	Radio Éireann Light Orchestra Wexford Festival Chorus Dermot O'Hara (Conductor) Powell Lloyd (Producer) Joan Denise Moriarty (Prima Ballerina)
1952 29, 30 October; 1,2 November **L'Elisir d'Amore** *by* Gaetano Donizetti	Elvina Ramella (Adina) Nicola Monti (Nemorino) Gino Vanelli (Belcore) Cristiano Dallamangas (Dulcamara) Patricia O'Keeffe (Gianetta)	Radio Éireann Light Orchestra Wexford Festival Chorus Dermot O'Hara (Conductor) Peter Ebert (Producer) Joseph Carl (Designer)
1953 28,29,31 October; 1 November **Don Pasquale** *by* Gaetano Donizetti	Cristiano Dallamangas (Don Pasquale) Nicola Monti (Ernesto) Afro Poli (Dr Malatesta) Elvina Ramella (Norina) N.N (A notary)	Radio Éireann Light Orchestra Wexford Festival Chorus Bryan Balkwill (Conductor) Peter Ebert (Producer) Joseph Carl (Designer)
1954 3,4,6,7 November **La Sonnambula** *by* Vincenzo Bellini	Marilyn Cotlow (Amina) Nicola Monti (Elvino) Franco Calabrese (Rudolpho) Thetis Blacker (Teresa) Halinka de Tarczynska (Lisa) Gwyn Griffiths (Alessio) Daniel McCoshan (A notary)	Radio Éireann Light Orchestra Wexford Festival Chorus Bryan Balkwill (Conductor) Peter Ebert (Producer) Joseph Carl (Designer)
1955 30 October; 1,3,5 November **Manon Lescaut** *by* Giacomo Puccini	Kevin Miller (Edmondo) Salvatore Puma (Chevalier des Grieux) Marko Rothmüller (Lescaut) Gwyn Griffiths (Geronte de Ravoir) Esther Réthy (Manon Lescaut) Geoffrey Clifton (Innkeeper) Daniel McCoshan (Dancing master) Geoffrey Clifton (Sergeant of the Royal Archers) Daniel McCoshan (Lamplighter) Celine Murphy (A singer)	Radio Éireann Light Orchestra Wexford Festival Chorus Bryan Balkwill (Conductor) Anthony Besch (Producer) Peter Rice (Designer)

1955
31 October; 2,4,6 November
Der Wildschütz
by Albert Lortzing

Thomas Hemsley (Count of Eberbach)
Monica Sinclair (The Countess)
John Kentish (Baron Kronthal)
Elizabeth Lindermeier (Baroness Freimann)
Celine Murphy (Nanette)
Max Pröbstl (Baculus)
Heather Harper (Gretchen)
Richard Day (Pancratius)

Wexford Festival Chorus
Hans Gierster (Conductor)
Anthony Besch (Producer)
Peter Rice (Designer)

1956
28,30 October; 1,3 November
Martha
by Friedrich von Flotow

Gisela Vivarelli (Lady Harriet)
Constance Shacklock (Nancy)
Gwyn Griffiths (Sir Tristram Mickleford)
Marko Rothmüller (Plunkett)
Josef Traxel (Lionel)
Geoffrey Clifton (The sheriff of Richmond)

Radio Éireann Light Orchestra
Wexford Festival Chorus
Bryan Balkwill (Conductor)
Peter Potter (Producer)
Joseph Carl (Designer)

1956
29,31 October; 2,4 November
La Cenerentola
by Gioachino Rossini

Nicola Monti (Don Ramiro)
Paolo Pedani (Dandini)
Cristiano Dallamangas (Don Magnifico)
April Cantelo (Clorinda)
Patricia Kern (Thisbe)
Barbara Howitt (Angelina)
John Holmes (Alidoro)

Wexford Festival Chorus
Bryan Balkwill (Conductor)
Peter Ebert (Producer)
Joseph Carl (Designer)

1957
27,29,31 October; 2 November
La Figlia del Reggimento
by Gaetano Donizetti

Patricia Kern (The Countess of Berkenfeld)
Gwyn Griffiths (Ortensio)
Geraint Evans (Sulpizio)
Graziella Sciutti (Maria)
Mario Spina (Tonio)

Radio Éireann Light Orchestra
Wexford Festival Chorus
Bryan Balkwill (Conductor)
Peter Ebert (Producer)
Joseph Carl (Designer)

1957
28,30 October; 1,3 November
L'Italiana in Algeri
by Gioacchino Rossini

Paolo Montarsolo (Mustafa)
April Cantelo (Elvira)
Patricia Kern (Zulma)
Gwyn Griffiths (Haly)
Petre Munteanu (Lindoro)
Barbara Howitt (Isabella)
Paolo Pedani (Taddeo)

Wexford Festival Chorus
Bryan Balkwill (Conductor)
Peter Ebert (Producer)
Joseph Carl (Designer)

1958
26,28,30 October; 1 November
I Due Foscari
by Giuseppe Verdi

Paolo Pedani (Francesco Foscari)
Carlo del Monte (Jacopo Foscari)
Mariella Angioletti (Lucrezia Contarini)
Plinio Clabassi (Jacopo Loredano)
Philip Talfryn (Barbarigo)
Ellen Dales (Pisana)

Radio Éireann Light Orchestra
Wexford Festival Chorus
Bryan Balkwill (Conductor)
Peter Ebert (Producer)
Michael Eve (Designer)

1958
27,29,31 October; 2 November
Anna Bolena
by Gaetano Donizetti

Plinio Clabassi (Henry VIII)
Marina Cucchio (Anne Boleyn)
Fiorenza Cossotto (Jane Seymour)
Geoffrey Clifton (Lord Rochefort)

Wexford Festival Chorus
Charles Mackerras (Conductor)
Peter Potter (Producer)
Michael Eve (Designer)

Gianni Jaia (Lord Richard Percy)
Patricia Kern (Smeton)
Philip Talfryn (Sir Hervey)

1959
25,27,29,31 October
Aroldo
by Giuseppe Verdi

Nicola Nicolov (Arnoldo)
Mariella Angioletti (Mina)
Aldo Protti (Egberto)
Trevor Anthony (Briano)
John Dobson (Godvino)
Griffith Lewis (Enrico)
Elizabeth Bainbridge (Elena)

Radio Éireann Light Orchestra
Wexford Festival Chorus
Charles Mackerras (Conductor)
Frans Boerlage (Producer)
Micheál MacLiammóir (Designer)

1959
26,28,30 October; 1 November
La Gazza Ladra
by Gioacchino Rossini

Trevor Anthony (Fabrizio)
Elizabeth Bainbridge (Lucia)
Nicola Monti (Giannetto)
Mariella Adani (Ninetta)
Paolo Pedani (Fernando)
Giorgio Tadeo (Gottardo)
Janet Baker (Pippo)
Griffith Lewis (Isacco)
Julian Moyle (Antonio)
Dennis Wicks (Gregorio)

Wexford Festival Chorus
John Pritchard (Conductor)
Peter Potter (Producer)
Osbert Lancaster (Designer)

1961
24,26,28,30 September
Ernani
by Giuseppe Verdi

Ragnar Ulfung (Ernani)
Mariella Angioletti (Elvira)
Lino Puglisi (Don Carlos)
Ugo Trama (Don Ruy Gomez di Silva)
Connall Byrne (Don Riccardo)
John Evans (Jago)
Elizabeth Rust (Giovanna)

Royal Liverpool Philharmonic Orchestra
Wexford Festival Chorus
Bryan Balkwill (Conductor)
Peter Ebert (Producer)
Reginald Woolley (Designer)

1961
25,27,29 September; 1 October
Mireille
by Charles Gounod

Andrea Guiot (Mireille)
Alain Vanzo (Vincent)
Johanna Peters (Taven)
Jean Borthayre (Ourrias)
Elizabeth Rust (Vincenette)
Franco Ventriglia (Ramon)
Morag Noble (Clemence)
Denis Wicks (Ambroise)
Laura Sarti (Andreloun)

Wexford Festival Chorus
Michael Moores (Conductor)
Anthony Besch (Producer)
Osbert Lancaster (Designer)

1962
21,23,25,27 October
L'Amico Fritz
by Pietro Mascagni

Nicola Monti (Fritz Kobus)
Veronica Dunne (Suzel)
Bernadette Greevy (Beppe)
Paolo Pedani (David)
Derick Davies (Henezo)
Adrian de Peyer (Federico)
Laura Sarti (Caterina)

Radio Éireann Symphony Orchestra
Wexford Festival Chorus
Antonio Tonini (Conductor)
Michael Hadji Mischev (Producer)
Reginald Woolley (Designer)

1962
22,24,26,28 October
I Puritani
by Vincenzo Bellini

Adrian de Peyer (Sir Bruno Robertson)
Mirella Freni (Elvira)
Luciano Saldari (Lord Arthur Talbot)
Franco Ventriglia (Sir George Walton)
Lino Puglisi (Sir Richard Forth)
Derick Davies (Lord Walton)
Laura Sarti (Queen Henrietta of France)

Wexford Festival Chorus
Gunnar Staern (Conductor)
Peter Ebert (Producer)
Reginald Woolley (Designer)

1963
20,22,24,26 October
Don Pasquale
by Gaetano Donizetti

Guus Hoekman (Don Pasquale)
Dino Mantovani (Dr Malatesta)
Alfonz Bartha (Ernesto)
Margherita Rinaldi (Norina)

Radio Éireann Symphony Orchestra
Wexford Festival Chorus
Antonio de Almeida (Conductor)
Michael Hadji Mischev (Producer)
Anna Hadji Mischev (Designer)

1963
21,23,25,27 October
La Gioconda
by Amilcare Ponchielli

Lino Puglisi (Barnaba)
Enriqueta Tarrés (La Gioconda)
Anna Reynolds (La Cieca)
Derick Davies (Zuàne)
Adrian de Peyer (Isèpo)
Giuseppe Gismondo (Enzo Grimaldo)
Franco Ventriglia (Alvise Badoero)
Gloria Lane (Laura)

Wexford Festival Chorus
Gunnar Staern (Conductor)
Peter Ebert (Producer)
Reginald Woolley (Designer)

1963
27 October
The Siege of Rochelle
by M.W. Balfe

Patricia McCarry (Clara)
Martin Dempsey (Captain Montalban)

Adrian de Peyer (Marquis de Valmour)
Brendan McNally (Count Rosenberg)
Derick Davies (Michel)
Anna Reynolds (Marcella)
Franco Ventriglia (The father guardian)
Angela Jenkins (First peasant girl)
Dorothy Wilson (Second peasant girl)

Wexford Festival Chorus
Jeannie Reddin and Courtney Kenny
  (Pianists)
Douglas Craig (Producer)
Reginald Woolley (Designer)

1964
24,26,29,31 October
Lucia di Lammermoor
by Gaetano Donizetti

Lino Puglisi (Lord Enrico Ashton)
Karola Agai (Lucia Ashton)
Giacomo Aragall (Sir Edgardo)
Franco Ventriglia (Raimondo Bidebent)
Laura Sarti (Alisa)
Alastair Newlands (Lord Arturo Bucklaw)
Edmund Bohan (Normanno)

Radio Éireann Symphony Orchestra
Wexford Festival Chorus
Antonio de Almeida (Conductor)
Michel Crochot (Producer)
Reginald Woolley (Designer)

1964
25,27,30 October; 1 November
Il Conte Ory
by Gioacchino Rossini

Pietro Bottazzo (Il Conte Ory)
Federico Davia (L'Ajo)
Stefania Malagu (Isoliero)
Walter Alberti (Roberto)
David Johnston (Un cavaliere)
Alberta Valentini (La Contessa
  Adele of Formoutiers)
Laura Sarti (Ragonda)
Deidre Pleydell (Alice)

Radio Éireann Symphony Orchestra
Wexford Festival Chorus
Gunnar Staern (Conductor)
Peter Ebert (Producer)
Reginald Woolley (Designer)
Francis Reid (Lighting)

1964
28 October; 1 November
Much Ado about Nothing
by Charles V. Stanford

Erica Bax (Hero)
Soo-Bee Lee (Beatrice)
Noel Noble (Don Pedro)
John MacNally (Don John)
Dennis Brandt (Claudio)
Richard Golding (Benedick)
Herbert Moulton (Leonato)
Edmund Bohan (Borachio)
Frank Olegario (Friar Francis)
Frank Olegario (Dogberry)
David Johnston (Seacole)
Tony Daly (Verges)

Wexford Festival Chorus
Courtney Kenny (Conductor)
Peter Ebert (Producer)
Reginald Woolley (Designer)

1964
31 October
Corno di Bassetto
*An entertainment devised by
T.J. Walsh based on the musical
criticism of* Bernard Shaw

Bernadette Greevy
Franco Ventriglia
Jeannie Reddin
John Welsh

1965
23,25,28,30 October
Don Quichotte
by Jules Massenet

Ivana Mixova (La Belle Dulcinée)
Miroslav Cangalovic (Don Quichotte)
Ladko Korosec (Sancho)
Deirdre Pleydell (Pedro)
Christine Wilson (Garcias)
David Johnston (Rodriguez)
Minoo Golvala (Juan)
Maurice Bowen (Ténébrun)
Guiseppe Sorbello (A bandit)
James Armstrong (First footman)
Dermod Gloster (Second footman)

Radio Éireann Symphony Orchestra
Wexford Festival Chorus
Albert Rosen (Conductor)
Carl Ebert (Producer)
Reginald Woolley (Designer)

1965
24,26,28,30 October
La Traviata
by Giuseppe Verdi

Jeannette Pilou (Violetta Valery)
Erich Vietheer (Dr Grenvil)
Patrick McGuigan (Marquis d'Obigny)
Gloria Jennings (Flora Bervoix)
Richard Golding (Baron Douphol)
Philip Langridge (Gastone de Letorières)
Veriano Luchetti (Alfredo Germont)
Robin Bell (Annina)
Octav Enigarescu (Giorgio Germont)
Dermod Gloster (Giuseppe)

Wexford Festival Chorus
Gunnar Staern (Conductor)
Peter Ebert (Producer)
Reginald Woolley (Designer)

1965
27,29,31 October
La Finta Giardiniera
by W.A. Mozart

Mattiwilda Dobbs (Onesti)
Federico Davia (Nardo)
Francis Egerton (Don Anchise)
Maddalena Bonifaccio (Arminda)
Birgit Nordin (Serpetta)
Ugo Benelli (Il Conte Belfiore)
Stefania Malagu (Il Cavaliere Ramiro)

Radio Éireann Symphony Orchestra Players
Gunnar Staern (Conductor)
Peter Ebert (Producer)
Judith Ebert (Designer)

1966
23,25,27,29 October
Fra Diavolo
by Daniel François Auber

Ugo Benelli (Fra Diavolo)
Antonio Boyer (Lord Cockburn)
Anna Reynolds (Lady Pamela)
Nigel Douglas (Lorenzo)
Paschal Allen (Matteo)
Alberta Valentini (Zerlina)
Enrico Fissore (Giacomo)
Renato Ercolani (Beppo)

RadioTelefís Éireann Symphony Orchestra
Wexford Festival Chorus
Myer Fredman (Conductor)
Dennis Maunder (Producer)
Reginald Woolley (Designer)

1966
24,26,28,30 October
Lucrezia Borgia
by Gaetano Donizetti

Ayhan Baran (Don Alfonso)
Virginia Gordoni (Lucrezia Borgia)
Angelo Mori (Gennaro)
Stefania Malagu (Maffio Orsini)
Alan Morrell (Liverotto)
Wyndham Parfitt (Gazella)
Patrick McGuigan (Petrucci)
Bruce Lochtie (Vitellozzo)
James Christiansen (Gubetta)
Francis Egerton (Rustighello)
Gordon Farrell (Astolfo)

Wexford Festival Chorus
Albert Rosen (Conductor)
Frith Banbury (Producer)
Reginald Woolley (Designer)

1967
21,23,26,28 October
Otello
by Gioacchino Antonio Rossini

Nicola Tagger (Othello)
Terence Sharpe (Doge)
Walter Gullino (Iago)
Pietro Bottazzo (Rodrigo)
Frederick Bateman (Lucio)
Silvano Pagliuca (Elmiro Barberigo)
Maria Casula (Emilia)
Renza Jotti (Desdemona)
Frederick Bateman (Gondolier)

RadioTelefís Éireann Symphony Orchestra
Wexford Festival Chorus
Albert Rosen (Conductor)
Anthony Besch (Producer)
John Stoddart (Designer)

1967
22,24,27,29 October
Roméo et Juliette
by Charles Gounod

Zuleika Saque (Juliette)
Anne Pashley (Stephano)
Pamela Bowden (Gertrude)
Jean Brazzi (Roméo)
Dennis Brandt (Tybalt)
Frederick Bateman (Benvolio)
Henri Gui (Mercutio)
Kenneth Reynolds (Paris)
Terence Sharpe (Grégorio)
Jaroslav Horáček (Capulet)
Victor de Narké (Frère Laurent)
Richard van Allan (Le Duc de Vérone)

Wexford Festival Chorus
David Lloyd-Jones (Conductor)
John Cox (Producer)
Patrick Murray (Designer)

1968
25,28,31 October; 2 November
La Clemenza di Tito
by Wolfgang Amadeus Mozart

Peter Baillie (Titus)
Hanneke van Bork (Vitellia)
Maria Casula (Sextus)
Delia Wallis (Annius)
Elaine Hooker (Servilia)
Silvano Pagliuca (Publius)

RadioTelefís Éireann Symphony Orchestra
Wexford Festival Chorus
Theodor Guschlbauer (Conductor)
John Copley (Producer)
Michael Waller (Designer)

1968
26,30 October; 1,3 November
La Jolie Fille de Perth
by Georges Bizet

Denise Dupleix (Catherine Glover)
Isabel Garcisanz (Mab)
John Wakefield (Henri Smith)
Henri Gui (Le Duc de Rothesay)
Roger Soyer (Ralph)
Silvano Pagliuca (Simon Glover)
Maurice Arthur (Un seigneur)
Brian Donlan (Le majordome)
Alexander Roy (dancer)
Christina Gallea (dancer)

Wexford Festival Chorus
David Lloyd-Jones (Conductor)
Pauline Grant (Producer)
Robin Archer (Designer)

1968
27,29,31 October; 2 November
L'Equivoco Stravagante
by Gioacchino Rossini

Richard van Allan (Gamberotto)
Renza Jotti (Ernestina)
Pietro Bottazzo (Ermanno)
Elfego Esparza (Buralicchio)
Mario Carlin (Frontino)
Maria Casula (Rosalia)

Aldo Ceccato (Conductor)
John Cox (Producer)
John Stoddart (Designer)

1969
24,26,30 October; 1 November
L'Infedeltà Delusa
by Joseph Haydn

Eugenia Ratti (Vespina)
Jill Gomez (Sandrina)
Alexander Young (Filippo)
Ugo Benelli (Nencio)
Eftimios Michalopoulus (Nanni)

RadioTelefís Éireann Symphony Orchestra
David Lloyd-Jones (Conductor)
John Copley (Producer)
John Fraser (Designer)
Mark Elder (Harpsichord Continuo)

1969
25,27,29,31 October; 2 November
Luisa Miller
by Giuseppe Verdi

Silvano Pagliuca (Count Walter)
Angelo Lo Forese (Rodolfo)
Bernadette Greevy (Federica)
Eftimios Michalopoulos (Wurm)
Terence Sharpe (Miller)
Lucia Kelston (Luisa)
Enid Hartle (Laura)
Stephen Tudor (A countryman)

Wexford Festival Chorus
Myer Fredman (Conductor)
John Cox (Producer)
Bernard Culshaw (Designer)

1970
23,26,30 October; 1 November
(Double Bill)
L'Inganno Felice
by Gioacchino Rossini

Jill Gomez (Isabella)
Ugo Benelli (Bertrando)
Robert Bickerstaff (Ormondo)
Federico Davia (Batone)
Elfego Esparza (Tarabotto)

RadioTelefís Éireann Symphony Orchestra
David Atherton (Conductor)
Patrick Libby (Producer)
John Fraser (Designer)

Giovedi Grasso
by Gaetano Donizetti

Federico Davia (The colonel)
Jill Gomez (Nina)
Malcolm Williams (Teodoro)
Elfego Esparza (Sigismondo)
Johanna Peters (Camilla)
Janet Hughes (Stefania)
Ugo Benelli (Ernesto)
Brian Donlan (Cola)

RadioTelefís Éireann Symphony Orchestra
David Atherton (Conductor)
Patrick Libby (Producer)
John Fraser (Designer)

1970
24,27,29,31 October
Lakmé
by Leo Delibes

Christiane Eda-Pierre (Lakmé)
Yvonne Fuller (Malika)
Carmel O'Byrne (Ellen)
Angela Whittington (Rose)
Gabrielle Ristori (Mistress Benson)
John Stewart (Gerald)
Jacques Mars (Nilakantha)
William Elvin (Frederic)
Malcolm Williamson (Hagi)
Lyn Walker (Dancer)
Anthony Bremner (Dancer)

Wexford Festival Chorus
David Lloyd-Jones (Conductor)
Michael Hadji Mischev (Producer)
John Fraser (Designer)
Oenone Talbot (Choreographer)

1970
25,28,31 October
Albert Herring
by Benjamin Britten

Milla Andrew (Lady Billows)
Johanna Peters (Florence Pike)
Patricia Reakes (Miss Wordsworth)
John Kitchiner (Mr Gedge)
Patrick Ring (Mr Upfold)
Elfego Esparza (Superintendant Budd)
Alan Opie (Sid)
Alexander Oliver (Albert Herring)
Delia Wallis (Nancy)
Enid Hartle (Mrs Herring)
Laureen Livingstone (Emmie)
Lillian Watson (Cis)
Robin McWilliams (Harry)

David Atherton (Conductor)
Michael Geliot (Producer)
Jane Bond (Designer)

1971
21,24,26,29 October
Les Pêcheurs de Perles
by Georges Bizet

Christiane Eda-Pierre (Leila)
John Stewart (Nadir)
Marco Bakker (Zurga)
Juan Soumagnas (Nourabad)

RadioTelefís Éireann Symphony Orchestra
Wexford Festival Chorus
Guy Barbier (Conductor)
Michael Geliot (Producer)
Anthony Bremner (Choreographer)

1971
22,25,28,31 October
La Rondine
by Giacomo Puccini

June Card (Magda)
Anne-Marie Blanzat (Lisette)
Beniamino Prior (Ruggero)
Alexander Oliver (Prunier)
Thomas Lawlor (Rambaldo)
Brian Donlan (Perichaud)
Harold Sharples (Gobin)
Gavin Walton (Crebillon)
Sara de Javelin (Yvette)
Susan Howells (Bianca)
Myrna Moreno (Suzy)
Gavin Walton (A steward)

Wexford Festival Chorus
Myer Fredman (Conductor)
Anthony Besch (Producer)
John Stoddart (Designer)

1971
23,27,30 October
Il Re Pastore
by Wolfgang Amadeus Mozart

Anne Pashley (Aminta)
Norma Burrowes (Elisa)
Anne Cant (Tamiri)
Richard Barnard (Agenore)
Jean Mallandine (Continuo)
Eduardo Valazco (Allesandro)

Kenneth Montgomery (Conductor)
John Cox (Producer)
Elisabeth Dalton (Designer)

1972
27,30 October; 2,5 November
Il Pirata
by Vincenzo Bellini

Marco Bakker (Ernesto)
Christiane Eda-Pierre (Imogene)
William MacDonald (Gualtiero)
Noel Drennan (Itulbo)
Hugh Richardson (Goffredo)
Mary Sheridan (Adele)

RadioTelefís Éireann Symphony Orchestra
Wexford Festival Chorus
Leone Magiera (Conductor)
Michael Geliot (Producer)
Jane Venables (Designer)
Robert Bryan (Lighting designer)

1972
26,29,31 October; 3 November
Oberon
by Carl Maria von Weber

John Fryatt (Oberon)
Louise Mansfield (Titania)
Janet Hughes (Puck)
Heikki Siukola (Huon)
Brent Ellis (Gerasmin)
Vivian Martin (Rezia)
Delia Wallis (Fatima)
Michael Beauchamp (Baibars)
Andre Page (Haroun)
John Flanagan (Hakim)
Susan Lees (A mermaid)

Wexford Festival Chorus
Kenneth Montgomery (Conductor)
Anthony Besch (Producer)
Adam Pollock (Designer)
Robert Bryan (Lighting designer)

1972
28 October; 1,4 November
Katá Kabanová
by Leoš Janáček

Jan Kyzlink (Savel Prokofjevic Dikoj)
Ivo Zidek (Boris Grigorjev)
Sona Cervena (Kabanicha)
Patrick Ring (Tichon Ivanyc Kabanov)
Alexandra Hunt (Katá)
David Fieldsend (Vana Kudrjas)
Elizabeth Connell (Varvara)
Christian du Plessis (Kuligin)
Susan Lees (Glascha)
Nellie Walsh (Fekluscha)

Wexford Festival Chorus
Albert Rosen (Conductor)
David Pountney (Producer)
Susan Blane (Designer)
Maria Bjornsen (Designer)
Robert Bryan (Lighting designer)

1973
25,28,31 October; 2 November
Ivan Susanin
by M.I. Glinka

Horiana Branisteanu (Antonida)
Reni Penkova (Vanya)
William McDonald (Sobinin)
Matti Salminen (Ivan Susanin)
Colin Fay (Sigismund)
Dennis O'Neill (Messenger)
Peter Forest (Russian warrior)
Tessa Jarvis (Dancer)
Anton Elder (Dancer)

RadioTelefís Éireann Symphony Orchestra
Wexford Festival Chorus
Guy Barbier (Conductor)
Michael Hadji Mischev (Producer)
Susan Blane (Designer)
William Bradford (Lighting designer)
Tessa Jarvis (Dance choreographer)

1973
26,30 October; 3 November
The Gambler
by Sergei Prokofiev

Sona Cervana (Baboushka)
Joseph Rouleau (The general)
Anne Howells (Pauline)
Arley Reece (Alexei)
Annabel Hunt (Blanche)
Bernard Dickerson (Marquis)
Richard Stilgoe (Mr Astley)
Dennis O'Neill (Nilsky)
Peter Forest (Potapitch)

Wexford Festival Chorus
Albert Rosen (Conductor)
David Pountney (Producer)
Maria Bjornson (Designer)
William Bradford (Lighting designer)

1973
27,29, October; 1,4 November
L'Ajo nell'Imbarazzo
by Gaetano Donizetti

Manuel Gonzalez (Il Marchese
    Giulio Antiquati)
Suso Mariategui (Il Marchese Enrico)
Silvia Baleani (Gilda Tallemanni)
Bernard Dickerson (Il Marchese Pippette)
Richard McKee (Don Gregorio Cordebone)
Johanna Peters (Leonarda)
Richard Stilgoe (Simone)

Wexford Festival Chorus
Kenneth Montgomery (Conductor)
Patrick Libby (Producer)
Adam Pollock (Designer)
William Bradford (Lighting designer)

1974
23,25,29 October; 1 November
Medea in Corinto
by Giovanni Simone Mayr

Eiddwen Harrhy (Creusa)
Lieuwe Visser (Creonte)
Arley Reece (Giasone)
Margreta Elkins (Medea)
Joan Davies (Ismene)
William McKinney (Egeo)
Robin Leggate (Tideo)
Alexander Magri (Evandro)

RadioTelefís Éireann Symphony Orchestra
Wexford Festival Chorus
Roderick Brydon (Conductor)
Adrian Slack (Director)
David Fielding (Designer)
James McCosh (Lighting designer)

1974
24,27,31 October; 3 November
Thaïs
by Jules Massenet

Lieuwe Visser (Palémon)
Thomas McKinney (Athanaël)
Jill Gomez (Thaïs)
Seán Mitten (Le serviteur)
Francis Egerton (Nicias)
Helen MacArthur (Crobyle)
Ann Murray (Myrtale)
Ruth Maher (Albine)

Wexford Festival Chorus
Jacques Delacôte (Conductor)
Jeremy Sutcliffe (Director)
John Fraser (Designer)
James Taylor (Lighting designer)

1974
26,28,30 October; 2 November
Der Barbier von Bagdad
by Peter Cornelius

Kevork Boyaciyan (Nureddin)
Joan Davies (Bostana)
Richard McKee (Abul Hassan Ali
    Ebn Bekar)
Helen MacArthur (Margiana)
Francis Egerton (The Kadi Baba Mustapha)
Antony Ransome (The Kalif)
Seán Mitten (Muezzin I)
Michael Scott (Muezzin II)
Harry Nicoll (Muezzin III)
Alexander Magri (A slave)

Wexford Festival Chorus
Albert Rosen (Conductor)
Wolf Siegfried Wagner (Director)
Dacre Punt (Set designer)
Alex Reid (Costume designer)
Jamie Taylor (Lighting designer)

1975
23,26,29,31 October
Le Roi d'Ys
by Edouard Lalo

Michel Vallat (Jahel)
Christiane Chateau (Rozenn)
Gillian Knight (Margared)
Stuart Harling (Karnac)
Antonio Barasorda (Mylio)
Juan Soumagnas (Le roi)
Juan Soumagnas (St Corentin)

RadioTelefís Éireann Symphony Orchestra
Wexford Festival Chorus
Jean Perisson (Conductor)
Jean Claude Auvray (Director)
Bernard Arnould (Designer)
James McCosh (Lighting designer)

1975
22 (modern première),
25,28 October: 1 November
Eritrea
by Francesco Cavalli

Ian Caddy (Boreas)
Jessica Cash (Iris)
Stuart Harling (Alcione)
Anna Benedict (Nisa)
James O'Neill (Itidio)
Philip Langridge (Eurimidonte)
John York Skinner (Dione)
Ann Murray (Laodicea)
Jessica Cash (Misena)
Anne Pashley (Eritrea)
Paul Esswood (Theramene)
Anna Benedict (Lesbo)
Ian Caddy (Niconida)
Matteo de Monti (Argeo)

Wexford Festival Baroque Ensemble
Jane Glover (Conductor)
Ian Strasfogel (Director)
Franco Colaveccia (Designer)
James McCosh (Lighting designer)

1975
24,27,30 October; 2 November
La Pietra del Paragone
by Gioacchino Rossini

Ian Caddy (Pacuvio)
Joan Davies (Aspasia)
James O'Neill (Fabrizio)
Iris Dell'acqua (Donna Fulvia)
Eric Garrett (Macrobio)
John Sandor (Giocondo)
Sandra Browne (Clarice)
Richard Barrett (Asdrubale)

Wexford Festival Chorus
Roderick Brydon (Conductor)
Adrian Slack (Director)
John Bury (Production designer)
Edward Lambert (Continuo)

1976
20,23,26,29 October
Giovanna d'Arco
by Giuseppe Verdi

Alexander Magri (Delil)
Curtis Rayam (Carlo VII)
Lajos Miller (Giacomo)
Erniko Maruyama (Giovanna)
Arnold Dvorkin (Talbot)

RadioTelefís Éireann Symphony Orchestra
Wexford Festival Chorus
James Judd (Conductor)
Jeremy Sutcliffe (Director)
David Fielding (Designer)
Graham Large (Lighting designer)

1976
21,24,28,31 October
The Merry Wives of Windsor
by Otto Nicolai
27 October concert performance
in White's Hotel

Catherine Wilson (Mistress Ford)
Anne Collins (Mistress Page)
Ian Comboy (Mr Page)
Keith Jones (Slender)
Seán Mitten (Dr Caius)
Maurice Arthur (Fenton)
Michael Langdon (Falstaff)
Alan Opie (Mr Ford)
Peter O'Leary (Townsman)
Sandra Dugdale (Ann Page)

Wexford Festival Chorus
Leonard Hancock (Conductor)
Patrick Libby (Director)
Adam Pollock (Designer)
Graham Large (Lighting designer)

1976
22,25,27,30 October
The Turn of the Screw
by Benjamin Britten

Maurice Arthur (The prologue)
Jane Manning (The governess)
Victoria Klasicki (Flora)
James Maguire (Miles)
Margaret Kingsley (Mrs Grose)
Lee Winston (Quint)
Anne Cant (Miss Jessel)

Wexford Festival Ensemble
Albert Rosen (Conductor)
Adrian Slack (Director)
David Fielding (Set designer)
James McCosh (Lighting designer)

1977
19,22,25,28 October
Hérodiade
by Jules Massenet
24 October concert performance
in Dún Mhuire Hall

Alvaro Malta (Phanuel)
Eilene Hannan (Salome)
Malcolm Donnelly (Hérode)
Jean Dupouy (John the Baptist)
Hilary Straw (La jeune Babylonienne)
Clair Symonds (Dancer)
Bernadette Greevy (Hérodiade)
Bonaventura Bottone (Une voix)
Glyn Davenport (Grand Pretre)
Michael Lewis (Vitellius)

RadioTelefís Éireann Symphony Orchestra
Wexford Festival Chorus
Wexford Children's Choir
Henri Gallois (Conductor)
Julian Hope (Director)
Domy Reiter-Soffer (Choreographer)
Roger Butlin (Designer)
John B Read (Lighting designer)

1977
20,23,26,29 October
Orfeo ed Euridice
by Christophe Willibald Gluck
27 October concert performance
in Dún Mhuire Hall

Kevin Smith (Orfeo)
Jennifer Smith (Euridice)
Anna Benedict (Amor)

Members of the Irish Ballet Company
Wexford Festival Chorus
Jane Glover (Conductor)
Wolf Siegfried Wagner (Director)
Joan Denise Moriarty (Artistic director)

1977
21,24,27,30 October
Il Maestro di Cappella
by Maffeo Zanon,
based on music by Cimarosa

Sesto Bruscantini (Il Maestro)

James Judd (Conductor)
Sesto Bruscantini (Director)
Tim Reed (Designer)

La Serva e L'Ussero
by Luigi Ricci

Sesto Bruscantini (Buontempo)
Ruth Maher (Marianna)
Carmen Lavani (Angelica)
Bonaventura Bottone (Roberto)
Michael Lewis (Andrea)

Jan Sendor (Lighting designer)

La Serva Padrona
by Giovanni Pergolesi

Carmen Lavani (Serpina)
Sesto Bruscantini (Uberto)
Angela Aguade (Vespone)

1978
25,28,31 October; 3 November
Tiefland
by Eugene d'Albert

Bonaventura Bottone (Nando)
Jon Andrew (Pedro)
Malcolm Donnelly (Sebastiano)
Mani Mekler (Marta)
Alvaro Malta (Tommaso)
Carmel Patrick (Pepa)
Aideen Lane (Antonia)
Caroline Tatlow (Rosalia)
Pat Sheridan (Moruccio)
Dinah Harris (Nuri)

RadioTelefís Éireann Symphony Orchestra
Wexford Festival Chorus
(Chorus master: Alan Cutts)
Henri Gallois (Conductor)
Julian Hope (Director)
Roger Butlin (Designer)
Victor Lockwood (Lighting)
Luke Pascoe (Costume designer)
Alison Meacher (costume designer)

1978
26,29 October; 1,4 November
Il Mondo della Luna
by Joseph Haydn

Ugo Benelli (Ecclitico)
Peter O'Leary (Scholar)
Gerard Delrez (Scholar)
Graham Trew (Scholar)
Greville O'Brien (Scholar)
Gianni Socci (Buonafede)

James Judd (Conductor)
Adrian Slack (Director)
Axel Bartz (Set designer)
Tim Reed (Costume designer)
Courtney Kenny (Continuo)
Victor Lockwood (Lighting)

Alan Watt (Ernesto)
Denis O'Neill (Cecco)
Elaine Linstedt (Clarice)
Helen Dixon (Flaminia)
Emily Hastings (Lisetta)

1978
27,30 October; 2,5 November
3 November (Prom performance)
The Two Widows
by Bedrich Smetana

Elizabeth Gale (Karolina)
Felicity Palmer (Aneska)
Joseph Rouleau (Mumlal)
Robert White (Ladislav)
Dinah Harris (Lidka)
Bonaventura Bottone (Tonik)

Wexford Festival Chorus
(Chorus master: Alan Cutts)
Albert Rosen (Conductor)
David Pountney (Director)
Sue Blane (Designer)

1979
24,27,30 October; 2 November
L'Amore dei Tre Re
by Italo Montemezzi

Alvaro Malta (Archibaldo)
Bonaventura Bottone (Flaminio)
Neil McKinnon (Avito)
Magdalena Cononovici (Fiora)
Lajos Miller (Manfredo)
Colette McGahon (Handmaiden)
Marie-Claire O'Reirdan (A young girl)
Wlliam Pugh (A young man)
Colette McGahon (An old woman)

RadioTelefís Éireann Symphony Orchestra
Wexford Festival Chorus
(Chorus master: Alan Cutts)
Wexford Children's Choir
(Director: Sister Mary Walsh)
Pinchas Steinberg (Conductor)
Stewart Trotter (Director)
Douglas Heap (Designer)
Graham Large (Lighting)

1979
25,28,31 October; 3 November
La Vestale
by Gasparo Spontini

Terence Sharpe (Cinna)
Ennio Buoso (Licinius)
Claire Livingstone (La Grande Vestale)
Mani Mekler (Julia)
Roderick Kennedy (Le Grand Pontife)
Pat Sheridan (Un consul)

Wexford Festival Chorus
(Chorus master: Alan Cutts)
Matthias Bamert (Conductor)
Julian Hope (Director)
Roger Butlin (Designer)
Sue Blane (Costume designer)
Graham Large (Lighting)

1979
26,29 October; 1,4 November
Crispino e la Comare
by Luigi and Federico Ricci

Pat Sheridan (Don Asdrubale)
Bonaventura Bottone (Contino del Fiore)
Sesto Bruscantini (Crispino Tacchetto)
Lucia Aliberti (Annetta)
Gianni Socci (Mirabolano)
David Beavan (Fabrizio)
Ruth Maher (Donna Giusta, La Comare)
Peter O'Leary (Bortolo)
Martin Shopland (A crier)
Colette McGahon (Lisetta)
Seamus Mahony (Trumpeter)
Jimmy Busher (Drummer)

Wexford Festival Chorus
(Chorus master: Alan Cutts)
James Judd (Conductor)
Sesto Bruscantini (Director)
Tim Reed (Designer)
Graham Large (Lighting)
Courtney Kenny (Continuo)

1980
22,25,28,31 October
Edgar
by Giacomo Puccini

Iris Dell'Acqua (Fidelia)
Nico Boer (Edgar)
Magdalena Cononovici (Tigrana)
Terence Sharpe (Frank)
Roderick Kennedy (Gualtiero)

RadioTelefís Éireann Symphony Orchestra
Wexford Festival Chorus
(Chorus master: Kim Mooney)
Bride Street Boys' Choir
(Director: Gerard Lawlor)
Robin Stapleton (Conductor)

Roger Chapman (Director)
Douglas Heap (Designer - sets)
Jane Law (Designer - costumes)
Graham Large (Lighting)

1980
23,26,29 October; 1 November
Orlando
by G F Handel

Roderick Kennedy (Zoroastro)
John Angelo Messana (Orlando)
Lesley Garrett (Dorinda)
Alison Hargan (Angelica)
Bernadette Greevy (Medoro)

James Judd (Conductor)
Wilfred Judd (Director)
Kandis Cook (Designer - sets)
Alison Meacher (Designer - costumes)
Graham Large (Lighting)

1980
24,27,30 October; 2 November
Of Mice and Men
by Carlisle Floyd

Curtis Rayam (Lennie Small)
Lawrence Cooper (George Milton)
John Winfield (Curley)
Seán Mitten (Candy)
Christine Isley (Curley's wife)
Padraig O'Rourke (Slim)
Brendan Cavanagh (Carlson)
Paul Arden-Griffith (Ballad singer)

Wexford Festival Chorus
(Chorus master: Kim Mooney)
John DeMain (Conductor)
Stewart Trotter (Director)
John Cervenka (Designer)
Graham Large (Lighting)

1981
21,24,27,30 October
I Gioielle della Madonna
by Ermanno Wolf-Ferrari

Marie Slorach (Maliella)
Angelo Marenzi (Gennaro)
Nuala Willis (Carmela)
Carlo Desideri (Rafaela)
Brendan Cavanagh (Biaso)
Harry Nicoll (Totonno)
Philip Creasy (Ciccillo)
Seán Mitten (Rocco)
Virginia Kerr (Stella)
Marian Finn (Serena)
Nicola Sharkey (Concetta)

RadioTelefís Éireann Symphony Orchestra
Wexford Festival Chorus
(Chorus master: Simon Joly)
Bride Street Boys' Choir
(Director: Gerard Lawlor)
Colman Pearce (Conductor)
Graham Vick (Director)
Russell Craig (Designer)
Graham Large (Lighting)

1981
22,25,28,31 October
Zaïde
by Wolfgang Amadeus Mozart

Lesley Garrett (Zaïde)
Neil Mackie (Gomatz)
Ulrik Cold (Allazim)
Curtis Rayam (Sultan Soliman)
Gordon Sandison (Osmin)

Nicholas Cleobury (Conductor)
Timothy Tyrrel (Director)
Dermot Hayes (Designer)
Graham Large (Lighting)

1981
23,26,29 October; 1 November
Un Giorno di Regno
by Giuseppe Verdi

Donald Maxwell (Cavaliere Di Belfiore)
Sesto Bruscantini (Barone Di Kelbar)
Lucia Aliberti (Marchese Del Poggio)
Angela Feeney (Giulietta Di Kelbar)
Ugo Benelli (Edoardo Di Sanval)
Gianni Socci (Tesoriere La Rocca)
Brendan Cavanagh (Conte Ivrea)
Tony Madden (Delmonte)

Wexford Festival Chorus
(Chorus master: Simon Joly)
James Judd (Conductor)
Sesto Bruscantini (Director)
Tim Reed (Designer)
Graham Large (Lighting)

1982
20,23,26,29 October
Sakúntala
by Franco Alfano

Evelyn Brunner (Sakùntala)
Richard Robson (Durvàsas)
Brian Kemp (Harita)
Harry Nicoll (A young hermit)
David Parker The king)
Rosamund Illing (Anusuya)
Anita Terzian (Priyàmvada)
Andrew Gallacher (The king's squire)
Armando Caforio (Kanva)
Brendan Cavanagh (A fisherman)

RadioTelefís Éireann Symphony Orchestra
Wexford Festival Chorus
(Chorus master: Simon Joly)
Albert Rosen (Conductor)
Nicholas Hytner (Producer)
David Fielding (Designer)
Mick Hughes (Lighting)

1982
21,24,27,30 October
Arianna a Naxos
by Josef Haydn

Bernadette Greevy (Ariadne)

Newell Jenkins (Conductor)
Guus Mostart (Producer)

L'Isola Disabitata
by Josef Haydn

Bernadette Greevy (Costanza)
Ursula Reinhardt-Kiss (Silvia)
Philip Gelling (Enrico)
Maldwyn Davies (Gernando)

John Otto (Designer)
Mick Hughes (Lighting)
Nigel Nicholson (Choreographer)

1982
22,25,28,31 October
Grisélidis
by Jules Massenet

Howard Haskin (Alain)
Richard Robson (Gondebaut)
Christopher Blades (The prior)
Sergei Leiferkus (Marquis de Saluces)
Rosemarie Landry (Grisélidis)
Joan Merrigan (Bertrade)
Günter von Kannen (The devil)
Rosanne Creffield (Fiamina)
(Little Löys)

Wexford Festival Chorus
(Chorus master: Simon Joly)
Robin Stapleton (Conductor)
Stephen Pimlott (Producer)
Ariane Gastambide (Designer)
Mick Hughes (Lighting)

1983
20,23,26,29 October
Hans Heiling
by Heinrich Marschner

Sergei Leiferkus (Hans Heiling)
Malmfrid Sand (The queen)
Constance Cloward (Anna)
Ingrid Steger (Gertrude)
Eduardo Alvares (Konrad)
Richard Lloyd-Morgan (Stephan)

RadioTelefís Éireann Symphony Orchestra
Wexford Festival Chorus
(Chorus master: Simon Joly)
Albert Rosen (Conductor)
Stephen Pimlott (Producer)
David Fielding (Designer)
Mick Hughes (Lighting)
Terry John Bates (Choreographer)

1983
21,24,27,30 October
La Vedova Scaltra
by Ermanno Wolf-Ferrari

Grant Shelley (Monsieur le Bleau)
Howard Haskin (Conte di Bosco Nero)
Neil Jansen (Milord Runebif)
Tom McDonnell (Don Alvaro de Castille)
Gordon Sandison (Arlecchino)
Jill Gomez (Rosaura)
Rosemary Ashe (Marionette)
Christopher Adams (Folletto)
Andrew Gallacher (Pedro)
Richard Lloyd-Morgan (Birif)
Marilyn Hunt (Lady)
Susan Lees (Lady)

Yan Pascal Tortelier (Conductor)
Charles Hamilton (Producer)
Tim Reed (Designer)
Mick Hughes (Lighting)
Terry John Bates (Choreographer)

1983
22,25,28,31 October
Linda di Chamounix
by Gaetano Donizetti

Jennifer Adams (Maddalena)
Brian Kemp (Antonio)
Gianni Socci (The Marquis di Boisfleury)
Brendan Cavanagh (The intendant)
Lucia Aliberti (Linda)
Anita Terzian (Pierotto)
Ugo Benelli (Carlo)
John O'Flynn (The prefect)

Wexford Festival Chorus
(Chorus master: Simon Joly)
Gabriele Bellini (Conductor)
Julian Hope (Producer)
Annena Stubbs (Designer)
Mick Hughes (Lighting)

1984
24,27,30 October; 2 November
Le Jongleur de Notre Dame
by Jules Massenet

Patrick Power (Jean)
Christian du Plessis (The prior)
Sergei Leiferkus (Boniface)
John Cashmore (A musician monk)
Richard Robson (A sculptor monk)
Peter McBrien (A painter monk)
Grant Shelley (A poet monk)
Brendan Cavanagh (A pardoner monk)
Richard Lloyd-Morgan (Man in crowd)
Virginia Kerr (An angel)
Alexander Mercer (An angel)
Tony Friel (Martin)

RadioTelefís Éireann Symphony Orchestra
Wexford Festival Chorus
(Chorus master: Martin Merry)
Yan Pascal Tortelier (Conductor)
Stefan Janski (Producer)
Johan Engels (Designer)
Mick Hughes (Lighting)
Terry John Bates (Choreographer)

1984
25,28,31 October; 3 November
Le Astuzie Femminili
by Domenico Cimarosa

Susanna Rigacco (Bellina)
Peter-Christophe Runge (Romualdo)
Raul Gimenez (Filandro)
Arturo Testa (Giampaolo)
Nuala Willis (Leonora)
Nancy Hermiston (Ersilia)

Gyorgy Fischer (Conductor)
Andy Hinds (Producer)
John McMurray (Designer)
Mick Hughes (Lighting)
Terry John Bates (Choreographer)
Courtney Kenny (Continuo)

1984
26,29 October; 1,4 November
The Kiss
by Bedrich Smetana

Marie Slorach (Vendulka)
John Ayldon (Paloucký Otec)
Eduardo Alvares (Lukáš)
Roger Howell (Tomeš)
Patricia Johnson (Martinka)
Richard Robson (Matouš)
Nancy Hermiston (Barče)
Grant Shelley (A frontier guard)

Wexford Festival Chorus
(Chorus master: Martin Merry)
Albert Rosen (Conductor)
Toby Robertson (Producer)
Bernard Culshaw (Designer)
Mick Hughes (Lighting)
Terry John Bates (Choreographer)

1985
23,26,29 October; 1 November
La Wally
by Alfredo Catalani

Josella Ligi (Wally)
John O'Flynn (Stromminger)
Ljubomir Videnov (Gellner of Hochstoff)
Lawrence Bakst (Hagenbach of Sölden)
Sunny Joy Langton (Walter)
Jean Bailey (Afra)
Richard Robson (An old soldier)

RadioTelefís Éireann Symphony Orchestra
Wexford Festival Chorus
(Chorus master: Ian Reid)
Albert Rosen (Conductor)
Stefan Janski (Producer)
Marie-Jeanne Lecca (Designer)
Mick Hughes (Lighting)
Terry John Bates (Choreographer)

1985
24,27,30 October; 2 November
Ariodante
by George Frideric Handel

Bernadette Greevy (Ariodante)
Pamela Myers (Ginevra)
Morag MacKay (Dalinda)
Cynthia Clarey (Polinesso)
Raul Gimenex (Lurcanio)
Petteri Salomaa (The king of Scotland)
Adrian Thompson (Odoardo)

Members of Irish National Ballet
Members of Wexford Festival Chorus
(Chorus master: Ian Reid)
Alan Curtis (Conductor)
Guus Mostart (Producer)
John Otto (Designer)
Mick Hughes (Lighting)
Terry John Bates (Choreographer)

1985
25,28,31 October; 3 November
**The Rise and Fall of the
City of Mahagonny**
by Kurt Weill

Nuala Willis (Leokadja Begbick)
John Gibbs (Trinity Moses)
Valentin Jar (Fatty the bookkeeper)
Sherry Zannoth (Jenny Smith)
Theodore Spencer (Jimmy Mahoney)
Julian Pike (Jack)
Richard Sutliff (Bill)
John O'Flynn (Alaska-Wolf Joe)
Brendan Cavanagh (Toby)

Members of Wexford Festival Chorus
Simon Joly (Conductor)
Declan Donnellan (Producer)
Nick Ormerod (Designer)
Mick Hughes (Lighting)
Terry John Bates (Choreographer)

1986
22,25,28,31 October
Königskinder
by Engelbert Humperdinck

William Lewis (King's son)
Daniela Bechly (Goose-girl)
Pauline Tinsley (Witch)
Sergei Leiferkus (Fiddler)
Curtis Watson (Wood-cutter)
Valentin Jar (Broom-binder)
Kathleen Tynan (Young girl)
John O'Flynn (Innkeeper)
Roisin McGibbon (Innkeeper's daughter)
Marijke Hendricks (Stable-girl)
Brian Donlan (City elder)
David Bartleet (Tailor)
Jonathan Veira (Gatekeeper)
Brindley Sherratt (Gatekeeper)

RadioTelefis Éireann Symphony Orchestra
Members of Wexford Festival Chorus
(Chorus master: Ian Reid)
Albert Rosen (Conductor)
Michael McCaffery (Producer)
Di Seymour (Designer)
John Waterhouse (Lighting)
Terry John Bates (Choreographer)

1986
23,26,29 October; 1 November
Also 4 November,
Queen Elizabeth Hall,
London
Tancredi
by Gioacchino Rossini

Kathleen Kuhlmaan (Tancredi)
Inga Neilsen (Amenaide)
Bruce Ford (Argirio)
Petteri Salomaa (Orbazzano)
Marijke Hendriks (Isaura)
Roisin McGibbon (Roggiero)

Wexford Festival Male Chorus
(Chorus master: Ian Reid)
Arnold Oestman (Conductor)
Michael Beauchamp (Producer)
William Passmore (Designer)
John Waterhouse (Lighting)

1986
24,27,30 October; 2 November
Mignon
by Ambroise Thomas

Cynthia Clarey (Mignon)
Curtis Rayam (Wilhelm Meister)
Beverly Hoch (Philine)
Teodor Ciurdea (Lothario)
Philip Doghan (Laerte)
John O'Flynn (Jarno)
Joseph Cornwell (Frédérick)
John O'Flynn (Antonio)

Wexford Festival Chorus
(Chorus master: Ian Reid)
Yan Pascal Tortelier (Conductor)
Richard Jones (Producer)
Richard Hudson (Designer)
John Waterhouse (Lighting)
Terry John Bates (Choreographer)

1987
21,24,27,30 October
La Straniera
by Vincenzo Bellini

Renata Daltin (Alaide)
Jake Gardner (Valdeburgo)
Ingus Peterson (Arturo)
Cynthia Clarey (Isoletta)
Mikhail Krutikov (Montolino)
Giancarlo Tosi (The prior)
Philip Doghan (Osburgo)

RadioTelefís Éireann Symphony Orchestra
Wexford Festival Chorus
(Chorus master: Roy Laughlin)
Jan Latham-Koenig (Conductor)
Robert Carsen (Producer)
Russell Craig (Designer)
John Waterhouse (Lighting)
Terry John Bates (Choreographer)

1987
22,25,28,31 October
La Cena delle Beffe
by Umberto Giordano

Mikhail Krutikov (Tornaquinci)
Oliver Broome (Calandra)
Fabio Armiliato (Giannetto Malespini)
Luis Giron May (Neri Chiaramantesi)
Philip Doghan (Gabriello)
Miriam Gauci (Ginevra)
David Barrell (Fazio)
Kathleen Tynan (Cintia)
Bruno Caproni (Lapo)
Giancarlo Tosi (Doctor)
Alessandra Marc (Lisabetta)
Brendan Cavanagh (Trinca)
Patricia Wright (Fiammetta)
Kate McCarney (Laldomine)
Philip Doghan (A singer)

Albert Rosen (Conductor)
Patrick Mason (Producer)
Joe Vaněk (Designer)
John Waterhouse (Lighting)

1987
23,26,29 October; 1 November
Cendrillon
Fairy tale in four acts
by Jules Massenet.
Libretto by Henri Cain, *after*
Charles Perrault (*sung in French*)

Pierre-Yves Le Maigat (Pandolfe)
Joan Davies (Madame de la Haltière)
Jane Webster (Noémie)
Therese Feighan (Dorothée)
Claire Primrose (Lucette)
Silvana Manga (The fairy)
Robynne Redmon (Prince Charming)
David Barrell (The Master of Ceremonies)
Brendan Cavanagh (Dean of the Faculty)
Patrick Donnelly (The first minister)
Oliver Broome (The king)
Anthony Morse (The herald)

Members of the Dublin City Ballet
Wexford Festival Chorus
(Chorus master: Roy Laughlin)
Stéphane Cardon (Conductor)
Seamus McGrenera (Producer)
Tim Reed (Designer)
John Waterhouse (Lighting)
Terry John Bates (Choreographer)

1988
20,23,26,29 October
The Devil and Kate
by Antonin Dvořák

Joseph Evans (Jirka)
Anne-Marie Owens (Kate)
Peter Lightfoot (Marbuel)
Joan Davies (Kate's mother)
Michael Forest (A musician)
Kathleen Tynan (A chambermaid)
Alan Fairs (The marshal)
Marko Putkonen (Lucifer)
Phillip Guy-Bromley (Gatekeeper)
Geoffrey Davidson (Hell guard)
Julie Wong (Solo dancer)
Kristine Ciesinski (The princess)

RadioTelefís Éireann Symphony Orchestra
Wexford Festival Chorus
(Chorus master: Roy Laughlin)
Albert Rosen (Conductor)
Francesca Zambello (Producer)
Neil Peter Jampolis (Designer)
Paul Pyant (Lighting)
Terry John Bates (Choreographer)

1988
21,24,27,30 October
3 November, Queen Elizabeth
Hall, London
Elisa e Claudio
by Saverio Mercadante

Lena Nordin (Elisa)
Janos Bandi (Claudio)
Alice Baker (Carlotta)
Plamen Hidjov (The Conte Arnoldo)
Bruno de Simone
   (The Marchese Tricotazio)
Olga Orolinova (Silvia)
Philip Doghan (Celso)
Marko Putkonen (Luca)

Wexford Festival Chorus
(Chorus master: Roy Laughlin)
Marco Guidarini (Conductor)
David Fielding (Producer)
David Fielding (Designer)
Bettina Munzer (Designer)
Paul Pyant (Lighting)

1988
22,25,28,31 October (double bill)
Don Giovanni Tenorio
or **The Stone Guest**
by Giuseppe Gazzaniga

Miroslav Kopp (Don Giovanni)
Balazs Poka (Pasquariello)
Norman Bailey (The commendatore)
Malmfrid Sand (Donna Anna)
Andrea Bolton (Donna Elvira)
Alison Browner (Maturina)
Joan Davies (Duke Ximena)
Finbar Wright (Duke Ottavio)
Alan Cemore (Biagio)
Philip Doghan (Lanterna)

Wexford Festival Chorus
(Chorus master: Roy Laughlin)
Simon Joly (Conductor)
Patrick Mason (Producer)
Joe Vaněk (Designer)
Paul Pyant (Lighting)
Terry John Bates (Choreographer)

Turandot
by Ferruccio Busoni

Milan Voldrich (Kalaf)
Balazs Poka (Barak)
Norman Bailey (The Emperor Altoum)
Kristine Ciesinski (Turandot)
Alison Browner (Adelma)
Bruce Brewer (Truffaldino)
Alan Cemore (Pantalone)
Phillip Guy-Bromley (Tartaglia)
Malmfrid Sand (The queen of Samerkand)
Julie Wong (Dancer)
Sarah Audsley (Dancer)

1989
26,29 October; 1,4,10 November
Der Templer und die Jüdin
by Heinrich Marschner

Paul Harrhy (Maurice de Bracy)
William Stone (Brian de Bois-Guilbert)
Mary Clarke (Rowena)
Björn Stockhaus (Cedric)
John Daniecki (Wamba)
Brian Bannatyne-Scott (Oswald)
Adrian Fisher (Friar Tuck)
Greer Grimsley (The Black Knight)
George Mosley (Locksley)
Anita Soldh (Rebecca)
Joseph Evans (Ivanhoe)
William Bankes-Jones (Isaac of York)
Peter Loehle (Lucas de Beaumanoir)

RadioTelefís Éireann Symphony Orchestra
Wexford Festival Chorus
(Chorus master: Jonathan Webb)
Albert Rosen (Conductor)
Francesca Zambello (Producer)
Bettina Munzer (Designer)
Kevin Sleep (Lighting)

1989
27,30 October; 2,5,11 November
8 November, Queen Elizabeth
Hall, London
Mitridate, Re de Ponto
by Wolfgang Amadeus Mozart

Martin Thompson (Mitridate)
Lena Nordin (Aspasia)
Cyndia Sieden (Sifare)
Luretta Bybee (Farnace)
Patricia Rozario (Ismene)
Paul Harrhy (Marzio)
Therese Feighan (Arbate)

Marco Guidarini (Conductor)
Lucy Bailey (Producer)
Peter J Davison (Designer)
Kevin Sleep (Lighting)
Charles Kilpatrick (Continuo)

1989
28,31 October; 3,6,12 November
The Duenna
(Betrothal in a monastery)
by Sergei Prokofiev

Neil Jenkins (Don Jerome)
Spiro Malas (Don Isaac Mendoza)
Sheila Nadler (The Duenna)
Thomas Lawlor (Don Carlos)
Amy Burton (Louisa)
James Busterud (Ferdinand)
Donald George (Antonio)
Paula Hoffman (Clara)
Brian Parsons (The masker)
William Rae (The masker)
Adrian Fisher (The masker)
Paul Arden-Griffith (Lopez)
Yvonne Brennan (Lauretta)
Kathleen Tynan (Rosina)
Andrew Forbes-Lane (Pedro)
Robert Burt (Pablo)
Garrick Forbes (Michael)
Brian Bannatyne-Scott (Father Augustine)
John Daniecki (Brother Elixir)
Geoffrey Davidson (Brother Chartreuse)
Björn Stockhaus (Brother Benedictine)
Ian Baar (Monastery doorkeeper)
Christopher Speight (Monastery doorkeeper)

Wexford Festival Chorus
(Chorus master: Jonathan Webb)
František Vajnar (Conductor)
Patrick Mason (Producer)
Joe Vaněk (Designer)
Kevin Sleep (Lighting)
Terry John Bates (Choreographer)

1990
25,28 October; 1,4,9 November
Zazà
Ruggiero Leoncavallo

Karen Notare (Zazà)
John Cimino (Cascart)
Claude-Robin Pelletier (Milio Dufresne)
Ludmilla Andrew (Anaide)
Theresa Hamm (Natalia)
Keith Mikelson (Courtois)
Yvonne Brennan (Floriana)
Wojciech Drabowicz (Bussy)
David Cumberland (Duclou)
Nigel Leeson-Williams (Michelin)
Brendan Cavanagh (Augusto)
Constance Novis (Claretta)
Elizabeth Hetherington (Simóna)
Regina Hanley (Madame Dufresne)
Nigel Leeson-Williams (Marco)

National Symphony Orchestra
Wexford School of Ballet and Modern
  Dance
Bruno Rigacci (Conductor)
Jamie Hayes (Producer)
Ruari Murchison (Designer)
Mark Pritchard (Lighting)
Terry John Bates (Choreographer)

1990
26,30 October; 2,6,10 November
The Rising of the Moon
by Nicholas Maw

Francis Egerton (Brother Timothy)
Gordon Sandison (Danal O'Dowd)
Pamela Helen Stephen (Cathleen Sweeney)
Lawrence Richard (Colonel Lord Jowler)
Peter-Christoph Runge (Major Max von Zastrow)
Keith Mikelson (Captain Lillywhite)
Pauline Tinsley (Lady Eugenie Jowler)
Annika Skoglund (Frau Elizabeth von Zastrow)
Marie-Claire O'Reirdan (Miss Atalanta Lillywhite)
Max Wittges (Corporal of Horse Haywood)
Mark Calkins (Cornet John Stephen Beaumont)
Elizabeth Bainbridge (The widow Sweeney)
Thomas Lawlor (Lynch)
Stephen Crook (Gaveston)
David Buxton (Willoughby)

Loch Garman Silver Band
Wexford Festival Chorus
(Chorus master: Jonathan Webb)
Simon Joly (Conductor)
Ceri Sherlock (Producer)
Richard Aylwin (Designer)
Mark Pritchard (Lighting)

1990
27,31 October; 3,7,11 November
La Dame Blanche
by François Adrien Boieldieu

Panaghis Pagoulatos (Gabriel)
Antoine Normand (Dikson)
Brigitte Lafon (Jenny)
Jorge de Leon (Georges Brown)
Gillian Knight (Marguerite)
Mariette Kemmer (Anna)
Andre Cognet (Gaveston)
David Cumberland (MacIrton)

Wexford Festival Chorus
(Chorus master: Jonathan Webb)
Emmanuel Joel (Conductor)
Jean-Claude Auvray (Producer)
Kenny MacLèllan (Designer)
Mark Pritchard (Lighting)

1991
24,27,30 October; 2,5,8 November
L'Assedio di Calais
by Gaetano Donizetti

Victor Ledbetter (Eustachio)
Alison Browner (Aurelio)
Ann Panagulias (Eleanora)
Ernesto Grisales (Giovanni d'Aire)
Frank Kelley (Giacomo de Wisants)
Hugh Mackey (Pietro de Wisants)
Nigel Leeson (Armando)
Kurt Ollmann (Edward III)
Elizabeth Woollett (Isabella)
Huw Priday (Edmondo)
Andre Cognet (Un Incognito)

National Symphony Orchestra
Wexford Festival Chorus
(Chorus master: Jonathan Webb)
Evelino Pidò (Conductor)
Francesca Zambello (Producer)
Alison Chitty (Designer)

1991
25,28,31 October; 3,6,9 November
La Recontre Imprévue
or **Les Pèlerins de la
Mecque**
by Christophe Willibald Gluck

Paul Austin Kelly (Ali, Prince of Balsora)
Christopher Hux (Osmin)
Richard Crist (The Calender)
Malcolm Walker (Vertigo)
Janet Williams (Rezia)
Kathryn Cowdrick (Balkis)
Sandra Dugdale (Amine)
Yvonne Brennan (Dardané)
Andre Cognet (Leader of the Caravan)
Huw Priday (The Sultan of Egypt)

National Symphony Orchestra
Wexford Festival Chorus
(Chorus master: Gavin Dorrian)
Richard Hickox (Conductor)
Jamie Hayes (Producer)
Ruari Murchison (Designer)

1991
26,29 October; 1,4,7,10 November
Der Widerspenstigen Zähmung
by Hermann Goetz

Wolfgang Babl (Baptista)
Marit Sauramo (Katherina)
Stefan Margita (Lucentio)
Peter-Christoph Runge (Hortensio)
William Parcher (Petruchio)
Hugh Mackey (Grumio)
Frank Kelley (A Tailor)
Huw Rhys-Evans (Major Domo)
Cara O'Sullivan (Housekeeper)
Julie Gossage (Hortensio's wife)
Lynda Lee (Baptista's wife)
Nellie Walsh (Katherina's maid)
Zsuzsanna Csonka (Bianca)

National Symphony Orchestra
Wexford Festival Chorus
(Chorus master: Jonathan Webb)
Oliver Von Dohnanyi (Conductor)
John Lloyd Davies (Producer/Designer)

1992
22,25,28,31 October; 3,6 November
Il Piccolo Marat
by Pietro Mascagni

Georgi Selesnev (L'Orco)
Karen Notare (Mariella)
Thomas Booth (Il Piccolo Marat)
Patricia McCaffrey (Princess de Fleury)
Keith Latham (Il Soldato)
Karl Morgan Daymond (La Spia)
Jose Garcia (La Tigre)
Johannes Von Duisburg (Il Ladro)
Richard Zeller (Il Carpentiere)
John Rath (Captain of the Marats)
Andrew Hammond (A bishop)
Fan-Chang Kong (A prisoner)
Robert Torday (An orderly)

National Symphony Orchestra
Wexford Festival Chorus
(Chorus master: Stuart Hutchinson)
Albert Rosen (Conductor)
Stephen Medcalf (Producer)
Charles Edwards (Designer)

1992
23,26,29 October; 1,4,7 November
Gli Equivoci
by Stephen Storace

Kip Wilborn (Eufemio of Syrcuse)
Kurt Link (Dromio of Syracuse)
Phillip Guy-Bromley (Aegeon)
Karl Morgan Daymond (Duke Solinus)
Christopher Trakas (Dromio of Ephesus)
Korliss Uecker (Adriana)
Sarah Pring (Luciana)
Gary Harger (Eufemio of Ephesus)
John Rath (Angelo)
Kate McCarney (Lesbia)
Jurgen O'Byrne (Little Dromio)

National Symphony Orchestra
Wexford Festival Chorus
Mark Shanahan (Conductor)
Giles Havergal (Producer)
Russell Craig (Designer)

1992
24,27,30 October; 2,5,8 November
Der Vampyr
by Heinrich Marschner

William Parcher (Lord Ruthven)
Ingo Kolonerics (Vampire Master)
Patricia McCaffrey (Janthe Berkley)
Phillip Guy-Bromley (Sir John Berkley)
Simon Preece (Berkley's servant)
Walter Mac Neil (Sir Edgar Aubry)
Daniela Bechly (Malvina Davenaut)
Alexander Malta (Sir Humphrey Davenaut)
Frances Lucey (Emmy Perth)
Jürgen Sacher (George Dibdin)
Johannes Von Duisburg (Blunt)
Jutta Winkler (Suse)

National Symphony Orchestra
Wexford Festival Chorus
Guido Johannes Rumstadt (Conductor)
Jean-Claude Auvray (Producer)
Kenny Mac Lellan (Designer)
Gavin Dorrian (Choreographer)

James Drummond Nelson (Gadshill)
Ingo Kolonerics (Green)
Nicholas Buxton (Scrop)

1993
14,17,20,23, 26,29 October
Cherevichki
by Peter Ilyich Tchaikovsky

Roman Tsymbala (Vakula)
Valentina Cherbinina (Solokha)
Leonid Boldin (The Devil)
Vladimir Matorin (Chub)
Marina Levitt (Oksana)
Keith Latham (The Mayor)
Wjacheslav Weinorovski
    (The Schoolmaster)
Rupert Oliver Forbes (Panas)
Anatoly Lochak (His Excellency Potemkin)
Paul Keohone (Woodsprite)
William Peel (Old Cossack)
Declan Kelly (Gentleman-in-waiting)
Andrew Hammond (Master of Ceremonies)
Ella Clarke (Ballerina)

National Symphony Orchestra
Wexford Festival Chorus
(Chorus master: Gregory Rose)
Alexander Annissimov (Conductor)
Francesca Zambello (Producer)
Bruno Schwengl (Designer)
David Colmer (Lighting Designer)
Gavin Dorrian (Choreographer)

1993
15,18,21,24, 27,30 October
Il Barbiere di Siviglia
by Giovanni Paisiello

Kjell Magnus Sandvé (Count Almaviva)
Mark Pedrotti (Figaro)
Frances Lucey (Rosina)
Enrico Fissore (Doctor Bartolo)
Gabriele Monici (Don Basilio)
Gerard O'Connor (Lo Svegliato)
Rupert Oliver Forbes (Giovinetto)
Keith Latham (A notary)
James Drummond Nelson (A judge)
Hanna Foley (Marcellina)

National Symphony Orchestra
Wexford Festival Chorus
Carla Delfrate (Conductor)
Lucy Bailey (Producer)
Simon Vincenzi (Designer)
David Colmer (Lighting Designer)

1993
16,19,22,25, 28,31 October
Zampa (ou La fiancée de marbre)
by Ferdinand Hérold

Mary Mills (Camille)
Bradley Williams (Alphonse de Monza)
Jutta Winkler (Ritta)
Antoine Normand (Dandolo)
John Daniecki (Zampa)
Valentin Jar (Daniel Capuzzi)
Tom McVeigh (A Corsaire)
Ella Clarke (Alice Manfredi)
Nicky Duggan (Lugano)

National Symphony Orchestra
Wexford Festival Chorus
(Chorus master: Gregory Rose)
Yves Abel (Conductor)
Tim Hopkins (Producer)
Charles Edwards (Designer)

1994
20,23,26,29 October; 1,4 November
The Demon
by Anton Rubinstein

Anatoly Lochak (The Demon)
Alison Browner (The Angel)
Marina Mercheriakova (Tamara)
Leonid Zimnenko (Prince Gudal)
Valery Serkin (Prince Sinodal)
Richard Robson (Old Servant)
Ludmilla Andrew (Nanny)
Wjacheslav Weinorovski (Messenger)

National Symphony Orchestra
Wexford Festival Chorus
(Chorus master: Gregory Rose)
Alexander Annissimov (Conductor)
Yefim Maizel (Producer)
Paul Steinberg (Designer)
David Colmer (Lighting Designer)

1994
21,24,27,30 October; 2,5 November
La Bohème
by Ruggero Leoncavallo

Magali Damonte (Musette)
Jean-Pierre Furlan (Marcello)
Jungwon Park (Mimi)
Patryk Wroblewski (Rodolfo)
Jonathan Veira (Schaunard)
Niamh Murray (Eufemia)
Guido Lebrón (Colline)
Valentin Jar (Gaudenzio)
Giancarlo Tosi (Barbemuche)
Frank O'Brien (Visconte Paolo)
Wjacheslav Weinorovski (Durand)
Ivan Sharpe (A Lad)
Simon Spencer Williams (Man from 1st floor)
Giles Davies (Clerk)
Emma Pollack (Clerk's wife)
Mary Rose Langfield (Widow)

National Symphony Orchestra
Wexford Festival Opera Chorus
(Chorus master: Gregory Rose)
Albert Rosen (Conductor)
Reto Nickler (Producer)
Russell Craig (Designer)
David Colmer (Lighting Designer)

1994
22,25,28,31 October;
3,6 November
Das Liebesverbot
by Richard Wagner

Robert Holzer (Friedrich)
Robert Swensen (Luzio)
Peter Srensson (Claudio)
Eric Ashcraft (Antonio)
Guido Lebrón (Angelo)
Marie Plette (Isabella)
Marit Sauramo (Mariana)
Gidon Saks (Brighella)
Jurij Kruglov (Danieli)
Majella Cullagh (Dorella)
Valentin Jar (Pontio Pilato)

National Symphony Orchestra
Wexford Festival Opera Chorus
(Chorus master: Gregory Rose)
Yves Abel (Conductor)
Dieter Kaegi (Producer)
Bruno Schwengl (Designer)
David Colmer (Lighting Designer)

1995
19,22,25,28,31 October;
3 November
Saffo
by Giovanni Pacini

Francesca Pedaci (Saffo)
Nicoletta Zanini (Saffo)
Carlo Ventre (Faone)
Roberto De Candia (Alcandro)
Mariana Pentcheva (Climene)
Gemma Bertagnolli (Dirce)
Aled Hall (Ippia)
Davide Baronchelli (Lisimaco)

National Symphony Orchestra
Wexford Festival Opera Chorus
(Chorus master: Lubomir Mátl)
Maurizio Benini (Conductor)
Beni Montresor (Designer)

1995
20,23,26,29 October;
1,4 November
Mayskaya Noch
by Nikolay Rimsky-Korsakov

Vladimir Matorin (Golova)
Vsevelod Grivnov (Levko)
Irina Dolzhenko (Hanna)
Frances McCafferty
  (Golova's sister-in-law)
Anatoly Lochak (Kalenik)
Maxim Mikhailov (The Clerk)
Wjascheslav Weinorovski (Distiller)
Marina Mescherlakova (Rusalka)
Annalisa Winberg (Waterspirit)
Pauline Bourke (Waterspirit)
Elena Guchina (Waterspirit)

National Symphony Orchestra
Wexford Festival Opera Chorus
(Chorus master: Lubomir Mátl)
Vladimir Jurowski (Conductor)
Stephen Medcalf (Director)
Francis O'Connor (Designer)
Guido Levi (Lighting Designer)
Kate Flatt (Choreographer)

1995
21,24,27,30 October;
2,5 November
Iris
by Pietro Mascagni

Michie Nakamaru (Iris)
Ludovit Ludha (Ósaka)
Roy Stevens (Kyoto)
Richard Robson (Il Cieco)
Carla Maney (Dhia)
Sergio Panajia (Un Merciaiolo)
Sergio Panajia (Il Cenciainolo)
Joy Constantinides (Ballet Dancer)

National Symphony Orchestra
Wexford Festival Opera Chorus
(Chorus master: Fergus Sheil)
Bruno Aprea (Conductor)
Lorenzo Mariani (Producer)
Maurizio Balò (Designer)
Guido Levi (Lighting Designer)
Kate Flatt (Choreographer)

1996
17,20,23,26,29 October;
1 November
Parisina
by Gaetano Donizetti

Alexandrina Pendatchanska (Parisina)
Monica Colonna (Parisina)
Amadeo Moretti (Ugo)
Roberto Serville (Azzo)
Richard Robson (Ernesto)
Daniela Barcellona (Imelda)

National Symphony Orchestra of Ireland
Wexford Festival Opera Chorus
(Chorus master: Lubomir Mátl)
Maurizio Benini (Conductor)
Roberto Polastri (Conductor; 29 Oct., 1 Nov.)
Stefano Vizioli (Director)
Ulderico Manani (Designer)

1996
18,21,24,27,30 October;
2 November
L'Étoile du Nord
by Giacomo Meyerbeer

Elizabeth Futral (Catherina)
Vladimir Ognev (Peter the Great)
Davina Takova (Prascovia)
Aled Hall (Danilowitz)
Christopher Maltman (Gritzenko)
Juan Diego Flórez (George)
Agnete Munk Rasmussen (Natalia)
Patrizia Cigna (Ekimona)
Robert Lee (Ismailoff)
Fernand Bernadi (Reynold)
Luis Ledesma (Yermoloff)

National Symphony Orchestra of Ireland
Wexford Festival Opera Chorus
(Chorus master: Lubomir Mátl)
Vladimir Jurowski (Conductor)
Denis Krief (Director)
Denis Krief (Designer)
Giovanni de Cicco (Choreographer)

1996
19,22,25,28,31 October;
3 November
Sárka
by Zdeněk Fibich

Svetelina Vassileva (Sárka)
Ludovit Ludha (Ctirad)
Denisa Slepkovská (Vlasta)
Anatoly Lochak (Prince Přemysl)
Richard Robson (Vitoraz)
Giuseppina Piuntl (Lybina))
Juliet Booth (Mlada)
Giselle Allen (Svatava)
Margareta Hillerud (Radka)
Kim-Marie Woodhouse (Hosta)
Cinzia de Mola (Castava)

National Symphony Orchestra of Ireland
Wexford Festival Opera Chorus
(Chorus master: Lubomir Mátl)
David Agler (Conductor)
Inga Levant (Director)
Charles Edwards (Designer)
Brigitte Reiffenstuel (Costume Designer)

1997
18,21,24,27,30 October;
2 November
La Fiamma
by Ottorino Respighi

Elmira Magomedova (Silvana)
Youri Alexeev (Donello)
Anatoly Lochak (Basilio)
Daniela Barcellona (Eudossia)
Giuseppina Piunti (Monica)
Paolo Pelliciari (Agnese di Cervia)
Carlo Lepore (Il Vescova)
Tereza Matlova (Agata)
Elena Belfiore (Lucilla)

National Symphony Orchestra of Ireland
Wexford Festival Opera Chorus
(Chorus master: Lubomir Mátl)
Enrique Mazzola (Conductor)
Franco Ripa di Meana (Director)
Edoardo Sanchi (Designer)
Steve Almerighi (Costume Designer)
Vincenzo Raponi (Lighting Designer)
Alessandra Panzavolta (Choreographer)

Joanna Campion (Sabina)
Doreen Curran (Zoe)
Dagmar Bundzova (Una madre)
Declan Kelly (Un cherico)

1997
17,20,23,26,29 October;
1 November
Rusalka
by Alexander Dargomïzhsky

Anna Maria Chiuri (Natasha/ Rusalka)
Maxim Mikhailov (Melnik)
Alessandro Safina (Knagi)
Annie Vavrille (Knagina)
Massimiliano Gagliardo (Svat)
Ljuba Chuchrova (Olga)
Katia Trebeleva (Rusalotchka)
Steven Boydall (A huntsman)
Declan Kelly (A villageman)

National Symphony Orchestra of Ireland
Wexford Festival Opera Chorus
(Chorus master: Lubomir Mátl)
Paul Mägi (Conductor)
Alexander Voloschuk (Conductor, 26,29 Oct)
Dimitri Bertman (Director)
Igor Nezny (Set Designer)
Tatyana Tulubieva (Costume Designer)
Vincenzo Raponi (Lighting Designer)
Alessandra Panzavolta (Choreographer)

1997
16,19,22,25, 28,31 October
Elena da Feltre
by Saverio Mercadante

Monica Colonna (Elena)
Nicola Ulivieri (Guido)
Cesare Catani (Ubaldo)
Stefano Rinaldi-Miliani (Sigifredo)
Elena Rossi (Imberga)
Luigi Petroni (Boemondo)
Lorenzo Muzzi (Gualtiero)

National Symphony Orchestra of Ireland
Wexford Festival Opera Chorus
(Chorus master: Lubomir Mátl)
Maurizio Benini (Conductor)
Sonja Frisell (Director)
Marouan Dib (Set and Costume Designer)
Vincenzo Raponi (Lighting Designer)

1998
15,18,21,24, 27,30 October
Fosca
by Carlos Gomes

Elmira Veda (Fosca)
Anatoly Lochak (Cambro)
Giuseppina Piunti (Delia)
Fernando del Valle (Paolo)
Tigran Martirossian (Gajolo)
Alessandro Guerzoni (Giotto)
Colin Iveson (Doge)

National Symphony Orchestra of Ireland
Wexford Festival Opera Chorus
(Chorus master: Lubomir Mátl)
Alexander Anissimov (Conductor)
Giovanni Agostinucci (Director)
Vincenzo Raponi (Lighting Designer)

1998
16,19,22,25, 28,31 October
Sarlatán
by Pavel Haas

Luca Grassi (Pustrpalk)
Louise Walsh (Rosina)
Ludovit Ludha (Bachelor)
Peter Wedd (Kyška)
Alessandro Guerzoni (Pavučina)
Julian Jensen (First student)
Alberto Janelli (Ohnižer)
Simon Wilding (Town Physician)
František Zahradniček (Snake charmer)
Jiři Vinklárek (2nd student)
Julian Tovey (3rd student)
Viktoria Vizin (Amaranta)
Leigh Melrose (Jochimus)
Alberto Janelli (Jochimus' servant)
Jeong Won Lee (Monster)
David Marsh (Král)
Radek Prügl (Jiný mŭz)

National Symphony Orchestra of Ireland
Wexford Festival Opera Chorus
(Chorus master: Lubomir Mátl)
Israel Yinon (Conductor)
John Abulafia (Director)
Fontini Dimon (Set and Costume designer)
Vincenzo Raponi (Lighting Designer)

1998
17,20,23,26,29 October;
1 November
I Cavalieri di Ekebù
by Riccardo Zandonai

Dario Volonté (Giosta Berling)
Francesca Franci (La Comandante)
Alida Barbasini (Anna)
Maxim Mikhailov (Suntram)
Victor Chernomortzev (Cristiano)
David Marsh (Samzelius)
Joseph Calleja (Liecrona)
Tea Demurishvili (Un'ostessa)
Irina Lasareva (Una fanciulla)
Julian Jensen (Rüster)
Peter Wedd (Julius)
Julian Tovey (Fuchs)
Colin Iveson (Rutger)
František Zahradniček (Everardo)
Simon Wilding (Wemburgo)
Alberto Janelli (Kenvellere)
Jirï Vinklárek (Kristoffer)
Jeong Won Lee (Berencreuz)

National Symphony Orchestra of Ireland
Wexford Festival Opera Chorus
(Chorus master: Lubomir Mátl)
Daniele Callegari (Conductor)
Gabriele Vacis (Director)
Francesco Calcagnini (Set Designer)
Hilary Lewis (Costume Designer)
Vincenzo Raponi (Lighting Designer)

1999
14,17,20,23, 26,29 October
Die Königin von Saba
by Karl Goldmark

Cornelia Helfricht (Königin von Saba)
Mauro Nicoletti (Assad)
Valerij Popov (Assad)
Max Wittges (König Salomon)
Piotr Nowacki (Itohepriester)
Inka Rinn (Sulamith)
Tereza Mátlová (Astaroth)
Vladimir Glushchak (Baal-Hanaan)

National Symphony Orchestra of Ireland
Wexford Festival Opera Chorus
(Chorus master: Lubomir Mátl)
Claude Schnitzler (Conductor)
Patrick Mailler (Director)
Massimo Gasparon (Set & Costume Designer)
Vincenzo Raponi (Lighting Designer)

1999
15,18,21,24, 27,30 October
Straszny Dwór
by Stanislaw Moniuszko

Zenon Kowalski (Miecznik)
Iwona Hossa (Hanna)
Viktoria Vizin (Jadwiga)
Dariusz Stachura (Stefan)
Jacck Janiszewski (Zbigniew)
Elizabeth Woods (Czésnikowa)
Zbigniew Macias (Old servant)
Piotr Nowacki (Skoluba)
Leszek Swidzinski (Pan Damazy)
Roberta Zelnickova (Marta)
Petr Frÿbert (Grześ)
Roberta Zelnickova (Stara Niewiasta)

National Symphony Orchestra of Ireland
Wexford Festival Opera Chorus
(Chorus master: Lubomir Mátl)
David Jones (Conductor)
Michal Znaniecki (Director)
Francesco Calcagnini (Set Designer)
Dalia Gallico (Costume Consultant)
Vincenzo Raponi (Lighting Designer)
Isadora Weiss (Choreographer)

1999
16,19,22,25, 28,31 October
Siberia
by Umberto Giordano

Elena Zelenskaia (Stephana)
Dario Volonté (Vassili)
Walter Donati (Gleby)
Claudia Marchi (Nikona)
Massimo Giordano (Il principe Alexis)
Eldar Alier (Walinoff)
Chloë Wright (La Fanciulla)
Darren Abrahams (Ivan)
František Zahradniček (Il Capitano)
Zbigniew Macias (Miskinsky)

National Symphony Orchestra of Ireland
Wexford Festival Opera Chorus
(Chorus master: Lubomir Mátl)
Daniele Callegari (Conductor)
Fabio Sparvoli (Director)
Giorgio Ricchelli (Set Designer)
Alessandra Torella (Costume Designer)
Vincenzo Raponi (Lighting Designer)
Isadora Weiss (Choreographer)

2000
19,22,25,28,31 October;
3 November
Orleanskaya Deva
by Pyotr Il'yich Tchaikovsky

Lada Birincov (Jeanne d'Arc
Youri Alexeev (King Charles VII)
Igor Tarassov (Lionel)
Aleksander Teliga (Thibaut d'Arc)
Ermonela Jaho (Agnès Sorel)
Ayhan Ardà (Raymond)
Igor Morozov (Dunois)
Andrei Antonov (Archbishop)
Sergio Foresti (Bertrand)
František Zahradníček (Lauret)
Katia Trebeleva (An Angel's voice)

National Symphony Orchestra of Ireland
Wexford Festival Opera Chorus
(Chorus master: Lubomir Mátl)
Daniele Callegari (Conductor)
Massimo Gasparon (Director)
Massimo Gasparon (Set &Costume Designer)
Rupert Murray (Lighting Designer)
Aniela Kadieva (Assistant Director)

2000
20,23,26,29 October;
1,4 November
Si J'étais Roi
by Adolphe Adam

Joseph Calleja (Zéphoris)
Iwona Hossa (Néméa)
Roberto Accurso (Le Roi)
Darren Abrahams (Piféar)
Tereza Mátlová (Zélide)
Igor Morozov (Kadoor)
Nicola Alaimo (Zizel)
Fiona O'Reilly (Une Choryphée)
Alés Mihálik (Atar)

National Symphony Orchestra of Ireland
Wexford Festival Opera Chorus
(Chorus master: Lubomir Mátl)
David Agler (Conductor)
Renaud Doucet (Director& Choreographer)
André Barbe (Set Designer)
Huguette Barbet-Blanchard(Cost. Designer)
Rupert Murray (Lighting Designer)

2000
21,24,27,30 October; 2,5 November
Conchita
by Riccardo Zandonai

Monica di Siena (Conchita)
Renzo Zulian (Mateo)
Agnieszka Zwierko (La Madre)
Katia Trebeleva (Estella)
Alison Buchanan (Dolores)
Joanna Campion (Rufna)
Fiona Murphy (La Sorregliante)
Aleksander Teliga (L'Ispettore)
Nicola Alaimo (Garcia)

National Symphony Orchestra of Ireland
Wexford Festival Opera Chorus
(Chorus master: Lubomir Mátl)
Marcello Rota (Conductor)
Corrado d'Elia (Director)
Fabrizio Palla (Set Designer)
Steve Almerighi (Costume Designer)
Rupert Murray (Lighting Designer)

2001
18,21,24,27,30 October;
2 November
Alessandro Stradella
by Friedrich Flotow

Stefano Costa (Alessandro Stradella)
Andrei Antonov (Bassi)
Ekaterina Morozova (Leonore)
František Zahradníček (Malvolio)
Declan Kelly (Barbarino)

National Philharmonic Orchestra of Belarus
Wexford Festival Opera Chorus
(Chorus master: Lubomir Mátl)
Daniele Callegari (Conductor)
Thomas de Mallet Burgess (Director)
Julian McGowan (Designer)
Giuseppe di Iorio (Lighting Designer)
Lynne Hockney (Choreographer
   and Movement Director)

2001
19,22,25,28,31 October;
3 November
Jakobín
by Antonin Dvořák

Valentin Pivovarov (Count Vilem of Harasov)
Markus Werba (Bohuš)
Alessandro Grato (Adolf)
Tatiana Monogarova (Julie)
Mirco Palazzi (Filip)
Michal Lehotsky (Jiří)
Alasdair Elliot (Benda)

National Philharmonic Orchestra of Belarus
Wexford Festival Opera Chorus
(Chorus master: Lubomir Mátl)
The Young Wexford Singers
Alexandre Voloschuk (Conductor)
Michael McCaffery (Director)
Paul Edwards (Designer)

Mariana Panova (Terinka)
Rebecca Sharp (Lotinka)

Giuseppe di Iorio (Lighting Designer)
Lynne Hockney (Choreographer and
Movement Director)

2001
20,23,26,29 October;
1,4 November
Sapho
by Jules Massenet

Giuseppina Piunti (Fanny Legrand)
Brandon Jovanovich (Jean Gaussin)
Agata Biénkowska (Divonne)
Massimíliano Gagliardo (Césaire)
Ermonela Jaho (Irène)
Luca Salsi (Caoudal)
Angel Pazos (La Borderie)
Nicolas Courjal (Le patron du restaurant)

National Philharmonic Orchestra of Belarus
Wexford Festival Opera Chorus
(Chorus master: Lubomir Mátl)
Jean-Luc Tingaud (Conductor)
Fabio Sparvoli (Director)
Giorgio Ricchelli (Set Designer)
Alessandra Torella (Costume Designer)
Giuseppe di Iorio (Lighting Designer)

2002
17,20,23,26,29 October;
1 November
Il Giuramento
by Saverio Mercadante

Serena Farnocchia (Elaisa)
Hadar Halevy (Bianca)
Manrico Tedeschi (Viscardo)
Davide Damiani (Manfredo)
Alessandra Panaro (Isaura)
Simeon Esper (Brunovo)

National Philharmonic Orchestra of Belarus
Wexford Festival Opera Chorus
(Chorus master: Lubomir Mátl)
Paolo Arrivabeni (Conductor)
Joseph Rochlitz (Director)
Lucia Goj (Set designer)
Silvia Aymonino (Costume Designer)
Giuseppe di Iorio (Lighting Designer)

2002
18,21,24,27,30 October;
2 November
Mirandolina
by Bohuslav Martinů

Daniela Bruera (Mirandolina)
Tereza Mátlová (Ortensia)
Elena Traversi (Deianira)
Massimiliano Tonsini (Fabrizio)
Simeon Esper (Servitore)
Simon Edwards (Il Conte d'Albafiorita)
Enrico Marabelli (Il Cavaliere di Ripafratta)
Simone Alberghini (Il Marchese di Forlim popoli)
Colm Lowney (Un legatore di gioie)

National Philharmonic Orchestra of Belarus
Wexford Festival Opera Chorus
Riccardo Frizza (Conductor)
Paul Curran (Director)
Kevin Knight (Designer)
Giuseppe di Iorio (Lighting Designer)

2002
19,22,25,28,31 October;
3 November
Manon Lescaut
by Daniel-François-Esprit Auber

Maryna Vyskvorkina (Manon Lescaut)
Alexandre Swan (Des Grieux)
Luca Salsi (Le Marquis D'Hérigny)
Matthieu Lé Croart (Lescaut)
Ermonela Jaho (Marguerite)
David Curry (Gervais)
Elena Traversi (Madame Bancelin)
Marco Nisticò (Monsieur Durozeau)
Steven Timoner (Un Sergent)
Marco Nisticò (Monsieur Renaud)
Joanna Burton (Zaby)
Petr Frybert (Bourgeois)
Martin Slavik (Bourgeois)

National Philharmonic Orchestra of Belarus
Wexford Festival Opera Chorus
(Chorus master: Lubomir Mátl)
Jean-Luc Tingaud (Conductor)
Jean-Philippe Clarace (Director)
Olivier Deloeuil (Director)
Greco (Designer)
Giuseppe di Iorio (Lighting Designer)

2003
16,19,22,25, 28,31 October
Die Drei Pintos
by Carl Maria von Weber/
Gustav Mahler

Robert Holzer
   (Don Pantaleone Roiz de Pacheco)
Peter Furlong (Don Gomez de Freiros)
Barbara Zechmeister (Clarissa)
Sophie Marilley (Laura)
Gunnar Gudbjörnsson (Don
   Gaston Viratos)
Alessandro Svab (Don Pinto de Fonseca)
Steward Kempster (Innkeeper)
Sinéad Campbell (Inez)
Ales Jenis (Ambrosio)

National Philharmonic Orchestra of Belarus
Wexford Festival Opera Chorus
(Chorus master: Lubomir Mátl)
Paolo Arrivabeni (Conductor)
Michal Znaniecki (Director)
Kevin Knight (Designer)
Nick Malbon (Lighting Designer)

2003
17,20,23,26,29 October;
1 November
María del Carmen
by Enrique Granados

Diana Veronese (María del Carmen)
Larisa Kostyuk (Concepción)
Silvia Vazquez (Fuensanta)
Jesús Suaste (Pencho)
Dante Alcalá (Javier)
Gianfranco Montresor (Domingo)
David Curry (Don Fulgencio)
Alberto Arrabal (Pepuso)
Stewart Kempster (Migalo)
Ricardo Mirabelli (Antón)
Robert Ashworth (Roque)
Nick Sharratt (Andrés)
Vicenç Esteve (Un cantaor huertano)
Ana Mariá Garciá Pérez (Una bailaora)

National Philharmonic Orchestra of Belarus
Wexford Festival Opera Chorus
(Chorus master: Lubomir Mátl)
Max Bragado-Darman (Conductor)
Sergio Vela (Director and Set Designer)
Cristiana Aureggi (Co-Set Designer)
Violeta Rojas (Costume Designer)
Nick Malbon (Lighting Designer)

2003
18,21,24,27,30 October;
2 November
Svanda Dudák
by Jaromír Weinberger

Matjaz Robavs (Svanda)
Tatiana Monogarova (Dorota)
Ivan Choupenitch (Babinskў)
Larisa Kostyuk (The Queen)
Alexander Teliga (The Magician)
Nick Sharratt (The Judge)
Pavel Kozel (The Executioner)
Alexander Teliga (The Devil)
Sean Ruane (The Devil's Servant)
Pavel Kozel (Hell's Captain)
Vicenç Esteve (1st Mercenary Soldier)
Richard Weigold (2nd Mercenary Soldier)

National Philharmonic Orchestra of Belarus
Wexford Festival Opera Chorus
(Chorus master: Lubomir Mátl)
Julian Reynolds (Conductor)
Damiano Michieletto (Director)
Robin Rawstorne (Designer)
Nick Malbon (Lighting Designer)

Index

by Brad Morrow